05-01

$4/5^{00}$

05-01

THE SCOTTISH PISTOL

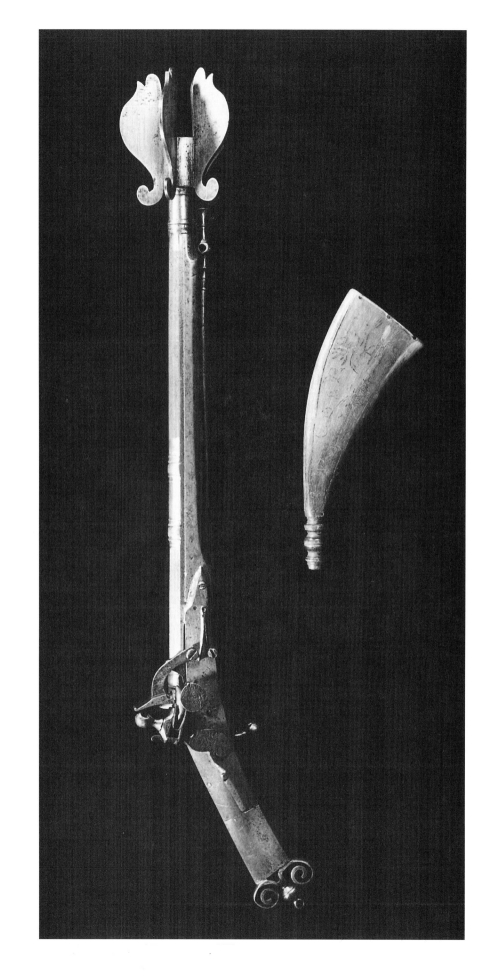

THE SCOTTISH PISTOL

Its history, manufacture and design

Martin Kelvin

FSA (Scot)

cygnus arts

London **Cygnus Arts**
Madison & Teaneck **Fairleigh Dickinson University Press**

Published in the United Kingdom by
Cygnus Arts, a division of Golden Cockerel Press
16 Barter Street
London
WC1A 2AH

Published in the United States of America by
Fairleigh Dickinson University Press
440 Forsgate Drive
Cranbury
NJ 08512

First published 1996

ISBN 1 900541 15 7
ISBN 0 8386 3745 0

British Library Cataloguing-in-Publication Data

Kelvin, Martin
    The Scottish pistol : its history, design and manufacture
    1.Pistols – Scotland – History
    I.Title
    683.4'32'09411
    ISBN 1900541157

Library of Congress Cataloguing-in-Publication Data

Kelvin, Martin.
    The Scottish pistol : its history, design, and manufacture/ Martin Kelvin.
        p.   cm.
    Includes bibliographical references and index.
    ISBN 0–8386–3745–0 (alk. paper)
     1. Pistols—Scotland.I Title.
    TS537.K44   1996
    683.4'32'09411—DC20   96–42417
                                      CIP

Printed and bound in Kranj, Slovenia, by Gorenjski Tisk.

Frontispiece

Mace pistol. This late snaphaunce pistol is dated on the fence, 1622. Overall length 23" (584mm), including mace head. *Gordon Collection, Marischal Museum, Aberdeen University.*

This book is dedicated to the memory of Charles E.Whitelaw,
the pioneer of research on the Scottish pistol.

The Blessing of Highland Arms

Gu'm beannaich Dia ar claidhean,
'S ar lannan Spàinteach geur ghlas,
'S ar lùirichean troma màclleach,
Nach gearrte le faobhar tais;
Ar lannan cruadhach,'s ar gòrsaid
'S ar sgiathan an-dealbhach dualach;
Beannaich gach armachd ga h'iomlan
Th'air ar n-iomchar 's ar crios-guaile.

Ar boghannan foinealach uibhair
'Ghabhadh lugha ri uchd Ausaid;
'S na saighdean beithe nach spealgadh,
Ann am balgan a bhruic ghruamaich,
Beannich ar biodag 's ar daga;
'S ar n-eile gasd ann na cruaichean,
'S gach trealaich cath agus còmhraig',
Tha'm bàrc Mhic Dhòmhnuill san uair so.

God's blessing be upon our swords,
Our keen grey brands of Spain,
Our heavy coats of mail on which
The sword-sweep falls in vain;
Our gauntlets and our corselets'
Our deftly-figured shields,
Whate'er our belts do carry,
Whatever warrior wields.

Our polished bows of yew-tree,
That bend in battle's din,
Our birchen shafts that split not,
Cased in badger's skin;
Bless our dirks and pistols,
Our good kilts in their folds;
And every kind of warlike gear
MacDonall's bark now holds.

Contents

List of Illustrations and Tables   viii
Preface   xi
Introduction   I

PART ONE   **HISTORICAL BACKGROUND**

Chapter 1   The History of Scotland   11
Chapter 2   The Highlander and the Clan System   20
Chapter 3   Weapons Associated with the Scottish Pistol   37

PART TWO   **HISTORY OF PISTOL MANUFACTURE**

Chapter 4   Natural Resources   55
Chapter 5   Shipping Lists   58
Chapter 6   The Hammerman Craft   62
Chapter 7   Gunsmithing Techniques   69
Chapter 8   Lock Mechanisms   73
Chapter 9   The Decoration of Scottish Pistols   78
Chapter 10   The Doune Pistol   91

PART THREE   **THE SCOTTISH PISTOL AND ITS MAKERS**

Chapter 11   Classification and Design   103
Chapter 12   A Survey of Scottish Pistols   145
Chapter 13   The Makers of Scottish Pistols   156

APPENDICES

1. Historical References   175
2. Scottish Pistols in Collections Abroad   208
3. The Care and Conservation of Pistols   211
4. Fakes and Reproductions   212

Glossary   219
Notes   221
Bibliography   226
Index   234

Illustrations and Tables

Frontispiece: mace pistol.

1. Portrait of Major James Fraser of Castle Leathers, c. 1715. 29
2. Portrait of Kenneth Sutherland, 3rd Lord Duffus, c. 1720. 30
3. Portrait of Lord Mungo Murray, c. 1680. 31
4. Portrait of Fearchar Shaw. 33
5. Portrait of Hugh Montgomerie, 12th Earl of Eglinton, c. 1760. 35
6. Basket-hilted backsword, c. 1745. 39
7. Scottish silver-mounted dirk, by William Ritchie of Perth, c. 1796. 42
8. Targe, probably from Perthshire, 1736. 44
9. Selection of Scottish powderhorns, of typical flattened form. 47
10. Another powderhorn, dated 1679. 48
11. The Arms of the Hammerman. 68
12. Snaphaunce lock – exploded view. 74
13. Interior of Highland lock. 76
14. Lock interior showing flintlock mechanism of English type. 76
15. Lower surface of pistol with stylised acanthus and wavy line engraving. 80
16. The barrel of a Christie pistol. 81
17. Celtic decoration on the butt and lockplate of a Christie pistol. 82
18. The obverse side of the Christie pistol of 1750. 83
19. Celtic scrollwork on the spine of a Scottish pistol. 87
20. Deeply incised engraving in the lemon-butt pistol by 'A.G.' 88
21. Restored workshop of Thomas Caddell in Doune. 93
22. Doglock pistol by Thomas Caddell, 1678. 94
23. Lockplate of John Campbell pistol. 96
24. Ramshorn-butt pistol by Alexander Campbell of Doune, c. 1740. 97
25. Fishtail-butt pistol with left-hand snaphaunce lock, 1619. 106
26. Pair of all-brass fishtail-butt snaphaunce pistols, by James Low, 1624. 109
27. Pair of all-brass lemon-butt snaphaunce pistols signed 'A.G.', 1634. 113
28. Obverse side of pistol signed 'I.O.', showing the fretted belt hook finial. 115
29. Heart-butt pistol, c. 1710, showing belt hook with long finial. 116
30. Close-up of barrel, showing silver and brass inlay, and silver barrel bands. 116

31. Early lobe-butt pistol, with left hand snaphaunce lock. Fence dated 1647. 119
32. Close-up of Murdoch signature, with characteristic flourish of the "R". 121
33. Obverse side of Murdoch lobe-butt. 121
34. Small Lobe-butt pistol by John Murdoch of Doune, c. 1775. 122
35. Pair of all-steel snaphaunce pistols of early ramshorn design, 1660. 125
36. Ramshorn-butt flintlock pistol by Patrick Buchanan of Glasgow, c. 1725. 126
37. Obverse side of Waters pistol. 129
38. Proof Marks of early Birmingham type. 130
39. Costume pistol by McNab of Rannoch. 135
40. Butt of percussion-dress pistol by Wighton, c. 1840–50. 138
41. Obverse side of late flintlock pistol by Macleod, c. 1820. 140
42. Lockplate of Macleod pistol. 140
43. The earliest-known Scottish pistols, 1598. 153

COLOUR PLATES between 110–111

1. Ramshorn-butt pistol by John Campbell (1st) of Doune, c. 1715–20.
2. Pair of ramshorn-butt all-steel pistols by John Christie of Doune.
3. Lockplate of Christie pistol.
4. Un-named heart-butt pistol, c. 1710.
5. Heart-butt flintlock pistol by 'I.O.' of Edzell, c. 1730.
6. Heart-butt pistol by James McKenzie of Brechin, c. 1730.
7. One of a pair of lobe-butt pistols by Thomas Murdoch of Leith, c. 1750–75.
8. Ramshorn-butt pistol by Thomas Caddell (3rd), c. 1710.
9. Lockplate of Caddell pistol.
10. Ramshorn-butt pistol by Thomas Murdoch of Leith, c. 1750–75.
11. Military pistol with bronze frame and kidney-shaped butt, c. 1780.
12. Ramshorn military pistol, un-named, but of Bissell type.
13. Detail of military pistol.
14. Pair of percussion dress pistols by Wighton of Edinburgh, c. 1840–50.
15. Lockplate of Wighton pistol.
16. Late flintlock Scottish pistol by Macleod, c. 1820.
17. Gold-mounted presentation pistol with ramshorn butt, by John Murdoch.

TABLES

I. Sources of Scottish Pistols 146
II. Statistical Analysis of Scottish Pistols 147
III. Makers of Scottish Pistols 157–60
IV. The Most Prolific Makers of Scottish Pistols 161
V. Geographical Locations of Scottish Pistol Makers 162

Preface

THE SCOTTISH PISTOL POSSESSES A NUMBER OF CHARAC-teristic features which immediately separate it from pistols of any other country. Although taken individually these characteristics might apply to weapons originating in many different countries, when they occur together, the end result is a pistol which is wholly and undeniably Scottish. Except in a few very rare examples, the Scottish pistol is entirely constructed from steel or brass, or a combination of these metals. The butt design conforms to certain well-recognised patterns which will be discussed in detail in a later chapter. The pistol itself is often embellished with silver inlay and engraving whilst the trigger is in the shape of a ball or sphere which lacks any guard. Lastly, a belt hook is fitted, which apart from its most obvious function as a means of suspension, allows the weapon to be displayed to its full advantage along its entire length, so fulfilling its secondary role as a badge of office for its wearer.

The frontispiece shows a magnificent ramshorn-butt pistol to which has been added a mace head. It is scarcely conceivable that this could have been intended for use other than as a symbol of authority and visible evidence of the rank of its bearer. By inspection of a man's pistols, clearly displayed on his person, the elegance of their lines and the beauty of their decoration, it was possible to determine an individual's rank in his clan. It was no accident that the chiefs chose the most elegant and flamboyant weapons for themselves.

Thus, the Scottish pistol is not the crudely-constructed, ill-functioning weapon which some students of antique firearms would have us believe. Rather, it is graceful, well-balanced and aesthetically-pleasing, at once a functional weapon and at the same time a badge of office and symbol of authority for its wearer. However, in order to fully appreciate the true grace and worth of a Scottish pistol, it is necessary to see beyond the weapon itself, placing it into its correct historical context and seeing, as it were, the man 'behind' the gun. This book attempts to give an accurate description of the development and use of the Scottish pistol throughout the two hundred and fifty years of its reign and, at the same time, to study the significant historical events of that time, having regard to industrial, commercial and economic influences during the period, making full use of all available primary source material from historical archive collections. In addition, this book provides a detailed analysis of over 750 pistols to be found in collections throughout the world.

From a wealth of historical material, a selection of more than one hundred incidents in which pistols are specifically mentioned, has been included, either because they are of historical interest, or of some humour, or where they appear as individual items in account books of the period. No incident has been included in which there is reasonable doubt that the pistols mentioned are not specifically Scottish.

It is at this point that reference must be made to the great Charles Whitelaw, to whom this work is dedicated. Whitelaw, a Glasgow architect, was a collector of antique weapons, having been given a pistol by his father in 1885, at the age of sixteen. This was the beginning of a lifelong interest in Scottish weapons—not just pistols but also powderhorns, dirks and targes—and resulted in the creation of a fabulous collection of these accoutrements of war, the like of which may never be seen again in private hands. Thus Whitelaw was able to build up a considerable knowledge of these weapons and of Scottish pistols in particular.

It must not be forgotten that Whitelaw was collecting mainly in the first quarter of this century when there were few collectors and few accessible collections. It was easier to acquire Scottish pistols at that time and prices, although high, were low compared to today. It is astonishing that, despite the scarcity of museum collections available for close study, Whitelaw was able to acquire so much knowledge on the subject. Much of his data cannot be improved on, even to this day. For example, he knew, seventy years ago, of the oldest extant pair of Scottish pistols and although nowadays there is a much wider dissemination of knowledge and many accessible museum collections throughout the world, no older pair has yet been found.

Whitelaw, it must be said, was a purist. He was primarily interested in early Scottish pistols and displayed a distinct lack of interest in weapons manufactured after the end of the eighteenth century. However nowadays, if knowledge is to be brought up to date, full consideration must be given to all examples of Scottish pistols, including the so-called 'Costume' and 'Percussion Dress Pistols', which were, to an extent, anathema to Whitelaw. Nor should we ignore military weapons of Scottish design, whether manufactured in Scotland or emanating from the workshops of Birmingham, and all these aspects have been included in this work. It is, in this respect, a matter of some personal amusement, that the cover of Whitelaw's *Scottish Arms Makers*, published thirty-eight years after his death, illustrates what can only be described as a pair of the very costume pistols which he himself held in such low esteem.

Whilst engrossed in the study of his own "small representative collection"—the words are his own—Whitelaw became increasingly frustrated by the absence of any gunmaker's name on his seventeenth century pistols, many of which had only initials impressed upon the lockplate. This led to a lifelong research into historical records, hammermen 'lockit-books', burgess rolls and minute books, town directories and inventories of estates, in order to determine, where possible, the full names of these early gunmakers. Unfortunately, Whitelaw died in 1939, his work unfinished and it was only in 1977 that his book was posthumously completed. It is a great achievement, but there is still a great deal of work to be done in this field to fill the remaining gaps in our knowledge. Incidentally, after Whitelaw's death, his collection was divided up and bequeathed to museums in both Edinburgh and Glasgow. Without this generous gift, the collections in each of the two museums involved would be sadly deficient. His 'modest' collection amounted to some twenty-four Scottish pistols, besides the broadswords, targes, dirks and powderhorns which also formed part of it, as well as a considerable number of antique firearms, which, while of Scottish manufacture, fall outside the scope of this book.

Although Charles Whitelaw had written the occasional article on Scottish weapons, his major contribution to the study of the Scottish pistol is contained in his *Treatise on Scottish Hand Firearms*, which appeared as a supplement to Jackson's *European Hand Firearms of the Sixteenth, Seventeenth and Eighteenth Centuries*, published in 1923. Thus, at the time of writing, there is no book devoted in its entirety to the Scottish pistol, leaving a large gap in our knowledge which should be filled, both for the sake of completeness and to the benefit of students and collectors.

Thus, more than seventy years after the publication of the *Treatise*, in order to produce a book worthy of the adjective 'definitive', it would be necessary to trace the development of the Scottish pistol from its earliest days, arising as it did in response to a demand from the Scottish people for a robust and flamboyant weapon, elegant yet functionally adequate and place it in its correct historical context. Consideration would have to be given to overseas trading from the Scottish east coast ports, by reference to shipping lists of the time, as well as to the industry, commerce and natural resources of Scotland itself, which determined the manufacture of the weapon. Finally, the study would not be complete without a detailed analysis of the weapons known to exist, both with reference to the different types and styles of the pistol and, lastly, the hammermen themselves, who produced the pistols in their primitive workshops in Doune and the coastal towns of east Scotland.

To write such a book, there have been many people and institutions I have had recourse to in a variety of ways and to whom acknowledgement is due. Firstly I would like to thank the following institutions for providing me with photographs of items in their collections: Glasgow Museums: Art Gallery and Museum, Kelvingrove; Historisches Museum, Dresden, Germany; Marischal Museum, University of Aberdeen; Musée d'Art et d'Histoire, Neuchatel, Switzerland; National Museums of Scotland, Edinburgh; Perth and Kinross District Council, Museum & Art Galleries Dept; Scottish National Portrait Gallery; The Board of Trustees of the Royal

Armouries. A work of this kind would not be complete without illustrations of the rarer examples of Scottish pistols, generally to be found only in museums, and the above institutions willingly provided these, and gave me every encouragement in pursuing my researches.

Several museums went even further, in permitting me to handle and photograph, if required, their entire collection of Scottish pistols, and I should like to acknowledge these separately. They were: Angus District Libraries and Museums Service; Art Gallery and Museum, Glasgow; Dundee Art Gallery and Museum; Inverness Museum and Art Gallery; Marischal Museum, University of Aberdeen; Smith Art Gallery and Museum, Stirling; West Highland Museum, Fort William. It is heartening and very gratifying to find that institutions of this kind are prepared to go to such lengths in order to further research into objects which, after all, form only a tiny part of their total collections. In particular I would like to record my gratitude to the staff of Glasgow, Inverness and Montrose Museums who endured my repeated photographic sessions with good grace and humour, dismantling display cases and giving up their valuable time on my behalf. All of these sessions were enjoyable as well as rewarding.

I am also deeply indebted to the many friends who allowed me access to their collections, and permitted me to examine and photograph individual items, and to reproduce them amongst the illustrations. My thanks are also freely given to the many libraries I visited during my researches, particularly the National Library of Scotland, which provided photocopies of several relevant manuscripts, the library of the Royal Armouries, John Rylands Library, Manchester, and Aberdeen University Library, as well as my local libraries in Stockport and Castle Douglas. Last but not least, I willingly acknowledge that without the unfailing support and active encouragement of my wife, Frances, this manuscript would never have been completed.

THE SCOTTISH PISTOL

Introduction

THE SCOTTISH PISTOL, DESPITE THE ROMANCE AND mystery with which it is enshrouded, cannot be regarded as the most important weapon in the Highlander's not inconsiderable armamentarium. This position undoubtedly belonged to the magnificent basket-hilted broadsword which he wore at his left hip, complemented by the dirk suspended from his waistbelt. These were the principal weapons on which the Highlander relied in battle. His pistols, with their limited range, must have been a second line of offence or defence, to be employed as the occasion demanded, whether due to restrictions of space precluding the use of the broadsword or for reasons which were purely opportunistic in nature.

The English footsoldier, commonly referred to as a Redcoat, was not equipped with pistols, his principal weapon being, from about 1715 onwards, the Brown Bess, a smoothbore musket which could be fired with its bayonet attached. Only the officers were equipped with pistols. Dragoons also carried pistols, a pair of 12″ Dragoon flintlocks, worn in saddle holsters slung across the horse's neck. Only the officers and men of the Highland regiments and the kilted militiamen from Argyll and else-where, wore the traditional Scottish pistol.

The Highlander, then, had a distinct advantage over the vast majority of his adversaries, although the claymore itself proved to be no match

INTRODUCTION

against the Brown Bess with fitted bayonet, as he found to his cost during the ill-fated Battle of Culloden.

While it is certainly true that the Scottish pistol is, in a sense, unique, it is nevertheless hardly surprising that a particular country should be associated with a specific type and design of pistol. The experienced collector of antique weapons can recognise, in many cases, pistols of French, Belgian, German, Dutch, Spanish, Italian, Turkish, American, Russian and even Japanese origin, since each of these countries has a particular style and design of pistol which appeals most to its national taste. Just as in any country there exists a preference for certain types of art, furniture, music, literature and even architecture, which is very often peculiar to that country alone, so this nationalistic preference is reflected in its choice of pistol.

French pistols, for example, have chiselled steelwork and much inlay of silver wire into the wooden stocks, a preference shared by the Italians, whose chiselled steelwork and furniture were even more elaborate. The Russians, on the other hand, displayed a preference, at one stage, for pistols sporting a large ivory pommel, whilst the Spaniards chose pistols fitted with micquelet locks, which had external mainsprings. Dutch pistols sometimes had stocks carved from ivory, the butt being in the shape of a warrior's head.

In the pistol originating in Albania, the so-called 'rat-tail' pistol, we see for the first time a pistol which approximates most closely to the Scottish pistol in many respects. It, too, is constructed of brass and steel, usually of thin texture covering a wooden stock. The brass and steelwork are engraved and silver ornamentation and even semi-precious stones, may be applied. The Albanian pistol can, like its Scottish counterpart, be seen as a badge of office for its wearer, at once a symbol of his status and authority.

Neither was the manufacture of a pistol entirely from metal the sole prerogative of the Scottish gunmakers, since all-steel pistols of German origin are not uncommon and Belgian as well as English makers also produced pistols fabricated entirely of steel. Taking the question of recognition a stage further, the experienced collector can sometimes identify not only the country of origin of a particular pistol, but also the pistol-maker himself, by virtue of a thorough knowledge of his individual idiosyncrasies in style and design. In this way, the skilled collector may identify the pistols of Keuchenreuter in Germany, Boutet in France and perhaps Rigby in

Ireland, whilst collectors of English pistols can sometimes identify more readily, the work of Mortimer, Wogdon, Egg, or Manton. Scottish pistols are no different in this respect and the discerning collector can soon identify specimens by Alexander and John Campbell, John Stuart, James McKenzie, Thomas Murdoch and one or more members of the Caddell dynasty of gunsmiths.

Thus we are able to put Scottish pistols into their proper perspective. They were selected by national choice as being the weapons most desirable and pleasing to those interested in acquiring and using them. Scotland, as will be shown, was a very warlike nation and the male population was in arms throughout the seventeenth and half of the eighteenth centuries, the period with which we are principally concerned. In addition, there was a strong mercenary tradition there and thousands of Scots fought as such in foreign wars, particularly with the army of Gustavus Adolphus of Sweden during the Thirty Years' War. Thus, there was a great demand for arms and, because of the very nature of Scottish warfare, robust arms were essential.

Pistols, during the matchlock era, were not at all practical, especially for use on horseback. Yet even in the mid-seventeenth century, most footsoldiers were still armed with matchlock muskets and this was certainly true, as will be shown, of the Covenant army. With the advent of the wheellock, however, pistols became a practical proposition for the first time and the cavalry, or horse dragoons, were often armed with a brace of pistols.

There is no evidence for the manufacture of wheellock pistols in Scotland and, indeed, the Scots preferred to use flintlocks, or at least snaphaunces (the earliest form of the flintlock) and declared so in 1668, when the Marquis of Atholl protested against arming the Perthshire Highlanders with matchlocks, as they were "altogether unacquainted with the use of any other gunne but fyrelocks".[1] Thus it must be assumed, that in all references to pistols in Scotland, it is invariably flintlocks which are being described, either snaphaunces until about the third quarter of the seventeenth century and true flintlocks after that date.

Consideration must now be given to the possible factors which influenced the Scots in adopting a pistol constructed almost always of metal rather than wood. There is no doubt that the guerrilla-type warfare which the Highlander preferred, demanded that his pistols stand up to very rough usage. The skirmishes in which the clansman habitually indulged, were fiercely-fought, hand to hand engagements, involving the use of dirk, broadsword and pistols and some damage to these weapons was almost inevitable. It was of great importance, therefore, that his pistols were able to withstand this hard usage and metallic construction was of great advantage. The outdoor life led by the Highlander increased the likelihood of damage to wooden-stocked pistols and this may have been an additional factor.

As later chapters explain, Scotland was deficient in forestry, even in the fourteenth century and a policy for the preservation of existing forests was in operation even at that time. Much of Scotland, as in England, had been denuded of timber and reference to the shipping lists of the time tells us that huge quantities were being imported, at enormous cost, from Norway and Sweden. The few wooden-stocked pistols to have survived to the present day, are stocked in 'brasil', or Brazil wood and perhaps rosewood, both of which had to be imported from South America.

This lack of available wood for gunstocks could well have been another factor influencing the Scots in determining the choice of metal rather than wood, in the construction of the Scottish pistol. Although iron also had to be imported in quantity in the early years of the gunmaking industry in Scotland, smelting of indigenous iron-ore deposits did take place on a small scale, until the establishment in the late eighteenth century of the ironworks at Falkirk, Furnace, and Taynuilt in Argyll. The more readily available iron in these critical early years of the gunmaking industry in Scotland may well have initiated the use of this material in the fabrication of gunstocks, establishing a trend which later became a national preference.

Yet another factor was that the gunmaking industry was in the hands of the hammermen themselves. Since the men of the Hammerman Craft worked in metal, it was natural that they would wish to employ the medium which they were most familiar.

Lastly, the exotic nature of the weapon, with its flamboyant and extravagant appearance, was appealing to the eye of the clansman. Like himself, it, too, was rugged, tough and unyielding and had to be equally capable of withstanding the hard usage to which it was subjected.

We now come to the vexed question as to which country had the greatest influence on the design of the Scottish pistol. This is one of the imponderable questions regarding the Scottish pistol which may never be satisfactorily answered. It has been possible to formulate the likely reasons why metal was chosen in preference to wood in the construction of the Scottish pistol, but to determine which country influenced the Scottish gunsmiths more than any other, is a much more difficult problem. Whitelaw believed that the Low Countries provided the model for the early Scottish gunsmiths, perhaps basing the idea on the fact that Scotland enjoyed extensive trade with Holland in the seventeenth and eighteenth centuries. However, when we examine Dutch pistols in detail, we find that there are few points of comparison between them and those of Scotland sufficient to substantiate Whitelaw's theory. A few examples of Dutch locks have cocks of flattened section, resembling, to some extent, the cocks of the early Scottish snaphaunce lock and sometimes one comes across an example of a Dutch snaphaunce lock which has a fence to the pan. However, the fence, in these cases, is usually either shell-shaped, or a round disc of convex section, bearing little resemblance to the round or hexagonal fence, of typically flat section, which is found in the Scottish snaphaunce lock. Also, although the snaphaunce lock itself was at one time believed to have originated in the Netherlands, there is little evidence that such locks existed there before 1600 and much earlier examples of this type of lock are known in Scotland, England and in Scandinavia.[2] These Dutch locks are clearly of later design than the Scottish locks and it seems much more likely that the Scottish pistol influenced the development of the Dutch lock.

No country had a monopoly on pistol design. For example, lemon-butt pistols of Dutch origin are known to exist, heart-butt pistols of French origin and even lobe-butt pistols of Belgian origin. In addition, individual customers could express a preference for a particular design of stock, which could then be manufactured by the gunmaker. This factor could account for a few odd-looking pistols which are occasionally encountered and to which it is difficult to ascribe a country of origin. The practice of restocking old weapons can be another confusing factor for the student or researcher.

Eaves has published details of another group of snaphaunce pistols, which he considers to be English and which resemble Scottish pistols more closely than those of any other country, having belt hooks and distinctive ball triggers, but lacking triggerguards.[3] The muzzles are moulded, much in the manner of the earliest Scottish pistols and the barrels have similar broad barrel bands. The lockplates and barrels are of brass and the lock terminals, in three of the four pistols, resemble monster heads, a feature thought to denote early English-made locks. Two of these pistols, which are displayed in the Palazzo Ducale in Venice, have fishtail butts, the remaining two having ball pommels. If Eaves's view is correct, Scottish pistols have more in common with English pistols of the period, than those of any other country, not at all having regard to decoration or lock style, but in respect of ball triggers, barrels and belt hooks. However, the locks of these pistols seem to bear more resemblance to the Dutch snaphaunce, rather than the Scottish and it could be argued that these pistols were to some extent influenced by the Scottish pistol, rather than the other way around.

It is also an inescapable fact that Scottish pistols bear a distinct resemblance to those of German origin, in several respects. Firstly, German-made wheellocks of all-metal construction are not infrequently encountered. Secondly, the fishtail butt is another feature of many wheellock pistols manufactured in Germany, some of which have all-metal stocks. The Scottish fishtail-butt pistol could easily have been inspired by this type of pistol, since Scotland traded extensively with Germany in the sixteenth and seventeenth centuries. Next, the lemon butt of the later Scottish pistols can be seen to be a natural development from the large round pommel of the German wheellock pistol, which became narrow and elongated, to give it its distinctive form and lemon-butt pistols of German origin are in existence.

It can be argued therefore that Scottish pistols have more in common with those of German origin than of any other country. It must, however, be realised, that a multiplicity of influences was responsible for the eventual adoption of a particular style of pistol by any one country. All nations with whom trade was established must have had some influence on pistol design and this would account for certain similarities occurring between pistols of one country and another.

Whatever the nature of these influences, the Scottish gunmakers produced a weapon which was different from all others made anywhere in the world. It had its own particular style of lock, uniquely decorated. The stocks, too, developed their own particular and distinctive butt shapes, while even the barrels evolved into a characteristic shape and style. The entire pistol was inlaid, usually in silver but sometimes in gold and engraved in a quite characteristic fashion.

This, then, is the origin of the Scottish pistol. Its features developed quite naturally by a process of evolution, a process which allowed it to emerge in the form in which we see it today, wholly and undeniably Scottish.

PART ONE

Historical Background

CHAPTER ONE

The History of Scotland

THE STORY OF THE SCOTTISH PISTOL IS INEXTRICABLY bound up with the history of Scotland itself. While it is neither feasible nor practical to attempt to condense such a turbulent period of Scottish history of nearly two hundred and fifty years into a few pages, it is nevertheless crucial to our understanding of the character, customs and way of life of the people who owned and used the Scottish pistol, that we have some knowledge of that history.

And turbulent indeed was life in Scotland at the end of the sixteenth century. James VI of Scotland, later to become James I of England and the son of Mary Queen of Scots, was on the throne. It was during his reign that the massacre of 200 Colquhoun clansmen took place, in 1603 at Glenfruin on the banks of Loch Lomond, an act which led to the proscription of the name MacGregor and the annihilation of anyone bearing that name.

Charles I was, like James, Scottish by birth but a confirmed Anglican. He attempted to change the Prayer Book in Scotland, so enraging the common people that when the Bishop of Brechin took services, he did so with a pair of loaded pistols laid in front of him, in full sight of the congregation.[1] We can confidently assume that these weapons were all-metal Scottish snaphaunce pistols, or dags, having lemon butts in the manner of those made by James Low or James Gray, both gunmakers in Dundee.

Nevertheless, it must have been as startling a sight then as it would be today, for a minister of religion to preach a sermon with a Bible in his hands and his pistols laid on the pulpit before him.

The seeds had been sown from which the Covenant would grow and with it, one of the blackest periods in Scottish history. The Covenanters were a group of strict Scottish Presbyterians, rigid in principle, living mainly in the Southwest of the country, to whom the tenets of Episcopalianism were absolute anathema. Thousands flocked to sign a Declaration, or Covenant, setting out their objections in detail, amongst them the Dukes of Montrose and Argyle. Montrose, however, soon changed his allegiance and raised an army of Highlanders, sending out the Fiery Cross over glen and mountain, to summon the clansmen to his standard and gaining victories over the Covenanters at Tippermuir, near Perth and again at the Battle of Kilsyth. He was finally defeated by a superior force under General David Leslie, at Philliphaugh, on the banks of the Ettrick and forced into exile. After the death of Charles, Montrose returned to Scotland in support of his son, Charles II, but was betrayed and captured. He was hanged, beheaded and quartered, in the barbaric manner of the time, in 1649.

Oliver Cromwell's army now invaded Scotland. The city of Dundee was walled at that time, so that many of the citizens of Edinburgh and other Scottish towns had sent their most valuable effects there for security and, indeed, many noblemen had taken refuge in the town, under the protection of its Governor, Major Sir Robert Lumsden of Bewhannie. In 1651, the town was stormed and Sir Robert and a few friends retired into the old church, which they defended for three days, "with sword and pistol", but were at last obliged to surrender, on promise of quarter for the Governor and his companions. General Monk, who had led the seige, nevertheless gave orders to execute the defenders and around 1300 men and 200 women were put to death. Monk had promised his soldiers the pillage of the town for twenty-four hours, of which they took full advantage, stripping the houses of £200,000 sterling in "bullion, silver plate, jewels, rings and watches and other precious things belonging to the town of Edinburgh—the best plunder of any gotten in the wars throughout the three nations."[2] After the sack of Dundee and the defeat of the Scottish army, Cromwell became Lord Protector.

There followed a period of relative calm, but rumours had begun to spread of enormous conventicles of armed Covenanters gathering in south-west Scotland, in order to hold religious services. Lauderdale, who was the King's representative in Scotland, decided to raise a vast army of Highlanders, in order to identify and eliminate the 'malcontent' Covenanters. This was the so-called 'Highland Host', raised in January 1678. It was given unprecedented powers in the execution of its duty: ". . . to take free quarter, to seize upon horses as deemed necessary". The Highlanders were given "complete indemnity against any action, civil or criminal, which might be brought up for any offence committed in the King's service by killing, wounding, apprehending or imprisoning such as shall make opposition to our authority, or by seizing such as they have reason to suspect . . ."[3]

The Highland Host of 1678 was composed of Highlanders, regulars and militia and comprised 7224 infantry and 750 horse, the latter being armed with pistols as well as swords.[4] The footsoldiers were armed with muskets, whose mechanism was matchlock, 'snapwork' being expressly forbidden, but it is likely that the Highlanders amongst them were armed with snaphaunces and flintlocks, since the Marquis of Athol in 1668 had vigorously protested against the more primitive matchlocks, stating that the Perthshire Highlanders were "altogether unacquainted with the use of any other gunne but fyrelocks".[5] Elder goes on to say that the matter had been referred to the King, but no clear decision had been reached. It is, however, highly improbable that the Highlanders would agree to adopt a musket which was both inferior and unfamiliar.

On the pretext of searching for arms and interrogating suspects, the clansmen devastated the Lowland countryside, stealing and plundering from innocents and malcontents alike and subjecting the entire populace to humiliation and violence. The Lowlanders adopted an attitude of passive resistance, but by the time that the clansmen returned to their homes the following April, the bitterness engendered by their brief but violent sojourn in the Lowlands had caused such a hardening of feeling, that the consequences would be to make the ensuing conflict of even greater acrimony. It was said that "many a man with but two cows, was eager to sell one of them for a pair of pistols."[6]

After the departure of the Highland Host, bitter battles were fought between the Covenanters and Government troops. At Drumclog in 1679, the Covenanters routed a superior force under the command of Graham of Claverhouse and later the Duke of Monmouth inflicted a heavy defeat on the Covenant army at the Battle of Bothwell Brig. In the same year, James Sharp, Archbishop of St Andrews and the highest prelate in Scotland, was murdered in broad daylight only a short distance from the town itself, by a party of Covenanters, who within a few months had paid the ultimate penalty for their action.[7] Known Covenanters were persecuted or shot. Both Graham of Claverhouse, later Viscount Dundee, and Grierson of Lag, were notorious for their harsh and callous treatment of the Covenanters during the 'killing times' of the 1680s.

Following the death of Charles II, James VII became King, but subsequently fled the country with the arrival on Scottish shores of William of Orange. Supporters of James became known as Jacobites, a name with romantic associations that was to have dire consequencies for its followers. Dundee raised an army to defeat William and at the Pass of Killiecrankie, the site of the famous Soldier's Leap, when an escaping Redcoat leapt across the stream to safety, Government troops under General Mackay were routed, although Dundee himself was killed. Following the victory at Killiecrankie in 1689, the highland army failed to take the town of Dunkeld, guarded by a regiment of Cameronians and retired with their booty to their homes. Defeated the following year at the Battle of the Boyne, James was forced into exile.

With James in France, all the Highland chiefs were enjoined to take an Oath of Allegiance to King William, by 31 December 1691 at the latest. All but a few took the Oath, but one in particular, the elderly MacIan Macdonald of Glencoe, laird of a small but troublesome sept of the Macdonalds, waited until virtually the last minute before appearing in Inverary on 31 December. Finding no-one there who could officiate, it was another six days before Macdonald could make his Oath of Allegiance. It was decided to make an example of the Macdonalds, and MacIan in particular, and an order was despatched on 12 February 1692 to Robert Campbell of Glenlyon, heading a detachment of Campbell troops who were in the meantime enjoying the hospitality of the Macdonalds. The orders, signed by Major Duncanson read as follows:

> for the good and safty of the Country . . . you are hereby ordered to fall
> upon the Rebells, the McDonalds of Glenco and putt all to the sword
> under seventy. You are to have a speciall care that the old ffox and his
> sonds doe upon no account escape your hands . . . ffeb 12 1692 [8]

On the morning of 13 February, the Campbells fell upon their unsuspecting hosts, killing forty of their number and scattering the remainder into the hills, where many more were to die of cold or starvation. This incident is now known as the Massacre of Glencoe.

The death of Queen Anne in 1714 left the way open for James's heir, known as the Pretender and his Jacobite supporters, to press his claim to the throne. Many of the Scottish clans, including the Camerons, Macleans and Macdonalds, rushed to his standard, which was raised by the Earl of Mar. The latter was ill-equipped to lead an army in rebellion and after the battle of Sheriffmuir, which both sides claimed as a victory, the Jacobite forces surrendered at Preston and the rebellion of 1715 was over. James Francis Edward fled firstly to France and later took up residence in Italy. A second rebellion in 1719 met with a similar fate.

On 23 July 1745, Prince Charles Edward Stuart, the Pretender's eldest son, landed with seven companions, but with very little in the way of arms and supplies, at Eriskay and set up his standard at Glenfinnan, on the shores of Loch Shiel. Despite the absence of a supporting army of French troops, many of the clan leaders were persuaded to join the cause, including Cameron of Lochiel and the Stewart of Ardshiel, as well as the clansmen of the Macdonalds of Keppoch, Glengarry and Clanranald.

The Highland army, consisting by now of 1500 men, marched to Perth and, having captured the city, advanced on Edinburgh and took possession of the capital. An English army, led by General Sir John Cope, was routed at Prestonpans, then known as Gladsmuir.

Charles delayed too long in Edinburgh, before crossing the Border and advancing towards London. By the time he had reached Derby, many of his Highlanders, pining for their native glens and unwilling to march any further into England, had returned to Scotland with their booty, leaving his army seriously depleted. Reinforcements from the ranks of the English and Welsh Jacobites failed to materialise and Lord George Murray, son of the exiled Duke of Atholl and Lieutenant-General of the Prince's army, advised the Prince to return to Scotland and this he reluctantly agreed to, knowing that several armies were building up against him. At Falkirk, another battle was fought against English forces and although the English army was once more put to flight, the Scots failed to capitalise on their victory, allowing their enemies to escape relatively unscathed. Their generosity was to prove their undoing.

The Duke of Cumberland advanced to meet Charles's army at Drummossie Moor, near Nairn. The ground was eminently unsuited to the Highland army's tactics in battle, being uneven and boggy. In addition, shortage of food and supplies meant that the army was starving and many of the Highlanders, it has been noted, were without targes. Further, much of the Highland army was scattered and neither the Macphersons, under Cluny, nor the Grants of Glenmoriston, had received the summons in time. A large body of Frasers was still awaited and, in all, only about five thousand men, out of a possible seven or eight thousand were on the field.

In an effort to surprise the Duke of Cumberland, it was decided by the Prince's generals to launch a night attack on Cumberland's army, camped about ten miles away. Two columns of men set out, but, due to the difficulties in travelling at night over unfamiliar ground, they failed to reach the encampment before a call to muster and had to return to their own lines, exhausted and starving.

Opposing the clansmen were not only regular and pressed redcoated dragoons of Cumberland's army, but the Campbell militiamen from Argyll, for long in the Government service in Scotland. The battle lasted a mere sixty minutes and, despite the heroic efforts of the clansmen, ended in a complete rout of Charles' army. The Chevalier himself was almost killed during the battle. When it was over, the Redcoats systematically butchered and stripped the clansmen who lay wounded in the field. Harsh treatment was also meted out to any suspected of having taken part in the battle.

After five months in hiding, travelling with a few loyal companions in conditions of appalling depredation, the Prince escaped at last to France, accompanied by Lochiel and others of his generals, several of whom were later appointed to high positions in French and other foreign armies.

Following the defeat of Bonnie Prince Charlie, there occurred a massive and relentless recriminatory campaign against the clans. Any man who had been 'out' in the '45 was either shot on sight, beheaded, hanged or imprisoned. If he was fortunate, he might be sent to the Plantations for seven years, that is, if he survived the journey there. Any clan chief who had fought in the ranks of the 'rebels', had his estates forfeited and, often, his castle put to the torch. Those suspected of Jacobite allegiance were enjoined to take the following oath:

> I, _____ , do swear and as I shall have to answer to God at the Great Day of Judgement, I have not nor shall have in my possession, any gun, sword, pistol, or arm whatsoever; and never use any tartan, plaid, or any part of the Highland garb; and if I do so, may I be cursed in my under-takings, family and property – may I never see my wife and children, father, mother and relations – may I be killed in battle as a coward and lie without Christian burial, in a strange land, far from the graves of my forefathers and kindred; may all of this come across me if I breck my oath.[9]

The landscape was denuded by what would today be called a scorched earth policy. Crops and homes were burned, cattle impounded and prop-erty and land confiscated. The Disarming Act of 1746 imposed severe penal-ties for bearing or concealing arms, as well as for wearing the kilt, or any other tartan garment. Houses where arms were found were burned to the ground. If found concealed underground, all adjacent fields and houses were to be destroyed. The penalties were six months imprisonment for a first offence, seven years transportation for a second.

In Inverness, following the Battle of Culloden on Drummossie Moor, an illicit trade in contraband by the soldiers, resulted in the open sale of "all manner of plaids, broadswords, dirks and pistols . . . "[10] When the renowned Scottish poet Duncan MacIntire, a man who had fought against the Highlanders at the Battle of Falkirk, denounced the Government for its Proscription Act in a poem, he was immediately committed to prison.[11] The Act was partially repealed in 1782 and was only fully repealed in 1867.

As might be expected, the result of the Disarming Act was to deal a severe blow to the gunmaking industry in Scotland and, most importantly, to that area most commonly associated with the manufacture of Scottish pistols, namely, the village of Doune, in Perthshire. The Disarming Act of 1715, after the first Jacobite rebellion, had resulted in the surrender of a large number of rusty, obsolete and useless weapons. It appears that intelligence reports received after the 1745 rebellion indicated that precisely the same thing was happening again, throughout the Highland region and that the clansmen were holding their serviceable arms in readiness for another rebellion, with French assistance, long after the '45 was over. A report from Campbell of Airds to Lord Albemarle in 1746 reads: "They have still plenty of arms for, when they surrendered, they gave up some rusty, useless arms and still left the good fresh arms".[12] There was, of course, still a demand for weapons in the Lowlands and in the towns of the east coast, sustained in the main by the need to equip the officers and men of the Highland regiments, but gunmaking in Scotland was never again to achieve the prominence it had enjoyed before the outbreak of the '45 rebellion.

Many of those who had fought for the Pretender at Culloden escaped to become mercenaries in foreign armies and it is partly for this reason that examples of Scottish pistols are to be found in such collections as the Tojhusmuseum in Copenhagen, Livrustkammer in Stockholm and Skokloster Castle, also in Sweden. Following the formation of the Highland regiments, many Scots were fighting abroad. Scottish soldiers had a long tradition of service as mercenaries in foreign armies and the Kings of France, for example, had had a Scottish company in their bodyguard since 1440.[13]

During the Thirty Years' War, from 1618 to 1648, a large number of Scots fought in the army of the Swedish king, Gustavus Adolphus and by the end of the 1620s, the number had risen to 20,000 men. The Black Watch, originally the 43rd Regiment but later renamed the 42nd Regiment of the Line, was formed in 1740, fighting at Fontenoy and also saw service in England during the '45. Between 1749 and 1755, the regiment served in Ireland and in 1756 was sent to America to fight in the Seven Years' War. During this period as many as twelve thousand Highlanders were enlisted.[14]

Scottish lairds, anxious to regain estates forfeited during the 1745 rebellion, raised regiments in the service of the King. Fraser's Highlanders, the 71st, and Montgomeries Highlanders, the 77th, were formed in this way. Both regiments saw action in the Cherokee Rising of 1759. Keith's

Highlanders and Campbell's Highlanders, the 87th and 88th respectively, were yet more newly formed Highland regiments. In India, both Fraser's Highlanders and the 89th Regiment were in action. The 73rd Highlanders, later the Highland Light Infantry, was raised in 1777. In 1783, the Scottish Borderers fought at the seige of Gibraltar and in 1794 a regiment was formed which later became the Argyll and Sutherland Highlanders.

As related elsewhere, the Scottish pistol fell into disuse, from a military standpoint, around 1788 and after that time was no longer issued to the Highland regiments. Nevertheless, it is likely that the officers continued to supply their own all-steel Scottish flintlock pistols, even as late as the Napoleonic Wars, as many of the later flintlocks incorporated features as worthy as any offered by their English counterparts and had the added advantage of greater artistic beauty, arousing, no doubt, much-deserved admiration from their brother officers.

Many young Scotsmen were sent out to India for a few years, serving in the East India Company and such young officers would proudly sport their percussion dress pistols, worn with full Highland dress at mess parties or balls, but it is unlikely that many of these were ever fired in anger.

One last incident which must be related is that of the famous Appin murder, when Colin Campbell, factor on the forfeited estate of Ardsheall (Ardshiel), was ambushed in a wood near Ballachorlith (Ballachuillish), and fell, mortally wounded, from his horse. James Stuart of Aucharn was apprehended for the murder and was later hanged, on the eighth of November, 1752. He himself did not fire the fatal shot, but was believed to have instigated the killing. It has never been determined who the real killer was and this has become one of the great highland mysteries, but many believe that the assassin was a man named Allan Brech.[15] The incident was immortalised by Robert Louis Stevenson in *Kidnapped!*

CHAPTER TWO

The Highlander and the Clan System

SINCE THE GREAT MAJORITY OF THE SCOTTISH PISTOLS which have survived until the present day were originally the proud possessions of the Highland clansmen, it is of some importance to the collector and student of these handsome weapons to have some understanding of the clan system and, through this, of the clansmen themselves.

The power and land ownership in the Highlands were vested in the clan chieftains or lairds, to whom the land belonged by ancestral right. This land and, indeed, the cattle it sustained, belonged to the chieftain himself, although he could permit his sons and close members of his family to use parts of the ancestral land in order to set up their own households and so form "cadet" branches. In addition, sections of clan land were leased or rented to certain privileged individuals, who were known as 'tacksmen'. In the event of war or feuds between the clans, these tacksmen would become junior officers, lieutenants, ensigns or sergeants. Tacksmen could, in their turn, rent a portion of their land to 'humblies', who were the ordinary folk at the lower end of the social stratum.

The clan piper, a personage of great importance, would be entitled to land of his own, as would the bard. Both of these played a privileged role in clan life, the bard being the entertainer, who would relate the clan's heroic ancestry, while the piper would perform his pibrochs. The latter's post was usually hereditary, succeeding generations of pipers playing before the Laird of the time. Another important member of the clan, who was also entitled to a grant of land from the chief, was the bladier or spokesman, of the chief, who would advise the chieftain on legal and military matters.

Every clan also had its own armourer, who was an important member of the clan community, holding a position of high rank. A special farm was allotted to him and these may still be traced by the name given to them, 'Baile a ghobainn' or 'Smith's town.'[1] Yet another hereditary office was that of standard-bearer. The chieftain would always lead his clansmen into battle, whilst the piper would play his pipes immediately behind.

It is implied that the chief was a man of great bravery and while it is true that the clan would not admire cowardice from its chief, succession was normally through the eldest son. 'Clann' is the Gaelic word for children and the clansmen followed their chief whatever the consequences, believing that they were ultimately descended from the same common ancestor.

Edward Burt, an Englishman who accompanied General Wade to the Highlands in the early eighteenth century in his capacity as engineer employed in the construction of the roads for which Wade is renowned, wrote a commentary on the Highlanders and their way of life in his *Letters from a Gentleman* published in 1754. He described the attitude of the ordinary clansman towards his chief:

> The ordinary Highlanders esteem it the most sublime degree of virtue to love their chief and pay him a blind obedience, although it be in opposition to the government, the laws of the kingdom or even to the law of God.[2]

Samuel Johnson, visiting the Highlands in 1773, put it this way:

> The inhabitants of mountains form distinct races and are careful to preserve their genealogies. Men in a small district necessarily mix blood by intermarriages and combine at last into one family, with a common interest in the honour and disgrace of every individual. Then begins that union of affection and co-operation of endeavours, that constitutes a clan.[3]

Strangely enough, the men of a particular clan did not necessarily bear the same surname and, in fact, surnames were not in general use in the

Highlands before the seventeenth century, patronyms being much in evidence before that time, i.e. Mac = son of, Macdonald = son of Donald, MacGregor = son of Gregor.[4] As the use of the surname became more popular, clansmen who accepted the protection and authority of the chief often adopted his surname.

The Laird himself was an educated man, whose children were themselves educated in the Lowlands or even in France. He wore the finest clothes and lived with his lady in the castle he built to defend his domain. He dined on venison from the deer which he hunted on his own land and drank freely of the finest imported French wines. Although he considered himself and was indeed considered by members of his own clan as a gentleman and a man of honour, he was at the same time capable of the cruellest and most barbaric behaviour. He was ruthless when provoked, especially towards neighbouring clans with whom he might have a blood feud or even with errant members of his own clan.

War between the clans was a common feature of clan life. Cattle thieving and daring raids into enemy territory, with pillaging, burning and looting, were a regular occurrence. In times of great emergency, however, a Gathering of the Clans would take place, when a 'fiery cross' was carried from glen to glen, to each remote sept of the clan, inviting their attendance at a proscribed clan meeting place. Thus, in 1689 the fiery cross was carried at the behest of Graham of Claverhouse, in order to raise an army against William of Orange, when a huge gathering of Camerons, Macdonalds, McLeans, McNeils and many others, took place at Mucomir, on the shores of Loch Lochy. In 1745, the fiery cross was sent out, probably for the last time, when Lord Glenorchy raised his clan against the Jacobites.[5]

All members of the clan, whether the sons of the chief or the humblie in his tiny windowless hovel, were proud and haughty men, sensitive to a degree regarding their honour and position and ready to defend them at a moment's notice.

The Lairds themselves and their kinsmen, could naturally afford the finest weapons and this can be confirmed, as will be shown, by a study of contemporary paintings. As far as the chieftains were concerned, their pistols were much more than mere firearms. They were badges of office, analogous to the *fasces* or axe, carried before the consul or magistrate in

Roman times, symbolic of the power vested in these authorities. The chiefs were inordinately proud of their pistols and their portraits reveal this in dramatic fashion, since they are rarely depicted unarmed. Frequently a single pistol is worn, rather than a pair and usually such pistols are scroll-butted and extensively inlaid with silver in flamboyant manner.

It is likely that tacksmen and other officers of the clan vied with one another regarding the quality and decoration of their own pistols, but even the ordinary clansmen must have regarded the acquisition of one or, better still, a pair, of Scottish pistols, as a mark of distinction.

It should be remembered that the clansman was a man of war, who had to be ready at all times to defend his property or go into battle behind his chief. While the most important items in these affrays were his target, his broadsword and his dirk, a pair of pistols was an invaluable asset which could be employed at a sudden call to action or even as a weapon of last resort. As a status symbol, the pistols must have had no equal.

That the ordinary clansman carried pistols is shown by a pamphlet from 1715, giving an account of the quelling of a MacGregor rising:

> [a group of] fourty or fifty stately fellows in their short hose and belted plaids, arm'd each of them with a well fix'd gun on his shoulder, a strong handsome target, with a sharp pointed steel, of about half an ell in length, screw'd into the navel of it, on his left arm, a sturdy claymore by his side and a pistol or two with a durk and a knife on his belt.[6]

Another account of the Highlander is given by Burt:

> When any one of them is armed at all Points, he is loaded with a Target, a Firelock, a heavy Broadsword, a Pistol, Stock and Lock of Iron, a Dirk; and, besides all these, some of them carry a sort of Knife, which they call a Skeen-ochles [*Sgian achlais*] from its being concealed in the Sleeve near the Arm-pit.[7]

According to Keltie, the Highlander's arms consisted of "a dirk with a knife and fork stuck in the side of the sheath and sometimes a spoon, together with a pair of steel pistols."[8] Another interesting description of the Highlander has been provided by an English spy, residing in Glasgow at the time of the Jacobite Rebellion of 1745:

> I lodge in the Gallowgate, so I could discern from my room every Highlander that passed. I stayed in my room the three days the Highland army entered the toon . . . The men are all pretty well armed, There is scarce any but has both gun, sword and pistoll. Some feu have bayonets and some feu targets.[9]

Lindsay of Pitscottie, writing in 1573, says: "Thair weapones ar bowis and dartes, with ane verie broad sword and ane dagger scharp onlie at the on syde."[10] Sacheverell, describing the Highlanders of Mull in 1688, refers to the sporran, which he deemed to be "a large shot pouch, with a pistol and dagger on either side, a target on their backs, a blue bonnet on their heads, in one hand a broadsword and a musket on the other."[11] Another government agent, John Macky, gives his account of Crieff Tryst, a fair held in 1720. Here he met Highland gentlemen, who had "a poinard, knife and fork in one sheath hanging at one side of their belt, their pistol at the other and their snuff mull before, with a great broadsword at their side."[12] Robinson tells us that "as for his arms they consist in a fusil, a broad sword, a dirk or dagger, an Highland pistol all of steel, hung on the other side of his belt, opposite to the dirk and a target."[13]

Grant gives us a characteristically colourful description of the arms of the Highlanders under Montrose:

> Their arms were the claymore, now basket-hilted and the dirk or armpit dagger; a target with a pike in its orb; a pair of steel pistols and frequently a long-barreled Spanish musket; a skene in the right garter was the last weapon to resort to, if under a horse's belly or grappling on the earth with the foe; and in addition to these were still occasionally used the pike and the tremendous Lochaber axe and even the bow and arrow.[14]

To complete this picture of the Highlander's arms, the following is the account of John Campbell, writing in 1752:

> . . . they wear a broad Sword, which they call a Clymore, a stroke of which, delivered from one of their Hands, would be sufficient to chop off the Head of the strongest Champion that ever lived; they wear a Pair of Pistols and a Durk, which resembles a Dagger, intended chiefly for stabbing; this weapon hangs before in a Scabbard, along with a Knife and Fork and a Purse for their Money, which they term a Sparren; next they

have a Large Powder Horn, that they sling across their Shoulders, with a small Belt full of Brass nails; and to finish the Dress, they wear a Target, composed of Leather, Wood and Brass and which is so strong, that no Ball can penetrate it and in the middle of this Target there is a Screw Hole, wherein is fix'd a brass Cup lin'd with Horn, which serves them to drink out of upon Occasion; and in the time of Action it serves for to fix a Bayonet in . . . Thus accoutred, they make a most splendid and glorious Appearance, it being esteemed by all Judges to be the most heroic and majestic habit ever worn by any nation . . .[15]

Duncan Forbes, the Lord President of the Court of Session, whose home was below the battlefield of Culloden, wrote the following in 1746, after the battle had been fought and the Highland army scattered:

What is properly called the Highlands of Scotland is that large tract of mountainous Ground to the Northwest of the Tay, where the natives speak the Irish language [i.e. Gaelic] The inhabitants stick close to their antient and idle way of life; retain their barbarous customs and maxims; depend generally on their Chiefs as their Sovereign Lords and masters; and being accustomed to the use of Arms and innured to hard living, are dangerous to the public peace; and must continue to be so until being deprived of Arms for some years, they forget the use of them.[16]

To the Highlander, his dress or habit, with its brightly coloured tartan plaid and short hose, his bonnet, his *philabeg* or 'little kilt', if he chose to wear one and his buckled brogues, were as much part of his proud heritage as were the heatherclad glens and mountains of his home and it was for this reason that the order was issued before the Battle of Culloden that every man must wear the kilt. It is likely that the early tartans were associated with districts rather than with individual clans, who were distinguished by the clan badges which they wore on their bonnets.

Portraits of the Clan Grant reveal that no two setts were alike, a fact confirmed by other clan portraits. In a dramatic portrait by David Morier of an incident at Culloden, the Highlanders are depicted wearing at least seventeen different tartans, although this may simply be due to artistic licence. Following the Disarming Act, with its concomitant banning of tartan clothes, the survival of the tartan was due, in large measure, to the formation of the Highland regiments. They were allowed to use the proscribed garment resulting in a uniformity of design, each regiment having its own tartan. This uniformity was adopted by the clans when the Act was repealed thirty-six years later.

Just as an appreciation of the clan system provides an insight into the way of life in the highlands in the warlike times of the past, contemporary accounts of the dress worn by the Highlanders is also of great value in establishing, not only the mere fact that pistols were worn, but that they were a significant part of his attire, as ready to hand as his dirk or broadsword. A man so fully armed could be a formidable enemy. Burt, with his ill-concealed bias, described the Highlander's dress:

> The Highland dress consists of a bonnet made of thrums without a brim, a short coat, a waistcoat, short stockings and brogues. Over this habit they wear a plaid, which is usually three yards long and two breadths wide and the whole garb is made of chequered tartan or plaiding; this, with the sword and pistol, is called a full dress . . . The common habit of the Highlander is far from being acceptable to the eye. With them a small part of the plaid which is not so large as the former, is set into folds and girt round the waist to make of it a short petticoat that reaches halfway down the thigh, the rest is brought over the shoulders and fastened before, below the neck often with a fork and sometimes with a bodkin or sharpened piece of stick, so that they make pretty nearly the appearance of the poor women in London when they bring their gowns over their heads to shelter themselves from the rain. This dress is called the quelt and for the most part they wear the petticoat so very short, that in a windy day. Going up a hill or, stooping, the indecency of it is plainly discovered.[17]

Although the common Highlander was attired in the belted plaid described by Burt or in a short philabeg, the Chief himself often wore tartan trousers, known as trews. Stewart of Garth, in his description of the dress of the Black Watch, embodied at Taybridge in 1740, wrote:

> . . . At night the plaid served the purpose of a blanket and was sufficient covering for the Highlander. These were called belted plaids from being kept tight to the body by a belt and were worn on guard, reviews and on all occasions when the men were in full dress. On this belt hung the pistols and dirk when worn.[18]

A common misconception amongst historians describing the Highlanders' conduct of battle, concerns the belief that the clansmen abandoned their kilts and charged into the fight in their shirt-tails, sometimes, depending on the particular account, tying them first, between their legs. This ludicrous notion stems from the wearing of the philabeg or short kilt, in addition to a separate shoulder plaid, which was worn loosely across the shoulders. As the latter was an obvious encumbrance in battle, since it restricted vision and could impede the use of the sword arm, it was consequently abandoned, along with the musket and retrieved after the battle. The belted plaid, on the other hand, so well described by Burt, was a one-piece garment, which was pinned to the shoulder and could consequently be worn during battle without hindrance. Sir Walter Scott explained it in his *Notes on Highland Discipline*:

> There were different modes of disposing the plaid, one when on a peaceful journey, another when danger was apprehended; one way of enveloping themselves in it when expecting undisturbed repose and another which enabled them to start up with sword and pistol in hand on the slightest alarm ...The manner of handling the pistol and dirk was also part of the Highland manual exercise, which the author has seen gone through by men who had learnt it in their youth.[19]

In response to a question put by Bonnie Prince Charlie to a clansman shortly after landing in Scotland, regarding the use of the plaid, the Highlander told him that "In such times of danger during a war we had a different method of using the plaid, that with one spring I could start to my feet with sword drawn and cock'd pistol in my hand without being in the least encumbr'd with my bedcloaths."[20]

The following list itemises the dress and equipment of a Highland chief, as printed in the memoirs of Charles Grant, Vicomte de Vaux, in 1796:

1. A full trimmed bonnet. (Crest, badge and 3 eagle's feathers)
2. A tartan Jacket, vest, kilt and crossbelt.
3. A tartan belted plaid,
4. A tartan pair of hose, made up (of cloth)
5. A tartan pair of stockings, with yellow garters.
6. Two pair of brogues.
7. A silver mounted purse (sporan) and belt.

8. A target, with spear.
9. A broadsword.
10.A pair of pistols, with bullet mould.
11.A dirk with knife, fork and belt.[21]

The observation and study of contemporary portraits of the Highland chieftains and gentry can also give us a great deal of information concerning the Scottish pistol, including the manner in which it was worn, its style at different points in its history and the other arms with which it was associated. It was quite usual, in these times, for the subjects of these vast family portraits to be depicted in martial array, sometimes clad in ancient armour, but more commonly wearing highland dress and carrying their most favoured arms. The pistols may be displayed in several different ways. The commonest method of suspension appears to have been from the waist belt, through which the belt hook is inserted, the exact position being determined by the choice of the wearer. Thus, the pistol may be worn either at the left hip, immediately in front of the sword, as in the painting of the redoubtable James Fraser of Castle Leathers (fig. 1) or close to the opposite hip, as in the painting of Kenneth Sutherland, 3rd Lord Duffus (fig. 2), both of which are in the Scottish National Portrait Gallery. In each case, the sword itself is hung from the swordbelt, which passes over the right shoulder, to permit its use by a right handed swordsman.

When two pistols are worn in the waistbelt, the second may be carried well back, at the right hip, as in the well-known portrait by John Michael Wright of Lord Mungo Murray, 5th son of the Marquis of Athole and now in the Scottish National Portrait Gallery (fig. 3). This painting, from around 1675–80, shows a youthful Lord Murray wearing a broadsword on the left hip, with his dirk worn in a central position, suspended, like his pistols, from the waistbelt. The pistols are early ramshorn dags of the period, having gold prickers, the ramshorns being extravagantly curled into spirals on either side. A powderhorn is suspended from a belt passing over the left shoulder and hanging from the same belt are three conical brass powder measures. Each of these contains an accurately-measured charge of gunpowder, which could then be poured directly down the gunbarrel when reloading. Scottish powderhorns do not usually incorporate any form of spring cut-off, which delivers a specific amount of gunpowder into the

FIG. 1. Portrait of Major James Fraser of Castle Leathers, artist unknown, c. 1715. His pistol is hung from the swordbelt. *On loan to the Scottish National Portrait Gallery from Mrs R. Townshend.*

FIG. 2. Portrait of Kenneth Sutherland, 3rd Lord Duffus, by Richard Waitt, c. 1720.
His pistol is suspended from a concealed waist belt. *Scottish National Portrait Gallery.*

FIG. 3. Portrait of Lord Mungo Murray, by John Michael Wright, c. 1680. Both pistols hang from the waist belt. *Scottish National Portrait Gallery.*

nozzle, unlike most nineteenth-century powder flasks, so that judging the correct amount of powder was somewhat arbitrary. The devices described above represented the first attempt to surmount this problem. Lord Mungo is also carrying a long-barrelled Spanish musket.

In *The Costume of the Clans*, the Stuart brothers describe the wearing of these accoutrements:

> Upon the breast of the belt, in the manner used by the foot-soldiers of all countries, from the sixteenth to the end of the seventeenth century, are suspended three gilt "bandaliers" or measures for holding the powder charge, universal among all harquebusiers and hagbuttiers before the introduction of cartridges and their receptacle the cartouche.[22]

A second method of wearing two pistols can be seen in a portrait of the Duke of Perth, Lieutenant-General of the Highland Army in 1745, which is at Drummond Castle and shows both pistols slipped, one above the other, into the swordbelt. Two paintings by the Victorian artist Robert Ronald McIan depict gentlemen of both the Forbes and Ogilvie clans equipped in this manner. MacIan stated that "The latter are stuck in the swordbelt; rather an unusual mode of carrying them, but an authority is found for it in a portrait at Drummond Castle of James, Duke of Perth, lieutenant-general in the Highland Army of 1745.[23]

In 1845, Robert Ronald McIan published a series of portraits representing the clans of Scotland, with an accompanying text written by James Logan, author of *The Scottish Gael*. This book was dedicated to Queen Victoria and it was no accident that the date of publication coincided with the centenary of the Jacobite Rebellion. The book heralded a massive resurgence of interest in the Scots and Scottish Highlands, which had begun with the writings of Sir Walter Scott, continued with the visit of King George IV to Edinburgh in 1822 and was further enhanced by Queen Victoria's holiday in Scotland in 1842 and the building of Balmoral Castle in 1848.

In some portraits, such as those by McIan of a member of Clan Chisholm and of Campbell of Breadalbane, the pistols are worn much closer together in the waistbelt, although on either side of the belt buckle. Dennis Dighton's famous watercolour of George IV's triumphal visit to Scotland in 1822, also shows the King wearing his pistols in this manner.

The Queen's collection contains another portrait of George IV, by Sir David Wilkie, showing the monarch in highland dress and wearing a different pair of pistols from the ones shown in the Dighton painting. The portrait presents the King armed with gold-mounted pistols, thrust into the waistbelt on either side of the belt buckle. The right pistol has been turned through 180°, kinking the leather belt, in order to point the ramshorn scrolls towards one another, perhaps to make the portrait aesthetically more pleasing. This must have been quite uncomfortable for the sitter, as the pressure exerted by this pistol can be quite clearly seen. In a second version of this portrait, which is in Bowhill in the Scottish borders, the King is

FIG. 4. Portrait of Fearchar Shaw by R. R. McIan. His pistol is worn in the typical military fashion, suspended from a short strap passing over the right shoulder. *Pan Books.*

wearing only his left pistol in his waistbelt, the ramshorn scrolls of his second pistol being visible in the left armpit position. This painting is said to have been presented to the 5th Duke of Buccleuch, when the King was staying at Dalkeith on the occasion of his visit to Scotland in 1822.

This wearing of a pistol in the left armpit position is encountered in other portraits, perhaps the most famous of which is the painting of 1714 of a Grant Piper by Richard Waitt, who painted many Grant family portraits. The pistol worn is a heart-butt and is suspended by a strap passing over the right shoulder. The painting itself, now in the Scottish National Portrait Gallery, formerly hung at Castle Grant, alongside those of the Grant family, indicating, as has already been shown, the elevated status enjoyed by the piper in clan society.

Another McIan portrait (fig. 4) shows the sitter Fearchar Shaw wearing his pistol in the normal manner for a soldier in the Highland regiments, that is, suspended by a short strap passing over the right shoulder, the pistol butt lying comfortably in the left armpit position, a method similar to that adopted by the Grant piper above.

Fearchar Shaw was one of three chosen to be executed for desertion from the Black Watch in 1743. The regiment had been marched to London and it was rumoured that it was to be sent abroad on active service. Shaw and his fellow mutineers attempted to return to Scotland, but were ambushed in a Northamptonshire wood and forced to surrender. McIan produced this work from an older portrait. Logan described the manner of wearing the pistol: "The pistol slung as here shown formed part of the highland arms of this period and those who chose might carry a dirk."[24] Other portraits of gentlemen, mostly officers in Highland Regiments, confirm this particular method of wearing the pistol. These include Hugh Montgomerie, 5th Earl of Eglinton (fig. 5), Charles Campbell of Lochlane and John Murray, 4th Earl of Dunmore.

opposite FIG. 5. Portrait of Hugh Montgomerie, 12th Earl of Eglinton, by J. S. Copley, c. 1760. The Earl is dressed as an officer in his cousin's regiment, the Montgomerie's Highlanders. His pistol is worn in the left armpit position. *Scottish National Portrait Gallery.*

Hugh, 12ᵗʰ Earl of Eglinton

If two pistols were worn, the same short strap was employed, with the first pistol in the left armpit position, the second lying on the left breast. This is confirmed by a portrait by McIan of a Macnab clansman. Other portraits of Scottish officers, such as that of Captain Ewen MacPherson, chief of the Clan MacPherson in 1845, show the two pistols worn in a different manner, one suspended below the left armpit, the second tucked into the waistbelt on the right side of the belt buckle. More commonly, however, the lower pistol was inserted into the left side of the waistbelt.

In some paintings, the personalities concerned are not actually wearing their pistols, which may have been laid down on a rock or table close to the sitter. John Campbell of the Bank is the subject of one such painting and another, the Laird of Cluny Macpherson.

These paintings, as well as all others in which arms are displayed, reveal to us quite clearly the importance of these weapons in the eyes of the owner. Not only are we given an opportunity to study the salient features of all the arms depicted, but also we can understand the portraits' sitters assertion of his possessions and therefore power.

CHAPTER THREE

Weapons Associated with the Scottish Pistol

WHILE WE ARE PRIMARILY CONCERNED IN THIS BOOK with the Scottish pistol *per se*, in order to complete the historical background, some consideration should also be given to the other arms and accoutrements carried in warfare by the clansman, and worn about his person in addition to his pistols.

MUSKET

Few muskets of Scottish manufacture have survived until the present day. They are long-barrelled weapons, with deeply curving and fluted butts, sometimes referred to as paddleshaped, and barrels inlaid with gold or silver. Most muskets were imported, probably from Spain, since Spanish guns are frequently mentioned in historical accounts, as well as in poetry and song, and both Logan and Grant affirm that the majority of muskets were of Spanish manufacture: " . . . a two-edged sword in each hero's belt, And a Spanish gun was in his grasp."[1] Spanish, as well as French, firelocks, were specifically mentioned in orders issued after the Battle of Culloden, regarding the collection of firearms abandoned by the Highland army.

The clansman's flintlock musket according to accounts, would be fired at the commencement of action, and presumably retrieved at the end of the battle. There are numerous contemporary accounts of the Highlander's habit of discarding his musket after it had been discharged. Home gives as the reason for this practice that holding onto the musket would prevent him from using his other arms in the normal way: "On gaining a battle, they can pick them up again, along with the arms of their enemies; but, if they should be beaten, they have no occasion for muskets." [2]

BROADSWORD

The principal weapon of the Highlander, as has already been stated, was undoubtedly the basket-hilted broadsword, which he used to terrible effect in the battles in which he fought. The injuries inflicted by the use of this weapon can easily be imagined, and a graphic description of its effect during the Battle of Killiecrankie has been given by Grant:

> On the following morning of the field of battle, and the Garry as far as the pass, and the pass itself, presented the dreadful spectacle of hundreds of dead bodies fearfully mutilated by sword wounds; while interspersed amongst them, lay plumed hats, grenadier caps, drums, broken pikes, and swords which had been snapped asunder by the axe and sharp claymore. Swaying the latter with both hands clenched in the basket-hilt, the clansmen cut down many of Mackay's officers and soldiers through skull and neck to the very breast; some had their bodies and cross-belts cut through at one blow; pikes and swords were cut like willows; and whoe'er doubts this may consult the witnesses of the tragedy. As if they had been torn by cannon-shot, heads, hands, legs and arms lay every-where about, lopped from the bodies. [3]

Campbell observed that "a stroke . . . delivered from one of their Hands, would be sufficient to chop off the Head of the strongest Champion that ever lived." [4] The Chevalier de Johnstone remarked that after the Battle of Prestonpans, "the field of battle presented a spectacle of horror, being covered with heads, legs, arms, and mutilated bodies; for the killed all fell by the sword." [5] The Chevalier gives another instance of the use of the broadsword in battle:

> . . . They had frequently been enjoined to aim at the noses of the horses

with their swords, without minding the riders, as the natural movement of a horse, wounded in the face, is to wheel round, and a few horses, wounded in that manner, are sufficient to throw the whole squadron into such disorder that it is impossible afterwards to rally it.[6]

Controversy has arisen in the past concerning the application of the term 'claymore' to the Scottish broadsword, some experts believing that a claymore is a two-handed sword. Modern opinion, however, supports the view that both weapons come into the category of 'claymore'. The word itself comes from the Gaelic *claidheamh mor*, meaning 'great sword'.

The basket-hilted broadsword has a very distinctive appearance, and is readily recognisable, even by those unfamiliar with weapons of war. Its blade was around three feet in length, about two inches wide at the base and was double-edged, which permitted its use for cutting as well as thrusting. The basket hilt itself was sometimes plain, sometimes engraved, or pierced in the form of clubs, diamonds, or hearts. Some are stamped with the initials of both the maker and his town of origin, and in others the town of origin can be determined by the style and construction of the hilt. Many of the blades are engraved with the name Andrea Ferrara, which may be spelled in various ways, and may have originated in Ferrara in Italy, but Solingen in Germany was probably the true source of most, the blades being spuriously marked to satisfy the Highland demand for Ferrara blades. Such blades were often passed down from father to son, through successive generations of the

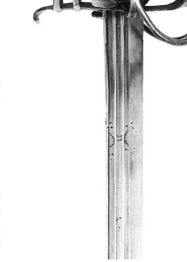

FIG. 6. Basket-hilted backsword with 36″ (914mm) blade, circa 1745. This sword is of superior quality, and would have been carried by a cavalry officer in a Highland regiment. The blade is single-edged, and its markings indicate that it was manufactured at Solingen, Germany. *Private Collection.*

same family. The claymore itself was slung in a scabbard from the swordbelt, and hung on the left side of the wearer.

Andrea Ferrara is thought to be of Italian, or, possibly, Spanish origin. He is said to have forbidden his apprentices to watch the final stage in the manufacture of his blades. One of his apprentices, determined to learn the secret, watched his master through a hole in the door of the foundry, and observed him sprinkling the blade with a white powder, after which it was hammered into the hot metal. The blade was then returned to the furnace, and the process repeated on the other side. When Ferrara discovered that he had been observed, he struck his apprentice with a heavy hammer, killing him instantly. Ferrara is alleged to have then fled to Scotland, in order to escape punishment, and there established a manufactory of his blades. This story has become something of a legend, and in all probability has no factual basis.

The broadsword, when matched against the Brown Bess with attached bayonet, with its far greater length, and therefore reach, may justly be regarded as the inferior weapon. However, that it was used to such deadly effect at Falkirk, Prestonpans, and Killiecrankie, indicates that another factor was involved in the battles between the disciplined English soldiers and the Highland army, namely, the terror induced by the very sight of the wild-looking Highlanders, with their strange attire, shouting their unintelligible clan slogans, and wielding their enormous swords, and this added factor is undoubtedly the reason for the early defeats sustained by the English army during the '45 Rebellion. This factor was recognised by the English commanders, and the Orders of the Day on Sunday 12 January 1745, read as follows:

> The manner of the Highlander's way of fighting, of which there is nothing so easy to resist, if officers and men are not pre-possessed with the lyes and accounts which are told of them. They commonly form their front rank of what they call their best men, or True Highlanders, the number of which being allways but few; when they form in battallions, they commonly form four deep, and these Highlanders form the front of the four, the rest being Lowlanders and arrant scum. When these battallions come within a large musket-shott, or three score yards, this front rank gives their fire, and immediately thro down their firelocks and

come down in a cluster, with their swords and targets, making a noise, and endeavouring to pearce the body, or battallion, before them, becoming 12 or 14 deep by the time they come up to the people they attack. The sure way to demolish them is at three deep to fire by ranks diagonally to the centre where they come, the rear rank first, and even that rank not to fire till they are within 10 or 12 paces; but if the fire is given at a distance, you will probably be broke, for you never get time to load a second cartridge; and if you give way, you may give yourselves for dead, for they, being without a firelock or any load, no man with his arms, accoutrements, & c, can escape them, and they give no quarters; but if you will but observe the above directions, they are the most despicable enemy that are.[7]

According to Home, the Highlanders brought down two men at a time, one with the dirk in the left hand, and another with the sword: "Their attack is so terrible that the best troops in Europe would with difficulty sustain the first shock of it; and if the swords of the Highlanders once come in contact with them, their defeat is inevitable."[8] Andrew Lumisden, private secretary to Bonnie Prince Charlie, writing about the Battle of Preston, says "The Highlanders threw down their muskets, drew their swords, and carried all before them like a torrent."[9] In that battle, fourteen hundred Highlanders, unsupported by horse or cannon, routed a regular army of two thousand foot and seven hundred dragoons, defended by a train of artillery.

DIRK

In its sheath suspended from the waistbelt in a central position hung the dirk, often referred to in contemporary accounts as the 'durk'. Its leather sheath often contains pockets, usually one above the other, for a small knife and fork. The dirk was developed from the ballock knife, which was in common use in England and Europe from the thirteenth century. By the late sixteenth century, this had become known as a dudgeon dagger, with a triangular section blade which was often inscribed with a text, and a slender hilt with haunches.

Writing in 1573, Lindsay of Pitscottie says: "Thair weapones ar bowis and dartes, with ane verie broad sword and ane dagger scharp onlie at the

FIG. 7. Scottish silver-mounted dirk, by William Ritchie of Perth, c. 1796. The scabbard mounts are of silver decorated with trophies of arms. This style of dirk was worn by the Reay Fencibles in 1794. Overall length 18″ (457mm). *Private Collection.*

on side."[10] Keltie speaks of "a dirk, with a knife and fork stuck in the side of the sheath, and sometimes a spoon."[11] Edward Burt also describes the dirk, as follows:

> The blade is straight, and generally above a foot long, the back near an inch thick; the point of the knife goes off like a tuck, and the handle is something like that of a sickle. They pretend that they can't well do without it, as being useful to them in cutting wood, and upon many other occasions; but it is a concealed mischief hid under the plaid, ready for the secret stabbing, and in a close encounter there is no defence against it.[12]

The blade is usually around eighteen inches long, while the handle is short, and is constructed of hardwood. The hilt itself is neatly and gracefully shaped, and is often carved with Celtic knotwork or basketweave. Occasionally it is studded with silver beads. The blade is sharpened on one side only, being flattened on the other, and is consequently wedge-shaped. The pommel is in the form of a round, flat, metal disc, which may be of brass or silver.

Many dirks are found, the blades of which were originally broadswords, and, having been broken, or possibly due to the prohibition of the wearing of swords following the Disarming Act of 1746, they have been shortened to dirk size, the dirk being more readily concealed than the sword. The dirk was an extremely effective weapon. It was held in the left hand, point downwards, and was used for stabbing, rather than cutting. Employed in conjunction with the broadsword, the overall result must have been devastating in its execution. One account of the use of the dirk in battle is given by the Chevalier de Johnstone:

> During the Battle of Falkirk, the Highlanders were attacked by the English cavalry, breaking their ranks and trampling under the feet of their horse. The Highlanders, stretched on the ground, thrust their dirks into the bellies of the horses, some seizing their riders by their cloths, dragged them down and stabbed them with their dirks, while several others used their pistols.[13]

The dirk figures prominently in Judiciary Records of the seventeenth century, being a favoured weapon in violent disagreements between individuals. In March 1664, Andrew Spalding, David Spalding and James Shaw were charged with:

> lying in wait for Andrew Fleeming, merchant in Dundee, as he was coming from Kirkmichel to Edinr., and there shooting him with a gun loaded with ball through the body, and thereafter wounding him with swords and durks in the head and other places of his body, and was cruelly murdered and killed.[14]

A common habit, amongst the Highlanders, was the practice of swearing an oath upon his dirk. Such an oath would never be broken, the penalty for any such breech being death by the point of the self-same dirk on which the oath had been sworn.

TARGE

The targe, or target, was a round, flat, or often convex shield, of under two feet in diameter. It was composed of two thin layers of oak or fir, covered with hide, and sometimes reinforced by brass or steel. The inner surface was covered with skin, while the exterior was often embellished by brass or steel cups, which were pierced, and sometimes engraved. The leather surface was tooled, and decorated by means of brass, or, rarely, silver studs, producing concentric patterns or rondels of very attractive form.

FIG. 8. Targe, probably from Perthshire, dated 1736. Diameter 18½″ (470mm).
Private Collection.

The targe had straps to allow its suspension on the back, the straps passing across the shoulders. In use, the left arm was passed through a leather or iron loop as far as the elbow, the left hand gripping a second iron loop. There was a central boss in the front surface of the targe, which could sometimes be unscrewed in order to insert a sharpened spike, forming an additional defence during battle. Thus the targe was a very effective shield against thrusts of pike and bayonet alike, and at the same time, its convex surface could deflect or absorb musket or pistol ball. Inside the removable form of central boss was contained a drinking cup made of horn.

There is an interesting description of the targe, which is contained in a letter written from one Mr Henry Fletcher to his brother:

WEAPONS ASSOCIATED WITH THE SCOTTISH PISTOL

Saturday 21 Januar 1716

In your last you desired a description of the Highland targe, which I shal give you according to the best Impersonation I have yet got, but is not perfect. The outward forme of ane Highland Targe is a convex circle, about 2 foot in diameter, but some have them oval; the innermost part of it nixt the man's breast is a skin with the hair upon it, which is only a cover to a steel plate, which is not very thick, for the whole is no great weight; on the inner side of this Steel plate, the Handle is fixed, which hath two parts, one that the left arm passes throw till near the elbow, the other that the Hand lays hold on: without the Steel plate there is a Cork which covers the Steel plate exactly, but betwixt the Cork and the Steel plate, there is Wooll stuffed in very hard: the Cork is covered with plain, well-wrought leather, which is nailed to the Cork with nails that have brass heads, in order round, drawing thicker towards the center. From the center sticks out a Stiletto (I know not the right name of it, but I call it so, because it is a sort of short poignard) which fixes into the Steel plate and wounds the Enemy when they close: about this Stiletto closs to the Targe ther is a peece of Brass in the forme of a cupelo about 3 inches over and coming half way out on the Stiletto and is fixed upon it. Within this brass ther is a peece of Horn of the same forme like a cup, out of which they drink their usquebaugh, but it being pierced in the under part by the Stiletto, when they take it off to use it as a cup they are obliged to apply the forepart of the end of their finger to the hole to stop it, so that they might drink out of their cup. The leather which has several lines impressed on it, the brass heads of the nails disposed in a regular way, the brass cupelo, and the Stiletto, which make up the outside of the Targe, give it a beautiful aspect. The Cork they make use of is ane excrescence of their Birk-trees which when green cuts like ane Apple, but afterwards comes to that firmness that a nail can fasten in it. The nails sometimes throw off a ball, especially when it hits the Targe a squint: but tho' a ball came directly upon it and miss the nail heads, piercing betwixt them, yet they reckon that the leather, the cork, the wooll so deaden the ball, that the Steel plate, tho' thin, repells it and lodges it in the wooll.[15]

45

SKENE-OCHLES

There are but two references to this weapon in archive material available to the author. The first of these is contained in a description given by Burt, in the first quarter of the eighteenth century, of the arms of the Highlander: ". . . and, besides all these, some of them carry a Sort of Knife, which they call a Skeen-ochles [*Sgian achlais*] from its being concealed in the Sleeve near the Arm-pit."[16] In the second, Grant refers to an "armpit dagger" in his description of Montrose's army.[17] The weapon itself is too large to be inserted into the dirk sheath, and in size lies somewhere between the dirk and its accompanying knife. Few examples appear to have survived.

SKEAN DHU

Whilst not coming into the category of a true weapon of warfare, mention should nevertheless be made of the *skean dhu*, or black knife (a reference to its black hilt). The weapon itself is a deadly knife whose blade is extremely sharp and pointed, being about 3½″ (89mm) in length and of wedge-shaped section. It is normally worn in the right garter as part of traditional Highland dress.

Mackay states that, after the Proscription Act, the Highlanders, as a substitute for the dirk, carried a short knife stuck in the side pocket of the breeches, or inserted between the garter and the leg, by those who ventured to wear the hose. Contemporary accounts have failed to confirm the wearing of the *skean dhu* in the garter before Victorian times, and the practice probably only began with the increase in popularity of the Highland dress, after the visit of George IV to Scotland in 1822.

THE POWDERHORN

The Scottish powderhorn, like the Scottish pistol, has a very distinctive appearance, which makes it both instantly recognisable and extraordinarily attractive. It is constructed from the horn of a neat, that is to say, from any bovine animal. The horn is first boiled in water until it becomes soft, after which it can be flattened to give it its characteristic shape. The bottom end

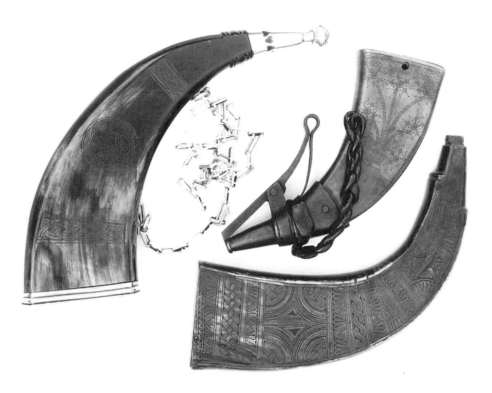

FIG. 9. Selection of Scottish powderhorns, of typical flattened form. One incorporates a spring cut-off, unusual in such horns. The original leather thong is still present. Another bears the date 1692, together with the initials of the owner. The third horn belongs to the period 1820–30. Bearing the crest and motto of Macdougall of Macdougall on its silver mounts, its stopper is adorned with a cairngorm, and is typical of the type of horn worn by the Scottish aristocracy on the occasion of George IV's visit to Edinburgh in 1822. *Private Collection*.

is then sealed, usually with hardwood, whilst at the spout end, lead or brass mounts may be attached. A wooden plug can then be inserted into the spout to seal it.

The wooden bottom is usually secured by means of tiny nails driven through the horn into the wood at regular intervals. Sometimes only one nail is used, inserted in a central position from one side to the other, and at other times there is no obvious fixing, the wood being such a tight fit into

FIG. 10. Another powderhorn, dated 1679. The decoration is quite characteristic, but a close examination reveals that the designs are incomplete. *Private Collection*.

the horn, assisted perhaps by some glue, that no further attachments are necessary.

The original stoppers or nozzles of these ancient powderhorns are seldom encountered, having been lost at some time past, since they were merely a push fit into the neck of the horn. The horns themselves were in all probability constructed and decorated by their original owners, to whom this must have represented a labour of love, and on occasion a powderhorn will be encountered in which the decoration is obviously incomplete. One can readily imagine the Highlander, sitting perhaps round the fire on a night raid, or safe with his family in his tiny cottage, whiling away his time by adding a little more decoration to his powderhorn with the point of his dirk. Perhaps the completed powderhorn would be passed round for critical appraisal by his friends, and comparison made with their powderhorns, discussing the relative merits of each.

Nevertheless, professional makers of powderhorns were in existence, and one such is mentioned in the *List of Persons Concerned in the Rebellion of 1745–46*, namely Marmaduke McBeath, whose occupation was given as

"Powder Flask Maker, of Canongate".[18] Most powderhorns are highly decorative, and many incorporate the name or initials of the original owner, sometimes together with a date, which is usually in the second half of the seventeenth century.

The earliest horns are usually quite large, and are elaborately decorated with animal or human figures. Other decorative motifs consist of intricate rondels and rosettes, sometimes overlapping to form very complicated patterns. Geometric designs also commonly occur, and other patterns include interlace, chequering, knotwork, S-forms, dentate, or herringbone designs, in typically Celtic fashion. The wooden stoppers, as has been indicated, are usually missing, since they lack any attachment to the body of the flask, but occasionally a genuine stopper is encountered.

Sometimes it is discovered that the owner has incorporated loops in the construction of the horn, to allow it to be suspended from a cord. These are usually situated in the concave, or upper, aspect of the horn. A short verse, or couplet, may be carved into the body of the horn. One such inscription, on a horn in the Museum of Antiquities in Edinburgh, reads: "I love thee as my wyffe I'll keep thee as my lyffe." This horn is dated 1689, and was illustrated in Drummond's *Ancient Scottish Weapons*. James Drummond was a collector of Scottish pistols and powderhorns, who produced a series of drawings of Scottish weapons, not only from his own collection, but from other well-known collections, including that of Sir Noel Paton, the famous artist, whose collection, along with that of Drummond himself, is now on display in the Museum of Antiquities, in Edinburgh. After Drummond's death, Joseph Anderson, who was Curator of the Museum at that time, published his drawings in 1881, having added his own commentary. Drummond's *Ancient Scottish Weapons* was the first serious attempt to produce a classification of the Scottish pistol.

Some powderhorns, particularly the smaller ones, are beautifully mounted in silver, with silver nozzles and bases, often elaborately engraved. Such horns were of the type worn with Scottish percussion dress pistols, to complete the Highland dress. Another feature occasionally seen, which is peculiar to powderhorns of Scottish manufacture, consists of a small sliding trap at one side of the base, which opens to permit the horn to be recharged. This feature is found only in powderhorns with metal bases, usually of silver. The stopper in silver-mounted horns sometimes takes the form of a ball surmounting the nozzle, which is attached by a short silver chain to the mount at the neck of the horn. Since the horn from which the Scottish powder flask was constructed is now some two to three hundred years old, it presents a most beautiful mellow coloration which is delightful to the eye.

The largest horns were worn across the back in the manner described by John Campbell: "... they have a Large Powder Horn, that they sling cross their Shoulders, with a small Belt full of brass nails."[19] A large horn of this type may be seen at the Marischal Museum in Aberdeen. The smaller horns could be suspended from a waist or shoulder belt, as can be seen, for example, in the portrait of Kenneth Sutherland, 3rd Lord Duffus (fig. 2), and in Denis Dighton's painting of George IV's visit to Edinburgh which shows the King and several members of his Guard of Honour wearing powderhorns supported by a chain passing over the left shoulder, the flask lying on the right breast. Many later powderhorns were embellished by the use of a large cairngorm set into it, much in the manner of dirks of the same period.

Scottish powderhorns are rarely seen nowadays other than in museum collections. Perhaps the best places to see them are the Scottish museums, particularly Glasgow Art Gallery and Museum, and the Museum of Antiquities in Edinburgh, where the beautiful examples which were formerly in the Drummond and Whitelaw collections, can also be seen. Blair Castle in Perthshire, has several powderhorns amongst its extensive arms collection. It is interesting that several examples of powderhorns which have survived to the present day, have originated in the Island of Mull, where they have been found, in time past, lying in the sand, dropped, it may be presumed, centuries ago, only to be revealed in relatively recent times, by the action of wind and waves on its shores, and powderhorns are still occasionally discovered on the sandy shores of Loch Linnhe, near Fort William.

AN ATTEMPT HAS BEEN MADE IN THE PREVIOUS THREE chapters to convey a general picture of the warlike status which prevailed in the seventeenth and eighteenth centuries in Scotland, highlighting the particular incidents which to this day can still arouse the strongest emotions and which have become part of the romantic legend of Scotland. The importance of understanding this historical background cannot be overemphasised if a full and true appreciation of the Scottish pistol, not just as an object to be admired but also as a weapon that played a part in that national history, is to be made. The following parts of this study will examine the specific history of the pistol itself, its manufacture and its design, and will present what is known of the pistols' makers.

PART TWO

History of
Pistol Manufacture

CHAPTER FOUR

Natural Resources

IRON, APART FROM A VERY PRIMITIVE WORKING OF BOG ores, was not mined or smelted in Scotland until long after the end of the sixteenth century.[1] Henry Kalmeter, who was an industrial spy working on behalf of the official body responsible for the Swedish mining industry, reported back to his employers in 1719, that the only ironworks to be found in Scotland, was one small foundry in Cannaby (Canonbie), close to the English border, where there was a smelting house and four forge hammers.[2] A few forge hammers were also in existence on the southern side of the Firth of Forth, but this smithy work was very slight. Virtually all the iron essential to the gunmaking industry was therefore imported, principally from Stockholm in Sweden and also from Dancig in Poland. Trade between these countries and Scotland had actually begun as far back as the fourteenth century and in the two years from 1474–76, as many as twenty-four Scottish vessels had entered Dancig harbour, a very large number in these days.[3]

During the first half of the eighteenth century, the iron industry in Scotland was relatively insignificant.[4] However, the scarcity of wood in England due to the demands imposed by the housebuilding and ship-building industries, resulted in the establishment of ironworks in Scotland, close to a hitherto untapped source of timber. Thus in 1727, William

Rawlinson of Furness in Lancashire, entered into an agreement with Macdonell of Glengarry for the exclusive use of his woods for a period of thirty-one years.[5] More furnaces were established in the Highlands, one in Taynuilt in Argyllshire and a second in 1775, at Furnace, on the western shore of Loch Fyne. The rising price of iron imported from Sweden and the huge financial burden of importing wood from Scandinavia, prompted Scottish manufacturers to experiment in the use of indigenous coal and ironstone deposits in central Scotland.

At this time, charcoal was used in the smelting process, to convert the iron ore into pig iron, from which wrought iron was produced in the forges. Kalmeter confirms the use of charcoal in several smelting processes in Scotland.[6] Smelting by the use of coke instead of charcoal was pioneered in Scotland in the early eighteenth century and in 1759, the Carron Ironworks was established near Falkirk, the first ironworks to smelt native iron ore with coal, and by the end of the century, several other ironworks were founded, although a few continued to use charcoal, believing that charcoal-iron was more suitable than coke-iron.[7] Cast iron, which formerly had had to be imported, was now exported in large quantities.[8]

The next improvement to have a major impact on iron production in Scotland, was the use of hot air in preference to cold, in the blast of the furnaces and the J. B. Neilson patent for the Neilson Hotblast in 1828, enabled the rich blackband iron ore resources of Scotland to be exploited and the area's splint-coal to be used uncoked.[9]

Thus, from 1830, there was a major expansion of iron production in Scotland, especially west-central Scotland, producing low cost pig iron essential to the gunmaking and other industries. The expansion of the iron industry in Scotland was paralleled by a similar growth in indigenous coal production to feed the blast furnaces. Coal production in Scotland, for example, rose from 40,000 tons during the period 1551–1560, to 475,000 tons during 1681–1690, a ten-fold increase.[10] The best coal to be found, at the beginning of the seventeenth century, was in Fife, according to Kalmeter, around "Wemys" and in particular at the harbour of "Metthle" (Methil). Being close to the sea, transport to the coastal saltworks was made easier, coal being essential to the production of this valuable commodity. At the same time, a good deal of the coal produced was exported from Fife to

Holland. Scottish coal was reckoned to be marginally better than that produced in England, due, as Kalmeter suggested, to its being "not so heavily impregnated with sulphur and therefore not so harmful to the chest."[11] The price of coal in the early eighteenth century was 10½ pence for eighteen stones when exported, but only sixpence when sold for the home market.

As far as forestation in Scotland was concerned, timber was in short supply even in the fourteenth century, when the few existing forests were carefully preserved.[12] Even in those days it was recognised that the disappearance of the natural timber forests in Scotland would have financial and domestic repercussions in the future and a policy for preserving the forests was implemented. In Fife, for example, Crown tenants were bound by special regulations to plant and preserve timber and a hundred years later, orders were issued for the preservation of the woods of Aberdeenshire, Elgin, Banff, Nairn and Forres.[13]

There was already a considerable trade with Scandinavia, importing timber of all kinds, including deal, oak, elm, burntwood, birch, timber boardings and short basonits. Kalmeter, as usual, had something to tell his employers about the timber supplies in Scotland, since the charcoal resulting from its incineration was vital to its use in such iron industry as existed at the time of his visit and to any future expansion of that industry. He reported that the deforestation had begun with the Romans and since then further tree-felling had been carried out, partly to remove natural hiding places for "robbers and highwaymen" and partly to improve the country for planting crops.[14] He also indicated that planting of firwoods had been commenced some time before, in the hope that Scotland would in the future be able to supply her own timber for use in her ironworks.

The policy for preservation of existing timber supplies in the sixteenth and seventeenth centuries may have had some bearing on the choice of iron in preference to wood. There were further factors determining this choice—the greater durability of metal, of considerable importance given the weapons' rough usage, and the aesthetic appeal of a flamboyant design with silver inlay or gilt brasswork being particularly attractive to the clansmen who carried the pistols.

CHAPTER FIVE

Shipping Lists

SHIPPING LISTS CONSTITUTE AN EXTREMELY VALUABLE source of information to the student researching into the early history of Scottish pistols, since they provide an insight into the overseas commerce of the port concerned, especially having regard to the import of goods connected with the gunsmithing industry. These lists were compiled by the Town Clerks, and formed the basis on which the harbour dues were assessed. Essentially they consist of details of the ship concerned, together with the name of the master, the goods carried, the names of the owner of the cargo, its port of origin, and the date of arrival. The master or clerk of the vessel was required to appear before the Baillies, and occasionally the Dean of Guild, in order to provide these details.[1]

Scotland's trade with Germany had begun even before the fourteenth century. As overseas trade expanded, Scottish vessels were landing their merchandise in Konigsberg, Stralsund, Elbing, and Lubeck, as well as Hamburg, Bremen, Rostock, and Weimar.[2] At about the same time, trade also existed with Poland, and in the years 1474–76, twenty-four ships had unloaded their cargoes in Dancig harbour. The Scottish ports of origin were mainly Leith and Aberdeen, but Perth, Dundee, and St. Andrews, also had a considerable share of overseas trading, as well as Inverness and Glasgow. During the sixteenth century, overseas trade continued to flourish. By the middle of the century, trade between Dancig and Aberdeen exceeded that between any other two ports, although trade between Dundee and Dancig was also at a very high level.

Aberdeen, in the year ending 1795, enjoyed trade with Granada, Denmark, Norway, Gibraltar, Greenland, Holland, Ireland, Italy, Poland, Portugal, Germany, Prussia, Russia, and Sweden, and in the year 1790, exported over five thousand tons of goods and imported half as much again. In the case of Dundee, which was an important centre of the gunmaking industry, we have been fortunate in that a complete list of all shipping entering its harbour during the period 1580–1618 has survived intact. This list, which comprises several volumes, was kept by the Clerk of Dundee, who was Sir Alexander Wedderburne, a Dundee merchant whose meticulous account books have survived to the present day, providing a remarkable source of information regarding the everyday commercial transactions of a seventeenth century merchant. The title page of one volume of the Shipping List reads "The Buik of ye entresis of Schippis arryvand at ye port and Heavin of Dundie Begun in ye moneth of March Anno Dni.1612."[3] The following are typical entries:

> Comperit James knight maister of ye schip callit ye princeiss contening
>   ye gudes following:
> david gipsone and Alexr.vannen ane last of gaid Iyrne, X br. of oisment
>   Iyrone.
> Allaster fargisone half ane last of gaid Iyrone
> Ritchert blyth ane br.of oismont Iyrone.[4]

> Vltimo die mensis August j anno dni 1614. Quhilk day comperit andro
> abircromby Maistr. vnder god of the schip of dundie callit the fox laitlie
> arryved from stockholm Contenand threttie sex last of Irone.[5]

The shipping lists tell us that a huge amount of iron was imported into Dundee in the early seventeenth century, the port of origin in most cases being Stockholm, in Sweden. A great deal of iron was also imported from Dancig in Poland. That it was necessary to import this commodity in such vast quantities and on such a scale, indicates that Scotland was unable to produce sufficient quantities of iron from her own resources, and that this had, in consequence, to be imported in order to make up the deficiency, iron being essential to the gunmaking industry. Kalmeter, writing in 1719, stated that no ironworks existed in Scotland other than one near the English border, all iron at that time being imported from Sweden.[6]

Two distinct types of iron are listed, gaid iron, and oismont iron, although precisely what the distinction was between them is not known.[7] Thus, in a later entry from the Shipping List of Dundee, we read:

James auchinleck iiij lastis ten br.of oisment jrone ten schip pundis of
    gaid Iyrone
to Jhone peirsone ten schip pundis gaid Irone
Robert Smyth achtein br.Iyrone ten schip pundis gaid Iyrone
margaret small XXj br.Iyrone ten schip pundis gaid Iyrone
Mr Jhone moncur iiij lastis and one half oismont Iyrone ane thrid of ten
    schip pundis gaid Iyrone
James Goldman half last of oismont Iyrone.[8]

The list reveals another important discovery regarding materials imported into Dundee. This concerns the huge imports of timber such as deal, oak, elm, burntwood, birch, short batons and timber boards, into Scotland during this period. The timber appears principally to have been imported from Norway. Clearly the import of such enormous quantities of timber in the sixteenth and seventeenth centuries indicates that Scotland at that time was very deficient in timber (as has been said, there existed even in the fourteenth century a policy for preserving the supplies of timber). This lack of available wood for gunstocks may have been a critical influence in the selection of iron, rather than wood, as the material of choice in the fabrication of the stocks. Although it is true that native iron was in equally short supply in the seventeenth century, there was probably sufficient to satisfy the dagmakers' requirements until the increase in demand for all-metal pistols later in the century necessitated imports of iron.

Another interesting factor to emerge from a close study of the shipping lists, is that the master or captain of a vessel often had a financial interest in the cargo. This is confirmed in the account book of David Wedderburne, in a note made on 3 October, 1597:

Send with John Scrymgeour merchant to Spane in the schip of St Andros,
Item: Ane pair of pistollatis cost me XIj lib Given him commissione to sell
the sam in Ingland or ony uther port he thinkis best to my proffitt.[9]

In attempting to decipher old shipping lists, various factors must be borne in mind. Firstly, since educational standards were considerably lower than they are today, spelling tends not only to be poor, but also inconsistent, so that, for example, the word 'iron' is spelled in three different ways by the clerk who made the above entry, namely, "Iyrone", "Irone" and "jrone", and "oismont" is spelled oisment, as well as oismont, in the same list. Proper names may be spelled with or without the initial capital letters, and sometimes the forename alone is spelled with a capital letter.

The entry of 7 September records a ship, "laittlie arryved frome stokhollome", and itemises its cargo thus:

Nyne last pteining to James man
Sevin last thrie schippund Irone pteining to Alexr boyture
Sex last twelve schippund Irone pteining to James symsone
Sex last xij schiplib Irone pteining to Alexr Jak
Thrie barrell Irone pteining to David murdy
ten brls. ij schiplib Irone pteining to James Downye
ten brls iij schiplib Irone pteining to Alexr.renkyne

Fyve last V brl.ii schip pund Irone	Rt moreis
Ane last VII br.Irone	Wm walker
br.Irone	Rot Symer
Fyve br.Irone	Wm kynlock
Ten br.Irone	Jon renkyne
Thrie br Irone	Walt durhame
Fyve br.Irone	Wm gulland
Sex br.Irone	Jon morgund[10]

The abbreviation "br." refers to barrels. Other measures of iron used consist of "lasts" and "schip punds" or "schip libs". Most of the above names cannot be identified with certainty as being gunsmiths living in the environs of Dundee, and it is most probable that the names are those of merchants, who acted as middlemen in the supply of iron to the gunmakers, armourers, and blacksmiths, whose individual requirements would probably be of very low order. Iron, of course, was equally essential to the armourers and blacksmiths in the manufacture of swords, dirks, and body armour, as to the gunsmiths in the fabrication of their pistols.

CHAPTER SIX

The Hammerman Craft

Our Art over all Mechanics hath renown,
Our Arms the Hammer and the Royal Crown,
Around this shield ten ovals you behold
Wherein ten several emblems stand in gold,
Deciphering ten distinct trades to be
All comprehended in our Deaconrie
And yet the ten have but one general name—
The generous ingenious Hammermen.

'The Hammermen's Arms of Aberdeen'[1]

THE HAMMERMAN CRAFT WAS AN INCORPORATION, THAT is, a union of members in an association, fraternity, or body of men voluntarily associated for certain purposes, under state sanction, and were derived from the Guilds of medieval times.[2] Guilds themselves can be defined as associations of persons exercising the same craft, formed for the purpose of protecting or promoting their common interest.[3] These guilds existed in Scotland prior to 1424, when an Act of Parliament of James I ordained that each craft should choose a wise man of the craft to be Deacon or Master over the rest, to govern and assay all work made by men of that craft, so that the King's lieges should not be defrauded, as in times past, by "untrue men of the crafts".[4] It was not uncommon for several crafts to band together, forming a composite association, such as the Wrights and Coopers Craft of Aberdeen, and the Wrights, Masons, Slaters Trade of Dundee.[5] In Glasgow, Perth, Stirling and many of the smaller burghs, the Incorporation of Hammermen was the premier craft guild.[6]

Thus the Hammermen comprised not only blacksmiths, armourers, dagmakers or gunsmiths, sword makers and cutlers, but also buckle makers, nailmakers, lorimers or saddle ironmongers, locksmiths and clockmakers, as well as pewterers, goldsmiths, silversmiths, and tinsmiths, who were workers in "white iron".[7] It was not unnatural that such groups of workers should join together, to their mutual benefit and protection, and to maintain the standards of their profession, whilst at the same time excluding outside competition. In order to obtain legal recognition, such associations of craftsmen had to apply for a Seal of Cause, or Charter, and these legal documents were granted by the Provost and magistrate of the burgh concerned.[8] The earliest such Seal of Cause was granted by the town council of Edinburgh in 1449, to the cordiners of that city, while the Edinburgh Hammermen were granted their charter in 1483. In 1536 the Hammermen of Glasgow achieved similar recognition. Once granted legal recognition, these incorporations were then empowered to discipline their members, such disciplinary measures prior to recognition being the responsibility of the burgh concerned, which was a more cumbersome and involved procedure. The Incorporation of Hammermen was, therefore, an association of craftsmen carrying on allied trades which involved the working or hammering of metal.

There was a religious element involved in the incorporation, the patron saint of all hammermen being St Eloy. Any craftsman breaking statutes was required to pay one pound of wax for the reparation of the altar and ornaments thereof, for each offence, and members setting up a booth within the burgh were required to pay for upholding divine service at the altar of 'St Eloyis'.[9]

The motto of the hammermen became "by hammer in hand all arts do stand". Membership was restricted to burgesses, that is to say, freemen resident within the town or burgh, and were admitted on submission of a test piece, or "essay".[10] In the case of a gunsmith, this might be a lock mainspring or gun lock, whilst an armourer might be asked to produce a broadsword mounting. On 24 January 1718, for example, Patrick Buchanan, a gunsmith in Glasgow, was asked to produce as his essay, "Ane side pistol with ane irone stock" and on 22 March 1711, John Simpson Yr., an armourer, produced as his essay "Ane broad hieland sword with hilt and mounting yrof". A fee was payable on admission to membership, the actual amount depending on whether the applicant was a stranger, son or son-in-law of a member, or an apprentice. Once the fee had been paid, the new entrant would take the Oath of Fidelity to his craft. A Master, later known as a Deacon, was elected from amongst the members, to serve for a period of one year as head of the craft. Apart from paying an entry fee, an additional contribution was demanded towards the purchase of mortcloths. These were funeral palls which were hired out by the craft. The new member was expected to serve a period of twelve months as Officer to the Incorporation.

In order to maintain standards, inspection of work carried out in the burgh was made by two or three respected members of the craft, on a Saturday afternoon, and any inferior or "insufficient" work was confiscated.[11] Members were required to attend monthly meetings of the incorporation, fines being imposed for non-attendance. Disputes between members were settled at such meetings, and disciplinary action taken when required. A duty of the Deacon or Master of the craft was to head the craft at the 'musters', or 'wapinschaws', which were held regularly, especially in times of strife, when "substancious and habill" men were obliged to provide a hagbut with "graith powder and bullet effeiring thereto", whilst those unable to do so might provide a long spear, a jack, steel bonnet, sword, and buckler. The burgesses also had duties as night watchers, to protect the town from attack, and its citizens from malefactors.[12]

From Incorporation funds, payments could be made to impecunious or distressed members, their widows or children, and contributions made to worthwhile charities.[13] The Minute Book of the Hammermen of Glasgow for 1730 reads: "To James and John Smith, Scotsmen who suffered by ye Turks 0-12-0", and in 1734, "To Margaret Cowper, a needie widow in strait 0-8-0", and again in 1745, "By cash paid porters for attending the masters in gathering shoes to the Highlandmen 0-1-0".

One important duty of the freemen, or masters of the craft, as they were sometimes called, was in the training of apprentices. These were indentured for a period of five years, after payment of a fee to the master. During the period of indenture, the apprentice lived with his master, and was fed and clothed by him. At the end of this time, the apprentice had to remain with his master for a further period of two years, for "meat and fee", that is, for board and a small wage.[14] Provided his master could furnish him with a satisfactory report, the apprentice was then permitted to apply for entry to the craft, by submission of his essay, and at the same time, to seek admission as a burgess or freeman of the town. The new member of the craft was required to practice his trade for a further two years, before taking on an apprentice of his own.

The craftsman worked in a booth set up at, or near, his home, producing and selling work to order. On market days and fairs, he would erect his booth at the Market Cross, in competition with other members of his craft, and with those 'out of town' craftsmen who were licensed to do so. Because of the unfair competition arising as a result of suburban craftsmen, unfreemen whose work was often inferior to that of the burgh craftsmen, selling their goods secretly in the town, and taking orders for such goods, many of the larger burghs issued licences to their suburban cousins, thus effectively bringing them under the control of the incorporations.[15] This was done in the case of Govan and Glasgow, and in Leith and Edinburgh.

Mention should be made of pendicle members of the trade or craft, who were admitted to the craft without essay, allowing the families of members to enjoy the charitable benefits of the incorporation, but being unable to practice the trade themselves until an essay had been submitted.[16]

Since the Incorporations of Hammermen comprised so many allied trades, demarcation disputes did arise, and an instance of one such dispute is recorded by the Hammermen of Glasgow as early as 1621. Again, in 1653, one Robert Robison, a brass smith, was accused of making "all sorts of black work", including the making of pistols, swords, gun mounts, and scabbards. He was enjoined to desist from this practice, on penalty of forfeiture of any other work than that which he was entitled to perform. Robison appealed against this decision, submitting that any hammerman might work at any branch of the craft, provided that he could "begin and sufficiently end the same" for the good of the lieges. The magistrates and council decided in his favour.[17] Following this decision, although demarcation problems were no longer a feature in craft disputes, the member could be asked to provide further essay pieces, as proof of his ability to produce "sufficient" work at his new craft. Despite this, other branches of the hammerman craft, including silversmiths as well as cutlers, were also involved on occasion in the manufacture of guns, particularly in the smaller towns and villages, which were remote from the influence of the craft.

Patrick Ramsay, who was a gunsmith in Dundee, and became Master in 1587, also worked as a silversmith, and Thomas Ramsay was another Dundee gunsmith who also worked in silver. In Montrose, William Lindsay was a silversmith of some repute, and in addition worked as a gunsmith. A pair of pistols by this maker has recently been returned to Scotland after many years. They were originally the property of Hay, who was secretary to the Old Pretender. A well-known Inverness silversmith, Robert Naughton, also produced Scottish flintlock pistols of quality.

As meticulous records were kept by the officers of the incorporation, in the craft "lockit book", these, where they have survived, have proved to be an invaluable source to the researcher, containing as they do, extensive lists of their members, together with the dates of their admission and the names of their apprentices. Difficulties in interpretation arise where more than one gunsmith has the same name, especially when a son succeeds his father, a not uncommon occurrence in the Hammerman Craft.

The earliest reference in the Incorporation of Hammermen of Glasgow to a dagmaker, was to one David McBen, who was admitted craftsman on 17 November 1621. After 1652, the term 'dagmaker' was no longer used, 'gunsmith' being adopted in its stead. The origin of the word 'dag' is obscure. The term itself refers to a pistol, and its use was not limited only to pistols of Scottish manufacture. The Gaelic word for pistol is certainly *dagge* or *dagga*, but *phiostal* is also used. The latter term was probably derived from the English, but it remains uncertain as to whether the derivation of dagge has similar origins, or whether the English word has derived from the Gaelic. It does, however, seem more likely, that the Highlanders referred to their pistols in their native language, as *dagga*, and that the Gaelic word became shortened by usage to 'dag'.

The Edinburgh Hammermen had been granted their charter in 1483. Records of the Incorporation, however, go back only as far as 1582.[18] The first mention of dagmakers was in July 1594. They were, at that time, joined with the locksmiths, and their essay was "a hackbut and a dag".[19] In October, 1621, the name 'gunsmith' replaced the old term 'dagmaker' and in the same year a gunsmith was admitted after submitting as his essay "a pair of sufficient pistols". Also in 1621, the gunsmiths extended their essay to "a mounted pistol, a carriban, a buckle, and an arrow head".[20] In Edinburgh, a common essay was "ane outred pistolet of irne"[21] or "ane compleit pistoll with ane timber stock and ane half bend lock".[22] In 1694, "a pistol with a bridged lock"[23] was added to the gunsmith's essay, and, in 1700, "the barrel forged"[24] was also included. Little makes an interesting observation in the following record:

> In 1586, a Beltmaker's essay was an Sword belt and ane belton belt . . . The first of these needs no explanation; but the last was used for two different purposes: In the first place, to keep the body firm; and in the second place, to hang the Side pistols upon.[25]

In Stirling, the Hammerman Craft was the Premier Craft Guild amongst the seven incorporated trades, which comprised, in addition to the hammermen themselves, weavers, tailors, shoemakers, fleshers, skinners, and bakers.[26] Qualifying for admission were no fewer than eighteen separate trades, including gunners, gunmakers or gunsmiths, armourers, dagmakers, and pistolmakers.[27] The first mention of a gunsmith in the records of the Incorporation, is on 26 October 1607, when David Maklein, gunmaker, was admitted "wt al of our consents".[28] John Christie is mentioned several times in the Hammermen records.

> 2 September 1751 Desired admission-granted, and he is to make a gunlock for his essay. Admitted 14 December.
>
> 7 December 1751 Christie, John, gunsmith in Down, admitted burgess and hammerman: paid £12.
>
> 28 May 1760 Petition of John Christie, gunsmith in Stirling, showing that by his marriage to a guild brother's daughter he is entitled to enter burgess but if he did so without previous agreement with the Hammerman incorporation he would not be able to carry on his present business. Besides employing himself that way he proposed also dealing in the merchant way and for the benefit of his family to enter with the Guildry it is customary in other trades of this place for tradesmen to continue the exercise of their employments after being admitted with the Guildry. Granted.
>
> son: William Christie, pistol maker, admitted freeman 1766.[29]

The box of the Stirling Hammermen has the arms of each of the Seven Incorporated Trades engraved on a brass plate. The present box, made of mahogany, was constructed in 1829, but the plate itself is believed to have been engraved by John Christie, gunsmith, and was probably removed from an older box.[30]

Between 1563 and 1611, a period of forty-eight years, no fewer than eighty-one hammermen were practising their art in Stirling, and even in 1749, three years after the Disarming Act, twenty-seven members were listed who had borrowed money from Incorporation funds.[31]

The records of the Hammermen of St Andrews go back as far as 1539, although the crafts were incorporated long before that time. The first reference to a gunsmith is recorded in 1585, when John Smith, himself a gunsmith, was Deacon of the craft in that year,[32] and in 1594, reference is made to "Alexander pryde, sone lawfull to James pryde", when he was "enterit prenteis to John Leirmonthe gunmaker".[33]

FIG. 11. The Arms of the Hammerman. Sandstone carving. New Abbey, Dumfriesshire.

CHAPTER SEVEN ✍

Gunsmithing Techniques

IT IS UNFORTUNATE THAT NO RECORDS ARE KNOWN TO exist describing in detail the techniques employed by the Scottish gunsmiths in the seventeenth and eighteenth centuries. However, a detailed examination of the Scottish pistols of that time does permit certain conclusions to be drawn regarding their method of construction. Such records of the period that do exist refer only to the making of Spanish gunbarrels, yet this may be of some relevance, since Spanish long guns were extremely popular amongst the Highlanders, reflecting some degree of satisfaction with the Spanish barrels, and it is quite possible that the Scottish gunmakers adopted the same techniques as their Spanish counterparts. It is perhaps unfortunate that the spy Kalmeter, who travelled widely in Scotland in the early eighteenth century, and reported in detail to his Swedish employers on, for example, the lead mining industry, did not visit and report in a similar way on the techniques of the Scottish gunsmiths of the period. Any discussion of these techniques must be partly conjectural.

In those days, gun barrels were manufactured by winding flattened strips of iron around a mandrel, which was a shaping rod of a size approximating to the desired bore of the weapon. This was done by application of heat in the forge and the edges were hammered together until heat welded. It is claimed by some that the iron was obtained from old horse-shoe nail stubs, which were first heated until a mass of molten steel was formed, which was then drawn out into bars. These bars were then flattened into the strips described above. This method was widely used in England, and the resulting barrels were termed 'stub twist', and were occasionally marked as such. It is not, however, known, whether this method was used to any extent in Scotland.

Bars of iron of square section around ¾″ to 1″ (19 to 25mm) thick, from whatever source, were employed to create the flat strips necessary for winding around the mandrel. However, the strength of the finished barrel could be increased by first twisting the squared section along its length before the flattening and winding process began, and it was even possible to employ two or three squared bars, each twisted in a similar way before being wound round together, and flattened into a single strip. Such barrels were extremely strong, and in addition produced a pattern of twist which was favoured especially by the Spaniards, although it is not known to what extent the Scots shared in this regard. However, it can be confidently assumed that the twist method was employed by the Scottish gunsmiths, although probably not to the extent of sophistication employed by their Spanish counterparts.

Once the barrel had been heat welded to form an iron or steel tube of the requisite length, boring tools were employed to create a uniform bore throughout its length. Differing sizes of drill were used to produce a relatively smooth bore. The breech end was then tapped and a breech plug inserted. The barrel was then filed to produce the broad barrel bands and create the moulded muzzle of the earlier weapons, or the octagonal swamped muzzle of the later varieties. Smoothing and polishing were then carried out using fine files. Since the tools of the period were much cruder than those used today, it is quite astonishing that such a high standard of finish was achieved by these primitive gunsmiths.

The following tools ('warklumes') were sold by the widow of a Stirling hammerman in 1549:

thre gret stedijs	[anvils]
thre lignettis of irne	[bars]
the gret scheris	[shears]
ane taingis	[tongs]

ane vice turkes	[screw pinchers]
the stule	[stool]
graitht perteinyn thairto	[graith]
hand halmeris	[hammers]
small hammeris	
filis	[files]
borrach	[brace]
fat	[vat]
stampis	
litill stedijs	
small warklumes[1]	

The stock of the pistol was formed from iron which had been flattened and rough-shaped in the forge. The forend was shaped around the mandrel, and the butt folded over and brazed at one side to form the ramshorn type of pistol, or the lobe butt. In the case of the latter, the terminal 'cap' was then brazed on. The ramshorns, in the earlier weapons, were formed as part of the butt, but later the horns were formed as a separate piece, which was then brazed on. The heart butt was created from two halves of shaped metal, which were then brazed together vertically to the upper part of the butt. Lemon butts were formed in a similar way, in two halves. This allowed greater freedom to create a pierced effect.

The barrels were fitted to the forend of the stock by means of a flange which penetrated a slot in the forend, whilst at the breech a tapped hole in the tang was secured by a round-headed screw passing through the stock from above. Only in the early wooden-stocked pistols is the English method of loop and pin fixing of the barrels found. Costume and percussion dress pistols employed a simple screw at the forend, passing from below to engage directly with the barrel.

Stud triggers were filed from solid metal, as were the triggers of the later flintlocks, and costume and percussion dress pistols. Ball triggers, which were in reality spherical, were formed in two halves, which were made in iron, silver, or an upper half of iron and a lower of silver. Sometimes brass was used instead. The lower end of the trigger plate was shaped into a thin metal rod, and the two demi-spheres of metal fitted over it. They were then brazed or silver soldered together, and the lower end of the rod peened over to secure the complete ball permanently. Prickers were formed in a similar manner, and were provided with an inch-long sharpened point, used to clear the vent of powder fouling.

The method of suspension of the trigger is worthy of some comment. In the early pistols, the suspension lies within the lock recess, and consists of a pin or screw which is not visible from outside. The Highland pistol is almost invariably fitted with an external screw which passes right through the stock, being filed flush with the stock on either side. Some makers, particularly Thomas Murdoch, preferred the old internal screw method, but this was not his invariable practice. Costume and percussion dress pistols had locks which employed the vertical sear, similar to English pistols. In most Highland pistols, the upper edge of the trigger plate pierces a rectangular slot in the butt. This then becomes a feature of the pistol, accentuated by a little line engraving round it, and some filing of the trigger plate to produce a wavy effect.

Foresights are rarely fitted, and even rear sights are not invariably found. When present, these are sometimes offset to correct a tendency to fire to the left. Highland pistols, usually emanating from Doune, are sometimes fitted with a disc or comb behind the cock. This is pierced in the shape of a star, and became the practice in pistols dating from around 1720–60.

The butts of most ramshorn pistols were slightly offset to accommodate the hand more easily. The earliest ramshorn pistols were fitted with right and left hand locks, and their butts were offset accordingly.

Engraving was probably carried out by the individual gunsmiths themselves, and was often extremely elaborate. The earlier pistols are more deeply engraved than the later varieties. Inlay was achieved by drawing the desired pattern on the pistols, deeply engraving the lines forming the pattern, and finally undercutting on each side of the engraved lines. Thin strips of silver were then hammered into position, held firmly in place by the technique of undercutting. Heat bluing of the pistols produced an effect which is only rarely seen today, most of this original finish having been removed by age, or by over enthusiastic cleaning and polishing.

CHAPTER EIGHT

Lock Mechanisms

SNAPHAUNCE LOCK

THE COCK OF THE SNAPHAUNCE LOCK IS OF FLAT SECTION, and has a comb which sweeps downwards and backwards from about the level of the top jaw. The top jaw itself locates into position in the comb by means of a slot, and is tightened by a bolt which is secured from below by a pin beneath the lower jaw, and a square nut above the top jaw. The inner faces of the jaws are convex, where the flint is held secure. There is no shoulder to the cock, whose fall is arrested by a buffer screwed to the front of the lockplate.

The pan has a rounded or octagonal fence at its peripheral margin and this frequently carries the year of its manufacture. The pan itself has a sliding cover, the striker being a separate entity, a metallic arm which operates under spring tension, the spring being mounted on the outside of the lockplate. The sear of the snaphaunce mechanism acts horizontally, its nose passing through an aperture in the lockplate, to engage below the projecting tail of the cock, holding it at full cock. The snaphaunce lock has no provision for half-cock. A rod on the inside of the lock connects the tumbler to the sliding pan cover.

To operate the snaphaunce mechanism, the pan is closed and the

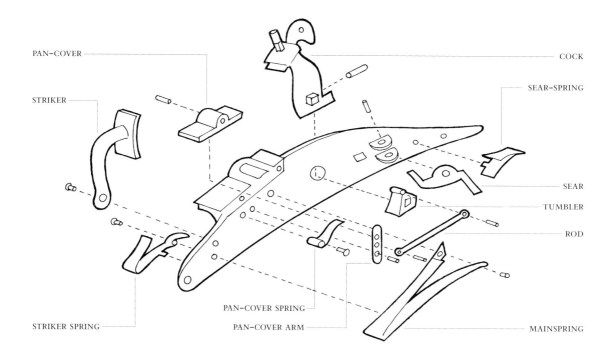

PAN-COVER

STRIKER

COCK

SEAR-SPRING

SEAR

TUMBLER

ROD

STRIKER SPRING

PAN-COVER SPRING

PAN-COVER ARM

MAINSPRING

FIG. 12. Snaphaunce lock, exploded view.

weapon cocked. The striker arm is then lifted forwards. When the trigger is pulled, the nose of the sear is withdrawn, and the cock springs forwards. As it falls, the rod connected to the pancover pushes the pan open; the flint hits the striker, knocking it back to its safety position. At the same time, a shower of sparks falls into the open pan, and the charge is ignited.

This type of snaphaunce lock is referred to as the Early Snaphaunce Lock. Later examples of this type of lock have the nose of the sear engaging in a rectangular aperture cut into the tail of the cock, rather than the method of engagement referred to above. As the snaphaunce mechanism developed, a shoulder was cut in the cock to arrest its fall on the upper surface of the lockplate, eliminating the need of a buffer, and the sear engaged in the tumbler, inside the lock, instead of passing through the lock-plate. This mechanism is known as the Late Snaphaunce Lock. Occasionally the sear nose engages in a recess cut into the inner face of the cock.

FLINTLOCK

In the flintlock mechanism, the pan cover and striker are incorporated in a single piece of metal, known as the frizzen. The frizzen has its own spring, secured, like the striker spring, to the outside of the lockplate. The earliest form of flintlock is called a doglock. Half-cock is achieved by the engagement of the sear on the tumbler, whilst at the same time a large dog-catch, pivoted on a pin at the lower edge of the lockplate, is manually operated to locate in a notch situated on the cock above the level of the spindle, in reinforcement of the lock half-cock position. The spindle and cock are forged from a single piece of steel, the tumbler being pushed onto the spindle and secured by a pin.

At full cock, the sear engages a flange on the tumbler, the exterior catch being disengaged by the backward movement of the cock. On pressing the trigger, the sear is disengaged, the cock falls forwards, striking the frizzen and knocking it forwards, towards the muzzle, thus exposing the powder in the pan to ignition from the resulting sparks. With this type of doglock, the fence was still a feature of the pan. Sometimes a smaller dog-catch is fitted, engaging the cock below the spindle, and a third variety can be encountered in which the dog-catch is pivoted from the top, again engaging the cock below the spindle. In each of the latter two varieties, the fence has disappeared entirely, the locks resembling ordinary flintlocks externally, but with the addition of dog-catches at the rear of the cock.

The Highland lock, common to all Doune pistols, has its own characteristics, being in some respects a reversion to the old snaphaunce mechanism, with a laterally-acting sear passing through the lockplate. This type of lock employs a separate tumbler, whose spindle passes through the lockplate. The cock fits over the squared spindle and is secured by a screw. There is no internal arrangement for half-cock, however, as there is in the doglock mechanism, the half-cock being achieved solely by the nose of the sear passing through a hole in the lockplate to hold the hammer breast. Full cock is attained by means of a projection at the rear of the sear, which engages with the tumbler as the cock is drawn backwards from the half-cock position. When the trigger is pressed, the sear is withdrawn through the lockplate and the cock springs forwards to strike the frizzen.

FIG. 13. Interior of Highland lock.

FIG. 14. Lock interior of heart–butt pistol showing flintlock mechanism of English type.

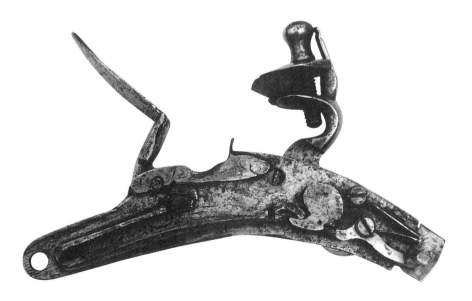

Late Flintlock Scottish pistols are in some instances fitted with Highland locks of this type, although refinements maybe added such as rainproof pans and roller frizzens, which incorporate a roller at the proximal end of the frizzen spring, in order to assist the speedy opening of the frizzen. Bridles to the frizzens make their first appearance in Scottish pistols of this type. In other cases the locks are English in type, with vertically-acting sears, half-cock and full-cock positions being achieved by means of slots in the tumbler. Bridles to the tumblers are only rarely fitted. Costume and Percussion Dress Pistols are invariably fitted with English style locks.

CHAPTER NINE

The Decoration of Scottish Pistols

THE DECORATION OF SCOTTISH PISTOLS IS A SUBJECT worthy of discussion in its own right. Many of these weapons, particularly those formerly in the possession of the Highland chiefs, were nothing less than works of art, each one hand-made by a single craftsman, who employed all his ingenuity and skills in order to produce a finished product that was not only functionally perfect, but would also excite the admiration of all who saw it. The owners of these pistols were justly proud of their possessions, whose beauty was in no small measure due to the embellishments which were lavished upon them by the gunsmiths.

These gunsmiths worked, either alone, or assisted by a single apprentice. Each pistol must have taken a considerable time to manufacture, and considerably longer to apply the decoration which was so important in establishing its status. The craftsman could not simply make the weapon, and leave it unadorned. He had, in addition, to learn the skills of inlaying silver, and of engraving, and while several excelled in these, there must have been many who did not.

Sometimes weapons can be encountered which have very little applied decoration, yet the pistols themselves are functionally perfect, and are beautiful examples of the art of the gunsmith. Added decoration was not essential to the manufacture and subsequent sale of a particular weapon.

Nevertheless, the gunsmiths in general were catering to a taste, and the public wish at that time, was for weapons embellished with silverwork and engraving.

The particular style of the embellishments was such that the pistol was immediately recognisable as being wholly and distinctly Scottish in origin. In Skokloster Castle in Sweden, there is a pair of snaphaunce lemon-butt pistols. These have barrels which are distinctly Scottish in appearance, ball triggers, and belt hooks. The lemon butts are hollow, pierced and fretted, yet, despite these features which they have in common with Scottish pistols, it is possible to say without hesitation, that the pistols are not of Scottish origin, not just because of the style of the locks but also because of the complete contrast between the decorative engraving on the pistols, compared to that on genuine Scottish pistols of the same period.

CELTIC ART

Celtic society is thought to have emerged in Central Asia around the period 500–450 BC. From here it expanded southwards into Italy, eastwards into the Balkans and Asia Minor, and westwards into France and the British Isles.[1] The art associated with Celtic culture incorporated elements which were often expressed in symbolic form. This symbolism is present in the decoration of surviving artefacts, including not only jewellery and pottery, but arms and armour and stone monuments, including both megaliths and gravestones. Geometric design, which was accomplished by the use of the compass, is quite common, and plant motifs, the so-called Vegetal style, are also frequently encountered.

The spiral, thought to represent eternal life, or the continuous creation and dissolution of the world, is another commonly occurring motif in Celtic art, and, yet another, a series of interlocking Ss.[2] This latter design is in reality a continuous spiral. It is frequently to be found in Scottish pistols and in early Celtic art is particularly encountered on bronze and iron sword scabbards. Knotwork, believed to symbolise the process of man's eternal spiritual growth, is frequently seen on powderhorns and targes, as well as dirk handles, but is not encountered on Scottish pistols.[3] Interlace, however, is a common element both in Celtic art and in Scottish pistols.

The early Christian gospels, dating from the seventh to the ninth century AD, such as the *Lindisfarne Gospel* and the *Book of Kells*, as well as the *Book of Durrow*, with its famous 'carpet page', exhibit many of the principal features of Celtic art, depicting the spiral in its many forms, and the manifold use of ribbon interlace and rectilinear design, including check, step, and key patterns, and diagonal fretwork.[4]

Many writers, when describing the decoration of Scottish pistols, mention the employment of Celtic design in the style of the engraving and the pattern of the silver inlay. Mayer, writing in 1934, considered this to be the result of a Celtic revival, that is, a revival of the ancient designs used centuries previously by the Celtic forebears of the dagmakers of the sixteenth, seventeenth and eighteenth centuries. Two years later, Finlay

FIG. 15. The lower surface of a ramshorn-butt pistol, showing stylised acanthus and wavy line engraving, both with origins in Celtic art. The conjoint Ss of the inner face of the butt is another feature of Celtic decorative art. The three transverse bands of engraved silver inlay are typical of pistols manufactured during the latter half of the eighteenth century.

disputed any Celtic revival and considered the Celtic decorative arts as applied to the Scottish pistol were the result of a continuing process passing down the generations. In his opinion, the designs had not been lost but had remained with the Scottish people throughout the intervening centuries. More recently, Caldwell has expressed the view that the decoration of Scottish pistols was more a late survival of Gothic and Romanesque design forms rather than Celtic. Whichever of these theories one accepts, it is perhaps best to regard the decoration of Scottish pistols as having been directly influenced in varying degree by Celtic designs. Where such designs do not at first appear to be of Celtic origin, although often a more prolonged and more detailed appraisal will result in a positive attribution, in most cases they can be seen, at the very least, to be derived from them.

In 1940, Joseph Meyer wrote a paper entitled 'Celtic Art on Scottish pistols'. In this erudite and fascinating article, Mayer described the common decorative motifs occurring on Scottish pistols, and in each case compared the design to a similar one occurring on Celtic artefacts, including the Christ Vine on the seventeenth century Bewcastle Cross, decorative motifs on the Lindisfarne Gospel, brooches, drinking cups and rock carvings.

Series of conjoined Ss are a well-known Celtic design, and interlacing scrollwork, so often encountered in Celtic monuments, is developed to a high degree in the Scottish pistols of the mid-eighteenth century. Inlaid

FIG. 16. The barrel of a Christie pistol, showing divergent scrolls, lobate and S-forms, as well as border and wavy line patterns.

FIG. 17. Celtic decoration on the butt and lockplate of a Christie pistol of 1750. Note the Lindisfarne-type engraving above the escutcheon, and the open-ended scrollwork derived from the Celtic spiral. The pierced star of the comb is yet another Celtic feature, and acanthus and borderline patterns also feature in Celtic art.

silver interlace usually takes the form of a single twisted strand, having four or more twists, intertwined with running loops which terminate in spirals. It is principally found on butts and butt spines.

The lyre shape was used by the Celts and is also a recurrent motif on Scottish pistols. It finds expression in the finials or base plates of belt hooks of some lobe-butt pistols of the eighteenth century. The star motif, engraved or fretted in the comb behind the cock of pistols of the second quarter of the eighteenth century, and echoed in the inlaid silver butt motifs of pistols of the same period, is also to be found amongst the jewellery of the early Celts. Lobate forms are also encountered, along with border engraving of many types, all of which have their counterparts in early Celtic art.

FIG. 18. The obverse side of the same pistol in fig. 17, shows engraving similar in style to that of the Lindisfarne Gospels. Punched dots are typical of Celtic art, and the double lyre-shape of the belthook finial also has Celtic origins.

The fishtail-butt pistol is quite typically Celtic in the design of its engraving. The border work is either of strapwork or diagonal key patterns. The butt is often engraved with the Celtic vine, in stylised form, and a similar device may be engraved on the striker arm.

Both chevrons and rondels were common motifs in Celtic art, and are found in Scottish pistols of the seventeenth and early eighteenth century. The typical punched decoration of the silverwork is also a feature employed extensively by the early Celts. The vine-like engraving on the butts of early eighteenth century Scottish pistols, can be found on the pages of the Lindisfarne Gospel, and can still be recognised, although now more stylised, in the deeply-chiselled engraving on the butts of pistols of the second half of the eighteenth century.

The divergent spiral is a frequent motif on the barrels of pistols of this period, and may be repeated on the lockplate. This spiral form has its origins in such Celtic monuments as the Newgrange megalithic tomb in County Meath, in Ireland, and may take the form of a leaf-scroll in spiral form. Sometimes a shell pattern is introduced, again in spiral form.

One rather unusual aspect of Celtic art, is the inclusion of a hidden face amidst the engraving, and this feature is occasionally encountered in Scottish pistols. The very practice of enchancing the silver inlay with punched dots, or of surrounding it with engraving or cross-hatching, and of covering the entire available surface in decorative work of one kind or another, is a characteristic of all Celtic art, and in fact, the more the student examines in detail the decoration of Scottish pistols, the more he will learn to recognise its Celtic derivations.

INTRINSIC DECORATION

Scottish pistols were, by their very nature, extremely decorative objects, not only because of the varied and unusual designs of the butt, but also having regard to their barrels. This was especially noticeable with the early pistols when barrels were usually long, and had heavy mouldings between the different stages. Many of these early pistols had six or seven stages, and this appearance, together with the 'belling', or 'swamped' effect of the muzzle (which often had, in addition, octagonal flats or facets round it) produced a dramatic impression. In addition, the proximal stage of the barrel was in itself often faceted, further enhancing the appearance of the weapon.

The ball triggers, and prickers if these were fitted, were also, to some extent, decorative features, which did much to improve the artistic impression of the pistol, while the belt hooks often had pierced and fretted finials, or end-pieces, which were attractive features to any prospective purchaser. The heavy baluster turnings of the early ramrods were an additional artistic feature, while lemon butts, being essentially hollow, were sometimes pierced and fretted, and at other times flattened into hexagonal or octagonal shapes. Yet another decorative feature is the comb found behind the cock in pistols of the second and third quarter of the eighteenth century. This was a pierced disc, often in the form of a star, with circular holes between its points.

BLUEING

There seems little doubt that Scottish pistols were originally blued. This idea seems strange to the modern collector, since almost all surviving specimens of Scottish pistols have been cleaned, and consequently present a bright overall appearance. Nevertheless it is not uncommon to find nineteenth-century Scottish pistols which retain all of their original blueing, and traces can be found in eighteenth and even seventeenth century examples.

Since most Scottish pistols of the seventeenth and early eighteenth century were extensively inlaid with silver, not only on the barrel, where the current fashion was for multi-staged barrels, each stage separated by a broad band of silver from its neighbour, but also on the butt and forend of the stock, the overall effect of the bright polished silver against a background of brilliant blue, must have been striking in its impact.

GILDING

As with blueing, evidence of gilding is occasionally found when examining Scottish pistols. It is likely that all brasswork was originally gilded, partly to prevent tarnishing, and partly to enhance the appearance of the pistol. Traces of this gilding can sometimes be identified in the early fishtail-butt pistols, but is most often found in presentation pistols of the late eighteenth and early nineteenth centuries.

BRASS

The use of brass in Scottish pistol did much to enhance its appearance. Brass was used in the construction of the barrels, and sometimes of the lockplate. The stocks of many of the earlier fishtail-butt pistols were constructed entirely of brass, and this metal was also frequently used in the manufacture of the later lobe-butt pistols. The earliest wooden-stocked fishtail-butt Scottish pistols were invariably fitted with engraved brass mounts, which served to protect the vulnerable extremities of that type of butt. Sometimes ball triggers and prickers were made of brass and frequently gilded, to both prevent tarnishing and to embellish.

INLAY

∞

Inlay was an important decorative feature of Scottish pistols, especially during the eighteenth century. This inlay was almost always of silver, but sometimes gold was used instead. On the barrel, inlay was applied to the broad barrel bands separating its different stages, and, as some of the early pistols had as many as seven different stages, the effect was very striking.

Barrel inlay usually took the form of rondels, diamonds, rectangles, squares, hearts, or simple lines. Similar decorative inlay was applied to the forend of the stock, where the chevron was sometimes employed. In this situation, interlacing scrollwork is commonly found, whilst another recurring motif is a type of ramshorn decoration, sometimes having a broad leaf between the horns. This pattern is most commonly encountered in the somewhat cruder pistols of around 1720–25, such as those made by Thomas Caddell and Patrick Buchanan. In pistols of this era, another common feature is a large silver heart inlaid into the butt, while pistols from 1725 onwards usually had an oval silver butt plaque in this situation, which was sometimes engraved with the initials or crest of the owner.

Another motif, inlaid into the butt, is a silver star, also a Celtic device, sometimes contained within a circle of engraved silver. The peripheral margin of the butt and sometimes also of the stock, were often inlaid with silver lines, and a variable amount of interlacing scrolls was interspersed throughout both butt and stock.

On the spine of the butt it is common to find interlacing scrollwork. The lower surface of the stock often has two or three parallel bands of engraved silver above and below the ball trigger. Heart-butt pistols often have a broad band of engraved silver at the junction of the base of the heart with the upper part of the stock. The ramshorn-butt quite commonly has a line of inlaid silver tracing the contours of the horns and base of the butt, and usually the silver is engraved in punctate fashion, an additional decorative feature. Most silver inlay was treated in this way, with tiny impressed dots following the lines of silver. The rose is a common feature and is almost always found as the decorative motif of the silver rondels. Heart-butts are sometimes decorated with the Dutch tulip, inspired by the succession of William of Orange.

Lobe-butt pistols have a particular form of inlaid silver on the butts. The steel pommel often has a silver rondel at its centre, with silver chevrons radiating outwards from it, so that, seen from below, the appearance is of a four-petalled flower. A silver plaque is sometimes inlaid into the upper part of the butt, behind the barrel tang screw, where the owner might engrave his family crest and motto. Yet another use of silver is in the construction of the hollow ball triggers and prickers.

FIG. 19. Celtic scrollwork on the spine of a Scottish pistol.

In the work of Alexander Campbell of Doune, in the mid-eighteenth century, we see the art of decorative inlay at its best. Pistols by that maker can be recognised at a glance by the elegance of their silver inlay. His use of interlacing scrollwork on the stocks and butts, as well as on the butt spines, gives his pistols the most beautiful and distinctive appearance. When it is considered that, in addition, the barrels were blued, the pistols must have looked magnificent indeed. John Christie of Stirling also excelled in the application of silver inlay to the stocks and butts of his pistols.

Inlay is occasionally found of copper or brass, sometimes of gold, the latter usually in presentation pistols of late design. There is no doubt that the extensive use of silver inlay in the decoration of the Scottish pistol contributed to its characteristic appearance, which distinguishes it so dramatically from pistols of other countries.

FIG. 20. Deeply incised engraving in the lemon-butt pistol by 'A.G.' Note the large central rose. *Marischal Museum, Aberdeen.*

ENGRAVING

This form of decoration was second only to the use of inlay in enhancing the appearance of the Scottish pistol. The first use of engraving was in the decoration of the brass mounts of the wooden-stocked fishtail-butt pistols of the late sixteenth and early seventeenth centuries. The fishtail terminal was usually engraved with two or three rosettes, whilst the other mounts were decorated with entwined foliage. Rosettes were also engraved wherever appropriate on other situations on the brass mounts. Entwined foliage was also applied to the lockplate, striker and cock of the pistol.

As this type of pistol became stocked entirely in brass, the decoration became more complicated. Again, the rosette is much in evidence, together with elements representing the Celtic vine, while the butt is frequently engraved with a symmetrical floral and foliate motif within a triangular panel. The forend also has borderline engraving, sometimes in the form of a modified Greek key pattern. Another form utilised is a simple fish scale, whilst interlace is also encountered.

Many heart-butt pistols have very little engraved decoration, this tending to be restricted to the cock breast and the tail of the lockplate. In the cruder weapons sometimes found in the first quarter of the eighteenth century, engraving tends to be limited to the silver inlay, with a little scroll-work on the cock and lockplate. With the Doune pistol, however, the art of the engraver reaches its peak, many being beautifully decorated with inter-lacing scrollwork, sometimes involving the entire pistol.

It should be noted that in eighteenth century pistols, the engraving is deeply incised, a feature not found in the engraving of the following century.

ETCHING

Etching was used in the decoration of the barrels and stocks of later flint-locks and percussion dress pistols. The process involved immersing the pistol in wax and allowing it to dry at which point a scriber drew the required pattern in the wax. Acid is then poured on top, and, after some time, bites into the metal following the pattern already created in the wax. In this way, complex designs can be produced, of animals, thistles, foliage, and one design frequently encountered, the figure of St. Andrew, patron saint of Scotland. This last is usually shown standing and holding the St. Andrew's cross in front of him. Trophies of arms are also frequently featured in etched stocks and barrels. Etching was a technique employed by gunsmiths around 1820, and is often combined with standard engraving.

GEMSTONES

Sometimes semi-precious stones are used to decorate Scottish pistols. This is usually a feature in percussion dress pistols of late type, around 1840–50. These have pommel-type butts, which allow the insertion of a cairngorm or similar stone. Occasionally a stone may be inserted into the side of the butt, or employed as the upper part of a thistle, in the thistle pricker usually found in this type of pistol. Such pistols as these are purely decorative objects, and were intended only as adjuncts to Highland dress.

NICKEL SILVER

This material was sometimes used in the construction of the stocks of percussion dress pistols of 1830–50. When brightly polished and engraved, with their barrels and locks of blued steel, the overall effect was very striking. Plate 14 shows a superb example of this type of embellishment. The pistols are constructed entirely of solid nickel silver, which is beautifully engraved overall, and the contrasting blued steel of the ramrods, locks, hammers, triggers and prickers can be clearly seen.

GOLD

Gold may occasionally be employed in the decoration of Scottish pistols. Ball triggers and prickers, as well as butt plaques, may be fabricated of gold, and may also be used instead of silver to create the scrollwork inlay on the butts and forends of the weapons. The precious metal was also often used to embellish the cocks, lockplates, and barrels, of presentation pistols. In the painting by John Michael Wright of a Highland Chieftain, although now positively identified as Lord Mungo Murray, he is wearing a pair of doglock ramshorn-butt pistols, each of which is fitted with a gold pricker, and we can presume that this metal was used also in the construction of the ball triggers, which cannot, however, be seen in the portrait.

CHAPTER TEN

The Doune Pistol

THE VILLAGE OF DOUNE IS SITUATED IN THE COUNTY OF Perthshire, northwest of Stirling, on the Stirling–Callander road. The ancient name of this parish is Kilmadock. Although only a tiny village, it was to become, throughout the eighteenth century, the principal centre in Scotland for the production of the Highland pistol.

Why the Highlanders held the craftsman gunsmiths of Doune in such high esteem that they chose to purchase their pistols from that source rather than the capital, Edinburgh, which was reasonably close to Doune, or Inverness, which was nearer to their homes, may never be known. Doune itself cannot even be considered to be situated in the Highlands of Scotland, being below the 'Highland Line', that is to say, south of the Great Glen, but, perhaps significantly, it lay on the route followed by the Highland drovers, taking their herds for sale to the cattle fairs of the Lowlands and the north of England. Archibald Campbell, in referring to the village of Doune, which he visited in 1802, makes no mention of gunsmiths.[1] He does, however, declare, that it derived considerable support from five Fairs held here during the year, and this in itself was probably an important factor in influencing the Doune gunsmiths to establish their trade in that village.

As each master of the craft took on apprentices, and as these apprentices became masters in their own right, the quality of work produced must have increased the demand for pistols from the Doune area, so that, as each newly-created master moved to his own premises in the village, the village itself, after a short time, became an important centre of the gunmaking industry in Scotland.

Highland pistols, or Doune pistols as they are commonly called, have a very distinctive style. Normally, they have scroll, or ramshorn butts, sometimes referred to in literature as 'claw' butts. Later examples, after about 1750, sometimes had lobe-butts. The principal characteristic of the Doune pistol is the laterally-acting, or horizontal, sear, which passes through a hole in the lockplate, to engage the breast of the cock in the half-cock position. The pistol is usually highly adorned with silver, having silver ball triggers and prickers, silver butt plaques of oval shape, and a variable amount of silver inlay and engraving. Sometimes the cock has a star-shaped comb behind its spur, a feature usually seen in pistols from around 1720-1760.

According to Logan, pistol-making was introduced to Doune by Thomas Caddell, a smith, in 1646, who had moved there from Muthil.[2] Caddell is traditionally credited with the establishment of the gun trade in Doune, and he was followed in his profession by successive generations of his family. *The Statistical Account of Scotland*, which was drawn up from the communications of the ministers of the different parishes by Sir John Sinclair, and published in twenty-one volumes in 1798, gives the following account of the gunmaking industry in Doune, which was provided by Mr Alexander MacGibbon:

> The only remains of any of the ancient branches of trade is the making of Highland pistols. The reputation of Doune for this manufacture, about the time of the German war, was very great.
>
> This art was introduced to Doune about the year 1646, by Thomas Caddell, who, having been instructed in his craft at Muthil, a village in Strathearn in Perthshire, came and settled in Doune.
>
> This famous tradesman possessed a most profound genius, and an inquisitive mind, and although a man of no education, and remote from any means of instruction in the mechanical arts, his study and persevering exertions brought his work to so high a degree of perfection, that no pistols made in Britain excelled, or perhaps equalled, those of his working, either for sureness, strength or beauty.

FIG. 21. The restored workshop of Thomas Caddell in Doune, Perthshire.

He taught the trade to his children, and several apprentices, of whom one was John Campbell, whose son and grandson carried on the business successfully with great repute.

While the ancient dress of Caledonia, that is, the philabeg, belted plaid, pistols and dirk was wore, the pistols made in Doune excelled all others, and acquired superior reputation over France, Germany, & C.

A pair of pistols, superbly ornamented, were fabricated by a tradesman taught in Doune, and, by the City of Glasgow, given in compliment to the Marquis de Bouillé.

The above Mr Campbell's grandson, who has now given over the business, made pistols to the first nobility in Europe, as Prince Ferdinand of Brunswick, the Duke of Cumberland, and others. The trade is now carried on by John Murdoch, also famous for his ingenuity in the craft, and who likewise furnished pistols to the first nobility of Europe.

These pistols were sold from 4–24 guineas a pair.

There is now very little demand for Doune pistols, owing, partly, to the low price of the pistols made in England, but the chief cause of

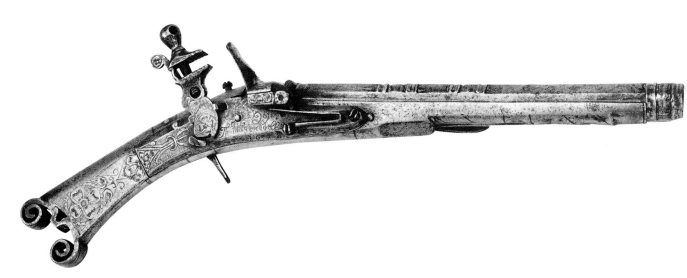

FIG. 22. Doglock pistol by Thomas Caddell, dated 1678. Note the generous curves of the ramshorn butt and the dog-catch behind the cock. The pricker and ramrod are missing and the trigger has been replaced. *Musée d'Art et d'Histoire, Neuchatel, Switzerland.*

> the decline is the disuse of the dirk and pistol as a part of the Caledonian dress; and, when Mr Murdoch gives over the business, the trade, in all probability, will become extinct.[3]

It is thus likely that Logan obtained his information regarding Thomas Caddell from the *Statistical Account*. That Thomas is referred to in the *Account* as a smith rather than a dagmaker or gunsmith, is hardly surprising, since at that time, most pistols were made by blacksmiths, dagmaking being only one aspect of the general stock-in-trade of the smith.

The manufacture of each pistol necessitated a great deal of work, and not every blacksmith was capable of producing consistent work of high quality. With the increasing demand for firearms, and pistols in particular, specialisation naturally occurred, and these early pistol makers were referred to as "dagmakers". Only after about 1650 does the term 'gunsmith' come into common parlance, and in Doune itself, not before 1702.

The earliest known pistol to be made by the hand of a Doune gunsmith is in the Museum of Art and History in the town of Neuchatel in Switzerland. The weapon is dated 1678, and is by Thomas Caddell. There is documentary evidence of the existence of a smith named Thomas Caddell, who was working in Doune in 1646, in the form of a receipt which has been found for ironwork on a coffin, made by him in that year.[4]

The earliest actual reference to a Doune gunsmith as such, is to be found in a tack granted by the Earl of Moray to a Thomas Caddell in 1702.[5] Arthur and Caldwell have proved the existence of four generations of Caddells known to have been gunsmiths in Doune, which, together with the smith thought to have originated the craft, makes a total of five generations.[6] Three of the four gunsmiths mentioned in a list of persons concerned in the rebellion of 1745–46 came from Doune. These were Robert Caddel, Thomas Caddel Senior and Thomas Caddel Junior. All were Jacobite supporters, Robert being imprisoned in Stirling in 1746, and pardoned in 1747.[7] The name of Robert Caddell was also included in a Muster Roll of Perthshire Horse (Strathallan's) drawn up by Oliphant of Gask on 7 February 1746. A witness who gave evidence in the trials against both Robert Caddell and Thomas Caddell Junior, was Alexander Campbell, named in the list as a "gunsmith in Down". Donald Campbell, referred to in the list as a gunsmith in Stirling, also gave evidence against one Will Oatt, another villager from Doune.[8] When the last Thomas Caddell died, around 1765, a John Caddell bought two pistols from his estate, valued at £7-4-0.[9]

One example of the work of Robert Caddell is known to have survived and is now in Glasgow Art Gallery and Museum. To Thomas Caddell, possibly the second, John Campbell was apprenticed, and, after the requisite period of seven years, he became a gunsmith in his own right. *The Statistical Account* mentions this apprenticeship, although stating that his master was the first Thomas Caddell, though he would have been by then very old. He was a gunsmith of great repute, whose long-barrelled pistols were engraved sparingly yet were elegant and well-balanced (see fig. 23 and plate 1).

John Campbell died in 1720 and was succeeded in business by his son Alexander. To the latter must go the distinction of being arguably the finest gunsmith in the history of the Doune pistol, producing work of incredibly fine quality, not only in the balance and design of his pistols, but in regard to the intricate scrollwork of inlaid silver with which he adorned the butts, spines and stocks of his pistols. Sometimes silver is used only sparingly, and

FIG. 23. Lockplate of a pistol by John Campbell (the first).

instead the engraving becomes very elaborate. Many beautiful examples of his work remain with us today, especially in Scottish museums. Alexander's son, John, representing a third generation of the Campbell family in Doune, also produced many fine examples of scroll-butt pistols.

On 3 August 1745, an entry in the Lockit Book of the Incorporation of Hammermen of Stirling reads:

> Daniel Campbell pistol maker in Doune admitted, the said Donald Campbell to pay only the sum of £30 Scots in regard there is none other of that business in this place, the essay to be a gun lock.[10]

Making due allowance for the clerk's error, it would appear that Donald Campbell was the same man who had given evidence in the trials following the '45 Rebellion and had practised as a gunsmith in Doune before moving to Stirling in 1745. No example of his work is known.

Another name famous for the manufacture of Doune pistols was that

FIG. 24. Ramshorn-butt pistol by Alexander Campbell of Doune, circa 1740. Here the application of silver inlay is brought to perfection. The star-shaped cock comb is always a sign of quality in Scottish pistols of this period, and a similar motif is inlaid in silver into the butt. Overall length 14¾″ (375mm), barrel 10″ (254mm), bore ¾″ (19mm).

Glasgow Museums: Art Gallery and Museum, Kelvingrove

97

of Murdoch. There were two Murdochs of repute, John and Thomas, and although contemporary with one another, they are not thought to be related. John Murdoch worked in Doune throughout the second half of the eighteenth century, and is specifically mentioned in the *Statistical Account* of 1798. He manufactured both lobe-butt and ramshorn-butt pistols, principally the latter. A superb pair of gold-inlaid ramshorn-butt pistols, signed only "Murdoch", and presented by his commanding officer to William Henry, Duke of Clarence, later to become William IV, were reputedly made by John Murdoch, who, the *Account* suggests, furnished pistols to the first nobility of Europe (see plate 17).

Thomas Murdoch, according to the *First Statistical Account*, was apprenticed in Doune and worked there during the third quarter of the eighteenth century. He is not specifically mentioned in the *Account*, but that the reference is to Thomas Murdoch can be deduced, as will be shown later. Thomas produced mainly lobe-butt pistols, and, indeed, was in all probability responsible for the design of the latter. Two Doune gunsmiths are known to have worked in collaboration with one another, in the lean times following the Jacobite Rising of 1745. These were Murdoch and Christie, and a pair of ramshorn butt pistols by these makers is in the Marischal Museum in Aberdeen and is marked on the lockplates 'Christie and Murdoch Duni *fecit*'. The insides of the lockplates are dated 1750.

Since John Christie did not move to Stirling until 1751, when he was admitted to the Incorporation of Stirling Hammermen, one can confidently assume that he was one of the partners. Thomas Murdoch, on the other hand, was christened in the year 1735, which makes him only fifteen or sixteen years old when the pistols were made. It is therefore more probable that John Murdoch was the second member of the partnership.

Following the defeat of the clansmen in 1746 and the subsequent decline in the Scottish arms industry in general, the Doune gunsmiths fell upon hard times and Thomas moved to Leith, near Edinburgh. He is recorded in the Edinburgh Directory for 1774 as being a pistol maker at Walkside, Leith.[11] Murdoch continued to manufacture pistols which were mainly of lobe-butt form, but also occasionally ramshorn. The lobe-butt may have appealed because of its resemblance to the conventional English butt, while at the same time retaining its Scottish characteristics—namely, its all-metal construction, its decorative style and the fitting of a Highland type of lock.

Two other Murdochs are known—William, who was the son of Thomas, and who carried on the business of pistolmaker at Walkside, Leith, after his father's death, and Alexander Murdoch.[12] Only one pistol manufactured by Alexander, a lobe-butt, is known to have survived, but William may have been the maker of three pistols which are marked only "Murdoch". Thomas Murdoch died in 1791. His obituary appeared in the *Edinburgh Evening Courant* on 22 September 1791:

> Yesterday died near Leith Mr Thomas Murdoch, an eminent pistol-maker. This gentleman brought that manufacture to great perfection. Some years ago, he was employed by the merchants of Glasgow to prepare a pair of pistols of great value, which were much admired, and sent as a compliment to the Marquis de Bouillé, as a proof of their high sense of his genteel behaviour at the capture of an island in the West Indies. Last year he sent, at his own expense, a pair of pistols of the old Highland construction, to his Royal Highness the Prince of Wales.

It is clear from this obituary that Thomas Murdoch was the "tradesman taught in Doune" who is referred to in Sinclair's *Statistical Account*.

Another maker who worked in Doune was John Christie, sometimes spelled 'Chrystie', who has been referred to above. Like Thomas Murdoch, he too, found it necessary to leave Doune, due, most probably, to the defeat of the Highland army and the subsequent Disarming Act. He established his gunsmithing business in Stirling, having been admitted to the Incorporation of Hammermen of that town on 7 December 1751. He should not be confused with James Christie who was a gunsmith in Perth during the period 1750–75. This latter had a son, also named James, who in turn became a Perth gunsmith in the first quarter of the nineteenth century.

Christie's pistols were beautiful examples of the art of the Doune pistolmaker. One of the finest examples of a Scottish pistol, which is in the Queen's collection at Windsor Castle, was made by John Christie in 1760 for King George III. A pair of ramshorn-butt pistols (see plate 2) also by Christie, were formerly in the collection of A. W. Cox of Glendoick in Perthshire, a notable collector of Scottish pistols in the early years of this century. One of this pair was illustrated by Whitelaw in his *Treatise on Scottish Hand Firearms*, when he described it, together with the gold inlaid pistol of George III referred to above, as "two particularly fine examples of the Highland pistol at its best." The lock of this pistol is stamped internally with the date '1750, NO 21', while the second pistol is marked '1751, NO 22'. The pistols are engraved and inlaid with silver in typically Celtic fashion, their cocks having particularly well-formed combs. The ball triggers and prickers are of silver. The pistols were exhibited at the Scottish National Exhibition held at Glasgow in 1911. Three cases of Scottish pistols were on display, amongst many other examples of the Hammerman Craft. A total of eighty-nine Scottish pistols was exhibited, several readily identifiable in present-day museum collections. Cox himself loaned thirty pistols to the exhibition, and Whitelaw a mere sixteen. All of Christie's pistols, other than those of military type, were stamped inside the lockplate with a serial number as well as the year of their manufacture, as described above. Christie is the only Doune gunsmith known to have followed this practice.

The signature 'Christie, London', on the lockplates of a pair of presentation pistols of hybrid design, dating from around 1820, appears to indicate the existence of another gunsmith of that name, who was active in the London area. These remarkable pistols are constructed of gilt copper or bronze, and are deeply chiselled and chased in rococo style. They have neither belt hooks nor ball triggers, but are fitted with conventional triggers and triggerguards, and have lobe butts which terminate in grotesque masks. The style employed in the decoration of these pistols is completely alien to that favoured by John Christie of Stirling, and, since they belong to a later period, it is likely that the Christie concerned was not the same man.

James Michie was another gunsmith who worked in Doune in the same period and in the latter part of the century a John Michie was active in Doune. John Stuart and James Paterson are less familiar names among Doune gunsmiths. The former signed his pistols "IO Stuart, *Duni fecit*". A pair of pistols by Paterson are now in the Victoria & Albert Museum in London. Further research may bring new names to light—sometimes the style of the pistol itself will suggest a Doune origin, but the best way to establish a Doune provenance is if the lockplate is engraved with the place of manufacture.

PART THREE

The Scottish Pistol and its Makers

CHAPTER ELEVEN

Classification and Design

THE EVOLUTION AND SUBSEQUENT DEVELOPMENT OF THE Scottish pistol are topics of immense fascination to the collector and student alike, and the time has now come to consider in turn, each of the different types and styles of pistol in our classification. Scottish pistols may be classified in a fashion similar to that used with antique pistols in general, by reference to the type of lock with which they are fitted. Thus we can recognise snaphaunce pistols, flintlock pistols, with, as a subdivision, doglock pistols, and percussion lock pistols.

The first attempt to classify the Scottish pistol was made by James Anderson, curator of what was then the National Museum of Antiquities in Edinburgh, in his descriptive text in Drummond's *Ancient Scottish Weapons*. Writing in 1881, he bases his classification on the shape of the butt and describes three varieties of form—the globose, the lobed and the ramshorn butt. Although a pistol illustrated in *Ancient Scottish Weapons* has a fishtail butt, Anderson did not describe it as such, and in fact believed that particular weapon to be of Spanish manufacture. He illustrated it only on account of its "close resemblance to the general form of Highland pistols". However, there is no doubt that the pistol is a Scottish one of early fishtail form.

Whitelaw, in his *Treatise on Scottish Hand Firearms of the XVIth, XVIIth, and XVIIIth Centuries*, published in 1923, classified Scottish pistols in a more traditional way, by reference to the type of lock fitted, relating each type to a specific butt style. Thus he recognised the early snaphaunce lock, the late snaphaunce lock, and the flintlock. Whitelaw, too, was the first person to designate a particular style of butt as fishtail. The Whitelaw classification can be tabulated as follows:

Early snaphaunce	Type A	Fishtail
	Type B	Globose
Late snaphaunce	Type C	Heartshaped
	Type D	Scrollshaped
Flintlock	Type E	Lobeshaped

Neither costume pistols nor percussion pistols are included in Whitelaw's classification as such, and are only mentioned in his notes on the evolution of the weapon. Nor does he refer to military pistols in his classification. A further discrepancy in Whitelaw's classification is in the overlap between, for example, a heart or scrollshaped butt when fitted with a flintlock mechanism, or when a lobeshaped butt has a snaphaunce lock.

The classification system used here is as follows:

1.	Pistols with Fishtail Butts	1600–1625
2.	Pistols with Lemon Butts	1625–1650
3.	Pistols with Heart Butts	1650–1730
4.	Pistols with Lobe Butts a) Early	1647
	b) Late	1750–1800
5.	Pistols with Ramshorn Butts	1649–1830
6.	Military Pistols a) Ramshorn	1739–1788
	b) Kidney-shaped	
7.	Costume Pistols	1820–1830
	incl. Percussion Dress Pistols	1830–1850
8.	Late Flintlock Pistols	1790–1820

This classification represents a reversion to Anderson's system, which has been extended in both directions—firstly, to include the fishtail butt which he had not recognised, and, secondly, to include military pistols and costume pistols as separate classes. The reason for this is that, to take military pistols first, there are two distinct types, one having a ramshorn butt, and the

CLASSIFICATION AND DESIGN

second a kidney-shaped butt. The latter term describes a butt shape which is not often encountered, and it was felt more appropriate to include this style of butt under the general class of military pistols, to which section it belongs, rather than create a wholly new class, the kidney-shaped butt being exclusive to military pistols alone.

In the case of costume pistols, it was felt that, although these are very often of ramshorn design, this is not always so, and that it was therefore preferable to create a separate class to include all such weapons, rather than to designate individual pistols as being costume or otherwise.

Percussion Dress Pistols, as a subheading, refers only to costume pistols fitted with percussion locks. They are, however, dignified with the somewhat grander title, since they almost always are of much better manufacture than ordinary costume pistols, are functionally more satisfactory, and the engraving and decoration are almost always of much better quality.

Lastly, the present classification includes a further type of pistol, namely, the Late Flintlock Pistol. Such pistols, formerly regarded as costume pistols, almost always have ramshorn or scroll butts, sometimes lobeshaped, but they are functionally and decoratively so superior to ordinary costume pistols, that their inclusion under that designation would be derogatory, hence a separate class has been created.

Thus, eight distinct types of Scottish pistol are recognised: fishtail butts, lemon butts (referred to in Anderson's classification as 'globose'), heart butts, lobe butts of both early and late design, ramshorn butts, military pistols with either ramshorn or kidney-shaped butts, costume pistols, including percussion dress pistols, and, finally, the late flintlock Scottish pistols.

When considering the dating of Scottish pistols, with regard to butt style, it must be recognised that some degree of overlap is bound to occur, as many gunsmiths worked in isolation, producing weapons perhaps to satisfy local demand for a particular style of pistol, long unfashionable elsewhere. The invention of the percussion system was not immediately accepted by all potential customers as being superior to the old flintlock system and it is likely that gunsmiths continued to supply flintlock weapons for some time after the new discovery until the new system had proved its worth. The same situation possibly prevailed at the changeover from

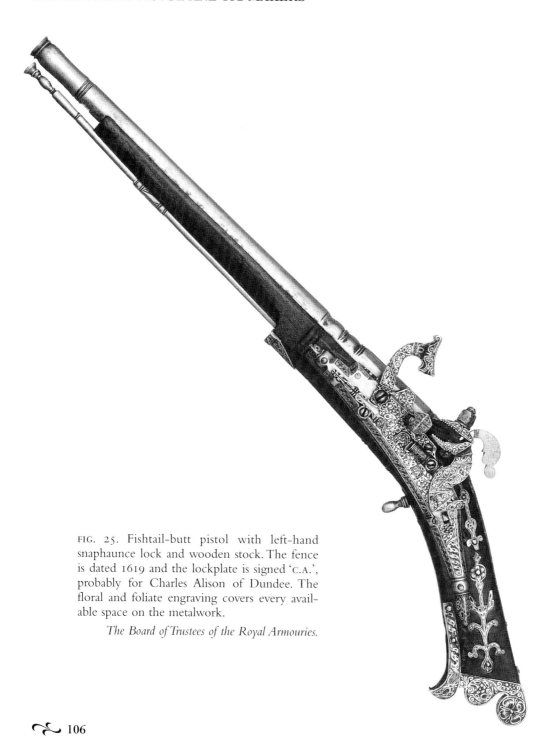

FIG. 25. Fishtail-butt pistol with left-hand snaphaunce lock and wooden stock. The fence is dated 1619 and the lockplate is signed 'C.A.', probably for Charles Alison of Dundee. The floral and foliate engraving covers every available space on the metalwork.

The Board of Trustees of the Royal Armouries.

snaphaunce to flintlock. The heart butt was more popular in the Lowlands, and its manufacture there probably continued long after the ramshorn butt had been adopted by the Highlanders, and at the same time, idiosyncrasies on the part of individual customers must have influenced the continued production of a particular style of butt against national or local trends. Therefore, the dates shown must be regarded as entirely arbitrary, and merely give guidance concerning general trends.

FISHTAIL-BUTT PISTOLS

The fishtail-butt pistol must be considered first, since the earliest known examples of Scottish pistols are of this type. The term 'fishtail-butt' was originally coined by Charles Whitelaw, and is quite an apt description, although more recently it has been suggested that the butt bears more resemblance to a bird's head than a fish's tail. It has already been mentioned that a pair of pistols is known which is dated 1598, and these can be seen in the Historisches Museum in Dresden. The initials of the maker are I.K., and may be those of John Kennedy, who is known to have been a dagmaker in Edinburgh in 1596.

Fishtail-butt pistols resemble most the butts of certain all-metal German wheellock pistols of contemporary manufacture. Reference has already been made to two pistols in the Palazzo Ducale in Venice, whose butts are of vaguely similar design, but the country of origin of these pistols cannot be assigned with absolute certainty, and it may well be that these pistols, as well Scottish fishtail-butt pistols, had a common ancestor in the German all-metal wheellock pistol.

These early fishtail-butt pistols had stocks constructed of wood, usually brazil wood, but sometimes walnut or rosewood, and the butts were inclined at a fairly pronounced angle to the barrels. As the projections at the upper and lower edges of the butt were vulnerable to damage, the stock was usually reinforced with brass mounts at these points. A variable amount of brass was inlaid into the stock and liberally applied with the engraver's art.

Pairs of fishtail-butt pistols are invariably fitted with left and right hand locks respectively, and the locks themselves are always snaphaunce. They are usually constructed of brass, but sometimes of steel, and are engraved overall. The lockplates are stamped with the initials of the dagmaker who constructed them, whilst the barrels may be inlaid at the breech with their date of manufacture. The barrels and forends of the stocks are flattened laterally, and are usually in several stages, but not to the extent of pistols constructed in the late seventeenth and early eighteenth centuries, being three or four in number. The muzzles may be elaborately moulded, sometimes flaring outwards at this point. This type of muzzle has sometimes been seen as bearing some resemblance to the Scottish thistle, but it is unlikely that it was intentionally created as such by the Scottish gunmakers.

The bore of the fishtail-butt pistol was of fairly small diameter, about ⅝″ (16mm), and it has been suggested that the pistol was intended to fire arrows rather than ball, although this too seems rather implausible.

The engraving of the metalwork of the fishtail-butt pistol is characteristic, and instantly recognisable, scrolling foliage being the predominant theme, and is to be found on the lockplate and external working parts of the lock, including the cock and striker. The butt mounts are engraved with two or perhaps three rosettes, and this motif may be found on other brass-work inlaid into the stock, whilst occasionally a thistle is encountered.

The topjaw is secured by a bolt which passes from below the lower jaw, through the upper jaw, to thread into a square nut above the upper jaw. The bolt itself is held in position below the lower jaw by a pin through its head, thus holding the flint securely between the jaws of the cock. In this way the Scottish snaphaunce differs from its English counterpart, in which the topjaw is secured by a single screw which passes through the topjaw from above, threading into a screwhole in the lower jaw, a system retained in the doglock mechanism. Behind the cock, an attractive plume-shaped comb sweeps downwards and backwards, providing additional security for the topjaw, as well as enhancing the appearance of the pistol.

In the snaphaunce lock, the striker and pancover are separate. There is no half-cock position, the pan being primed separately and the pancover

opposite FIG. 26. Pair of all-brass fishtail-butt snaphaunce pistols with right and left-hand locks, by James Low of Dundee. Dated 1624. Overall length 17″ (432mm), barrel 12″ (305mm), bore ⅜″ (9.5mm). *Glasgow Museums: Art Gallery and Museum, Kelvingrove.*

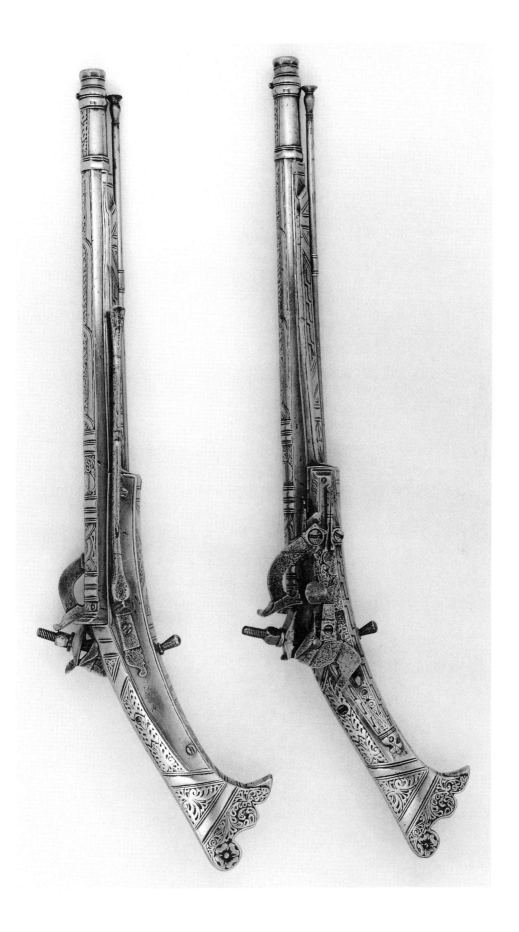

closed, before lifting the striker arm backwards, towards the cock, to prepare the weapon for firing. On pressing the trigger, the pancover is pushed open by a rod inside the lock, and, at the same time, the flint hits the striker, producing the sparks which result in the ignition of the charge. The lack of a half-cock mechanism, however, made the weapon unsafe to carry loaded, especially in view of the absence of a trigger-guard to protect the trigger, unless the striker arm was pushed forwards, away from the cock. It could then be returned to the firing position when necessary.

As in all Scottish pistols, whatever the butt style, a belt hook is fitted on the opposite side to the lock, and in the case of the fishtail-butt pistol, is relatively plain, lacking an elaborate finial, while the ramrod is constructed of wood and tipped with brass. The trigger is sometimes of the ball variety, but is commonly of a style more accurately referred to as a 'stud' trigger, being of elongated cylindrical form, wider and more rounded at its extremity. No pricker is fitted to fishtail-butt pistols.

Gradually over the years, the use of wood in the construction of the stock was abandoned in favour of brass, which readily lent itself to the art of the engraver. Brass fishtail-butt pistols are usually elaborately and deeply engraved overall, with a mixture of rosettes and scrolling foliage which may be a stylised representation of the Celtic vine. The same theme is repeated on the butts, which frequently exhibit a triangular panel on either side, containing flowers and foliage in an attractive symmetrical pattern. One example employs fish scale as an overall design, thus complementing the style of butt. Borderline engraving consists of simple lines, cable, interlace, stepwork or a Grecian key pattern.

The brasswork was normally entirely gilded, and the barrels, if of steel, blued, so that these fishtail-butt pistols were most beautiful weapons, which must have been highly prized by their owners. The ramrods of these all-brass pistols were constructed of brass or steel, and had heavy beaded baluster turnings.

A magnificent pair of all-brass fishtail-butt pistols dating from 1611 can be seen in the Museum of Antiquities in Edinburgh. These were formerly in the collection of King Louis XIII of France. Another superb pair of these pistols, dated 1624, is to be seen in Glasgow Art Gallery and Museum (see fig. 26). All are the work of James Low of Dundee.

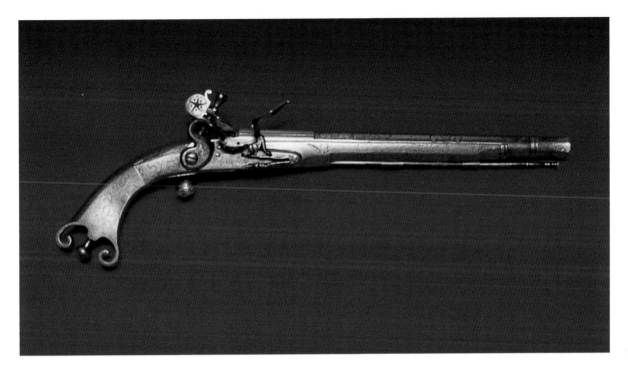

PLATE 1. Ramshorn-butt pistol by John Campbell (1st) of Doune, c. 1715–20. Campbell sometimes employed cannon barrels in his pistols and at other times used extensive silver inlays. This particular weapon is plain but has very graceful lines. Overall length 16″ (406.5mm), barrel 10¾″ (273mm), bore ½″ (13.5mm). *Private Collection*.

PLATE 2. Pair of ramshorn-butt all-steel pistols by John Christie of Doune, mid-eighteenth century. Note the star-shaped cock comb, the facetted pan and the coffin-shaped frizzen with its delicately-chiselled spring. These pistols represent the ultimate in Doune pistol manufacture. Overall length 13″ (330mm), barrel 8″ (203mm), bore ½″ (13.5mm). *Private Collection*.

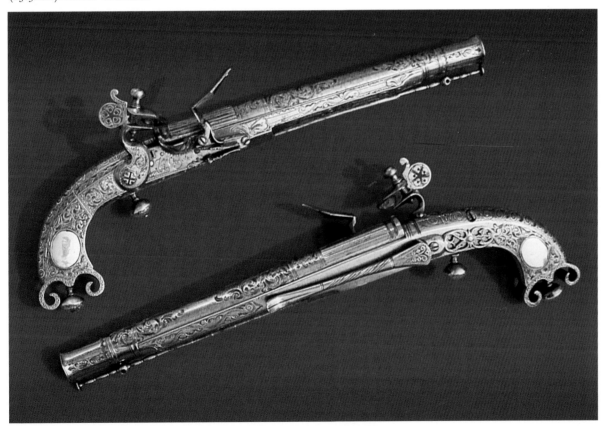

PLATE 3. Lockplate of Christie pistol, mid-eighteenth century (see plate 2).

PLATE 4. Un-named heart-butt pistol, c. 1710. Note the extensive silver and brass inlay on stock and barrel. The floral motif on the butt is thought to represent the Dutch tulip, commemorating the accession to the throne of William of Orange in 1689. Overall length 13″ (330mm), barrel 9½″ (241.5mm), bore ½″ (14.5mm). *Private Collection*.

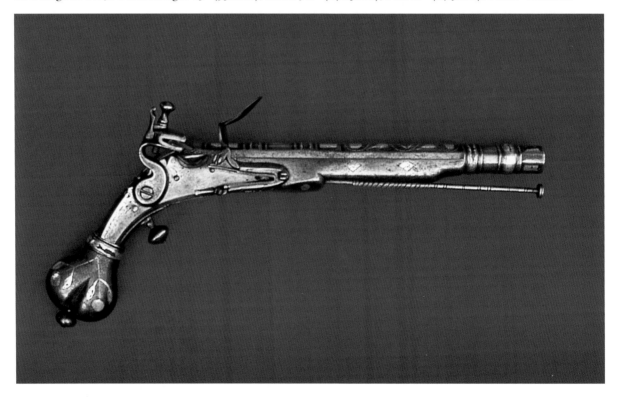

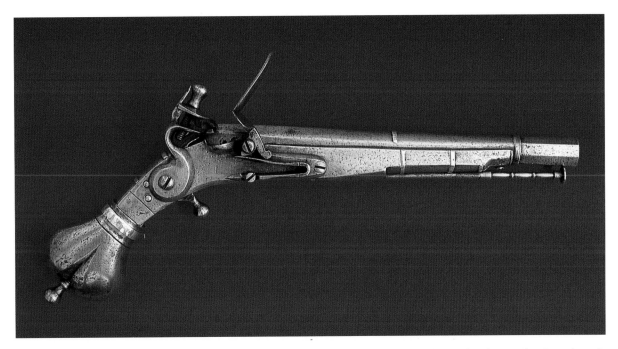

PLATE 5. Heart-butt flintlock pistol by 'I.O.' of Edzell, c. 1730. A similar pistol by this maker, but with a brass barrel, is in Glasgow Museum and Art Gallery. Overall length 13″ (330mm), barrel 9″ (228.5mm), bore ½″ (14.5mm). *Private Collection.*

PLATE 6. Heart-butt pistol by James McKenzie of Brechin, c. 1730. Note the short, stubby appearance and typical angular butt. Overall length 9.75″ (247.5mm), barrel 6″ (152.5mm), bore ½″ (15mm). *Angus District Libraries and Museum Service.*

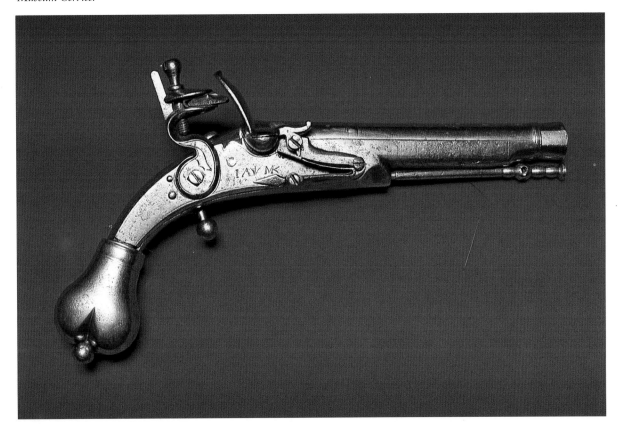

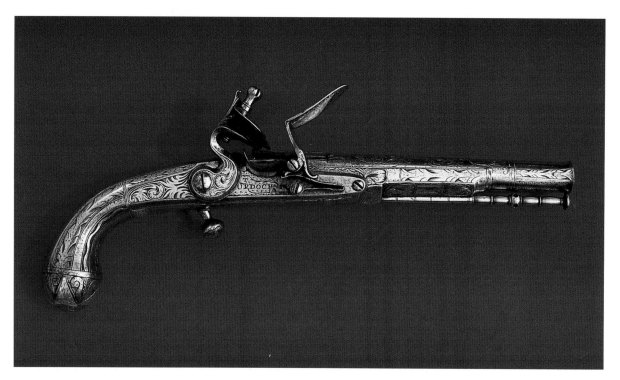

PLATE 7. One of a pair of lobe-butt pistols by Thomas Murdoch of Leith, c. 1750–75. Note the typical stylised acanthus and wavy line engraving of the butt. Overall length 12″ (305mm), barrel 7″ (178mm), bore ½″ (15mm). *Private Collection.*

PLATE 8. Ramshorn-butt pistol by Thomas Caddell (3rd), c. 1710. This pistol may have belonged to Lord Panmure, a Jacobite attainted after the rebellion of 1715. Note the extensive silver inlay on stock and barrel. The ramrod is not original. The pistol reputed to have belonged to Colonel John Roy Stuart is very similar to this weapon. Overall length 16″ (406.5mm), barrel 10½″ (266.5mm), bore ⅝″ (16mm). *Angus District Libraries and Museum Service.*

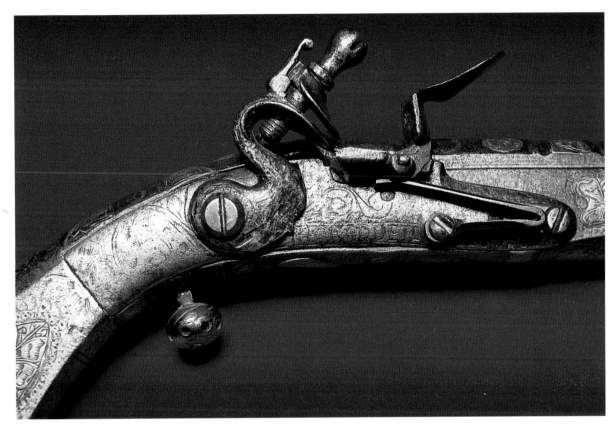

PLATE 9. Lockplate of Caddell pistol, c. 1710 (see plate 8). *Angus District Libraries and Museum Service.*

PLATE 10. Ramshorn-butt pistol by Thomas Murdoch of Leith, c. 1750–75, showing traces of original bluing. The butt plaques are engraved with the crest and initials of Sir Joseph Scott of Great Barr, Staffordshire. The pistol is in pristine condition but the ramrod has been replaced during its working life. Overall length 11½″ (292mm), barrel 7″ (178mm), bore ⅝″ (15mm). *Private Collection.*

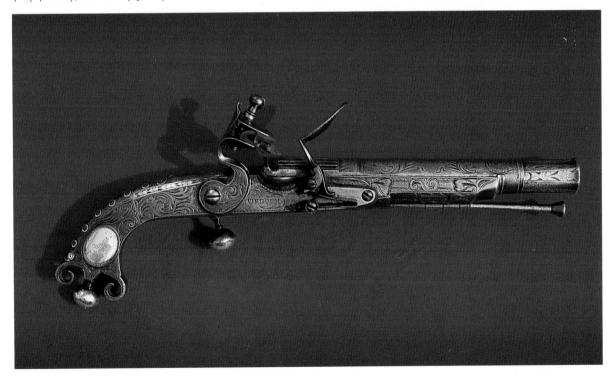

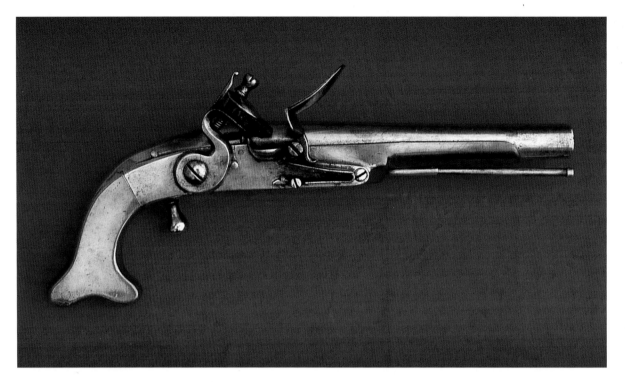

PLATE 11. Military pistol with bronze frame and kidney-shaped butt, by John Waters of Birmingham, c. 1780. Overall length 11½″ (292mm), barrel 7″ (178mm), bore ⅝″ (15mm). *Private Collection.*

PLATE 12. Ramshorn military pistol, un-named, but of Bissell type. Note the ring-neck cock, unusual for this type of pistol, the single stage barrel, and the daisy-pattern engraving on the butt. Overall length 13″ (330mm), barrel 8″ (203mm), bore ⅝″ (14mm). *Inverness Museum and Art Gallery.*

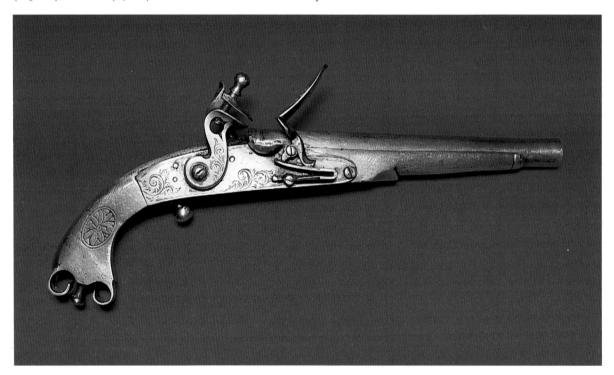

above PLATE 15. The lockplate of Wighton pistol, c. 1840–50 (see plate 14).

below PLATE 14. Pair of percussion dress pistols by Wighton of Edinburgh, c. 1840–50. Stocks and barrels are constructed from solid nickel silver; ramrods, locks, and triggers, of blued steel. The pistols are engraved overall with running leaf scrolls, and the English style locks incorporate safety bolts. Both pistols are engraved with the crest and motto of their original owner. Alexander G. Wighton is recorded in the Edinburgh and Leith Post Office Directory from 1839–51, his occupation being listed as Work Jeweller/Engine Turner. Overall length 11″ (279.5mm), barrel 6¾″ (171.5mm), bore ⅜″ (11.5mm). *Private Collection.*

above PLATE 13. Detail of military pistol showing plain belt hook finial, and Tower Proof and View Marks for private arms. *Inverness Museum and Art Gallery.*

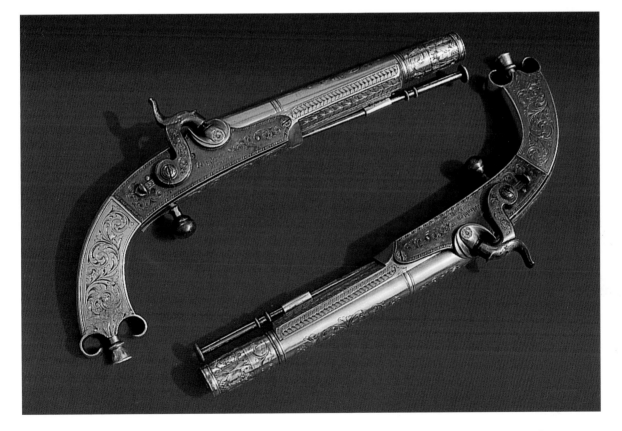

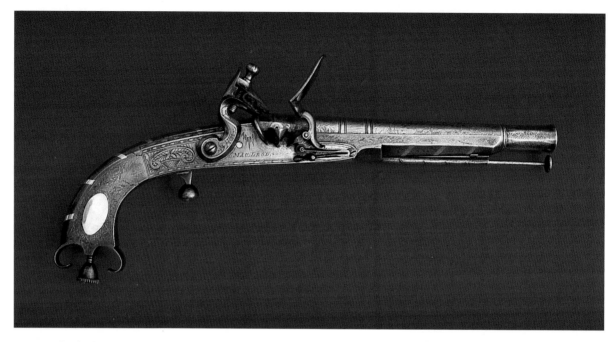

16. Late flintlock Scottish pistol by Macleod, c. 1820. Note the roller frizzen, rainproof pan, platinum-lined vent, and pigeon-breasted cock. Both stock and barrel are extensively etched, the former being inlaid with silver. Overall length 13″ (330mm), barrel 7¾″ (197mm), bore ⅝″ (15.5mm). *Private Collection.*

17. Gold-mounted presentation pistol with ramshorn butt, one of a pair by John Murdoch of Doune, late nineteenth century. Overall length 12½″ (317.5mm), barrel 8″ (203mm), bore ⅝″ (14.5mm). *Inverness Museum and Art Gallery.*

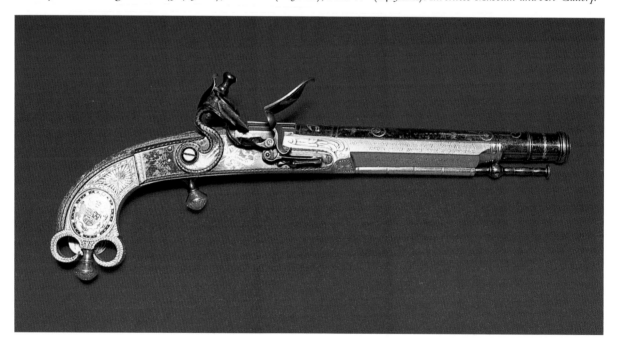

These early Scottish pistols were usually stamped with the initials of the dagmaker who constructed them. This mark is impressed upon the lockplate, and, in addition, a date may be inscribed on the fence, or on the barrel itself, giving the year of manufacture of the weapon. Unfortunately, in many cases it has proved impossible to determine the full names and towns of origin of the makers of these early weapons, due to the absence or loss of records, or to an insufficiency of historical documentation in burgh records, Hammermen minute books, or in town directories and other legal documents. Much of the work in this field was pioneered by Charles Whitelaw, and was published eventually in *Scottish Arms Makers*, but a great deal remains to be discovered regarding these early pistol makers. It is an enormous task, but a challenging one, and it is hoped that future researchers will eventually unravel its mysteries, and provide us with the key to the identity of these unknown craftsman of the seventeenth century.

LEMON-BUTT PISTOLS

This style is so called because of the approximation of its shape to that of a lemon. Many of these butts, however, have flattened or multifaceted sides, six or eight in number, and the butt may terminate in a sharp point, which is distinctly un-lemonlike in appearance. Nevertheless, the term is a good one in respect of the visual image it creates, and is worthy of retention. The lemon-butt pistol seems to be distantly related to the German wheellock, which was often fitted with a large ball pommel, and lemon-butt German wheellock pistols are themselves known to exist.

The lemon butt is usually fitted with a device called a pricker, this being a ball which unscrews to reveal a sharpened point, used to clear the barrel vent of powder fouling, and occasionally this item may be missing or absent, while the lemon terminal itself may be pierced and fretted, producing a most attractive appearance. Usually constructed of gilt brass, they were highly desirable weapons to the fortunate few who could afford them.

All lemon-butt pistols have locks of snaphaunce form, each pair being fitted with right and left hand locks. The belt hooks have plain finials, while the triggers are of the stud variety. The ball pricker is usually of steel or

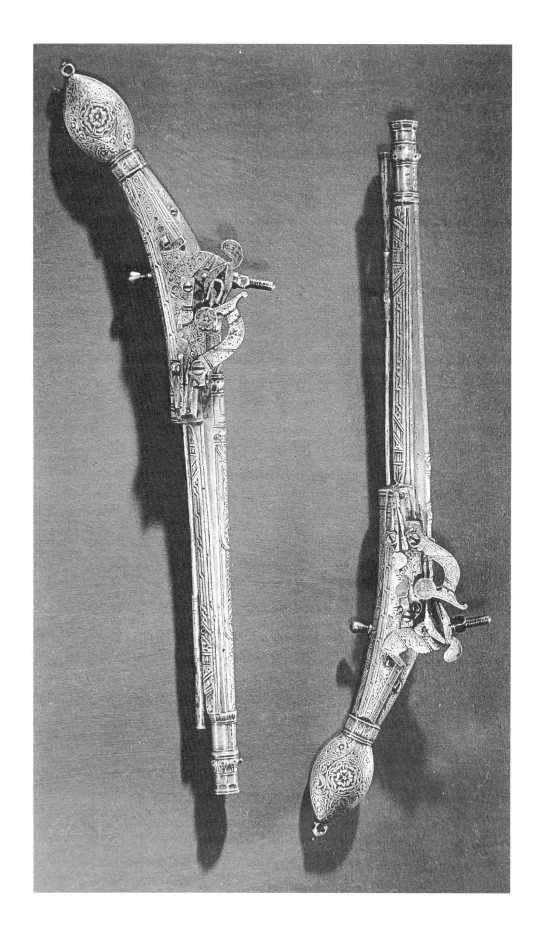

brass, and is often perforated with two holes, running at right angles to each other, a feature which may be repeated on the proximal ramrod bead. It is said that the ramrod could be inserted through the holes in the pricker in order to facilitate the removal of a tight pricker. It has also been suggested that the holes were made to allow a lanyard to be inserted, but essentially the holes are decorative in nature. Engraving, as with the all-brass fishtail butt pistols, is a combination of leaf scrolls and rosettes, with the occasional Scottish thistle, together with various patterns of borderline engraving.

Lemon-butt pistols tend to be long-barrelled weapons of narrow bore. The barrels usually have several stages, separated by broad barrel bands, having muzzles which were either moulded or of the octagonal swamped variety. One characteristic that emerged was a multi-faceted breech, so often to be found in Scottish pistols of the eighteenth century. Lemon-butt pistols may be constructed of iron, or, more rarely, of wood. An example of the latter is in the Museum of Antiquities in Edinburgh. This particular pistol was made by Robert Mosman of Canongate, and has a snaphaunce lock. Its lemon butt was formerly covered in brass plates, but these are now missing and only the holes remain in which were inserted the pins securing the plates. The pistol is dated 1625, across the breech of its brass barrel, and was formerly in Whitelaw's collection. It is fitted with a true ball trigger and was probably made to satisfy the requirements of an individual customer.

The fact that few wooden-stocked pistols have survived, compared to those stocked in iron or brass, may reflect, to some extent, the greater vulnerability of the former to accidental damage and to woodworm.

Many surviving examples of lemon-butt pistols are stamped 'I.L.' on the lockplate. These initials are thought to represent James Low of Dundee, who worked during the second quarter of the seventeenth century. A pair of pistols by this maker was sold at Phillips in London in 1987 for £28,000.

James Low was probably the most prolific maker of lemon-butt pistols in Scotland, judging by survival rates, and examples of his work can

FIG. 27. Pair of all-brass lemon-butt snaphaunce pistols, dated 1634 and signed 'A.G.', possibly representing Archibald Gibson of the Canongate. Overall length 16¾" (659mm). *Marischal Museum, Aberdeen.*

be seen, not only in museums in Scotland itself, but also in Denmark, Sweden, and France. Several of these may have been presented as gifts to foreign rulers, such was their quality. James Gray, another Dundee gunsmith, and Patrick Hamilton of Canongate, also made lemon-butt pistols.

HEART-BUTT PISTOLS

In the heart-butt pistol, the Scottish dagmakers created a weapon that was not only functionally excellent, but at the same time possessed of a degree of elegance surpassing that of the fishtail or lemon-butt pistols made in the first half of the seventeenth century. So-called because of the characteristic shape of its pommel, which bears some resemblance to the popular graphic representation of a heart, the heart-butt is flattened laterally and has a pricker screwed into its base, which is often hollow and pierced with two holes running at right angles to one another.

Like the lobe-butt pistols, the heart-butt evolved from the lemon-butt pistols of the second quarter of the seventeenth century. The main source of production of the heart-butt pistol was Dundee, on the east coast of Scotland, but other towns were also prominent in its manufacture, including Elgin, Montrose, Old Meldrum and Brechin. Since these towns are below the 'Highland Line', the weapons are sometimes referred to as being of 'Lowland type'. Scotland did not have a monopoly on the production of heart-butt pistols, and heart-butt pistols of French manufacture are known to exist, but these pistols did not achieve the popularity which they enjoyed in Scotland.

Early pairs of heart-butt pistols are fitted, in the style of the time, with right and left hand locks, the later versions having only right hand locks. In addition to this feature, we come across, for the first time, the offset butt, the angle of the butt to the vertical being offset to the left, in the case of the right hand pistol, and to the right, in the case of the pistol designed for use with the left hand. Whitelaw believed that this was in order to correct a tendency of the right hand pistol to fire to the left, due to the release of the tumbler when the trigger is pressed, whilst the opposite was true of pistols fitted with left hand locks. It is, however, difficult to see why forces operating inside the lock, whether from the mainspring, the lack of a bridle

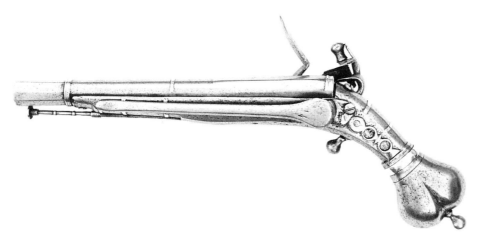

FIG. 28. Obverse side of pistol by 'I.O.' of Edzell, c. 1730, illustrated in plate 5, showing the fretted belt hook finial.

to the tumbler, or the laterally-acting sear, should affect the aim of a pistol, and it would seem more likely that trigger pressure and the force exerted by the cock on the striker or frizzen must have been more important in this respect than the release of the tumbler. However, the vast majority of heart-butt pistols have straight butts.

Regarding the question of sights in Scottish pistols, it must be remembered that they were not weapons which were intended to be used at long range, and sights themselves were really superfluous. Seldom does one find any foresight on a Scottish pistol, and the rear sight is of the open variety, being a semi-circular hole filed into the breech ridge. Whilst the use of this device for sighting in the absence of a foresight may seem a trifle arbitrary, a little practice indicates that the method used was actually quite a satisfactory one, it being necessary only to raise the barrel until the gap in the semi-circle is completely filled. As the pistol is so beautifully balanced in the hand, this result is easier to achieve than might be imagined.

An alternative explanation of the offsetting of the butt is that it allows the pistol to lie more comfortably in the hand, with the barrel in a central position and this makes for a better balance, and therefore greater accuracy. This can easily be confirmed by raising the hand as if to fire a pistol, with the forefinger around an imaginary trigger. If the inside of the hand is now examined, we can see that the area of the palm which grips the butt is wedge-shaped, becoming narrower from top to bottom, and it is self-evident that a butt of this shape would be accommodated more easily in the hand. In any event, this offsetting of the angle of the butt from the vertical in order to improve the aim, is a feature only encountered in Scottish pistols, and does great credit to the early Scottish gunmakers whose work is not infrequently denigrated by collectors of English pistols.

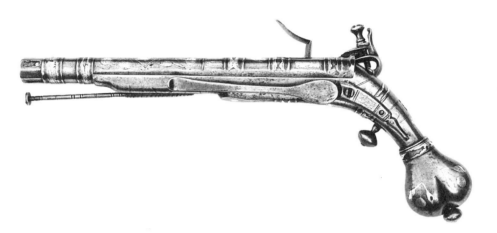

FIG. 29. Obverse side of heart-butt pistol, c. 1710, illustrated in plate 4, showing well-shaped belt hook, with long finial.

FIG. 30. View of the barrel, showing silver and brass inlay, and silver barrel bands.

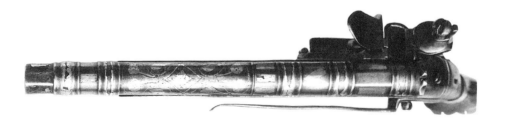

The earliest heart-butt pistols are fitted with snaphaunce locks, later examples being doglock or flintlock in type. Conversions from the earlier varieties to the later flintlocks will sometimes be encountered. The snaphaunce lock has an attractive pierced and fretted fence on the outside of the pan. This feature is sometimes repeated at the proximal end of the belt hook, before it splays out into a fretted finial, which was to be a popular feature throughout the following century.

The earliest snaphaunces have the nose of the sear passing through the lockplate to engage a projection at the tail of the cock in the full-cock position, there being no half-cock on these weapons. The arrest of the cock is achieved by means of a buffer screwed to the outside of the lockplate. Later snaphaunces involve the nose of the sear engaging a rectangular recess in the cock, whilst in some varieties of snaphaunce, the sear nose engages with a recess in the inner face of the cock, whilst at the same time the sear itself engages a slot in the tumbler.

Doglock as well as true flintlock heart-butt pistols are also encountered, including some Highland-type locks. The earliest flintlock heart-butt pistols have cocks which are of elegantly rounded section, whilst those of the later heart-butts are frequently flat. The barrels of heart-butt pistols may be long and multi-staged, having broad barrel bands between the stages, which may be inlaid with engraved silver. The muzzles are sometimes moulded, sometimes having flared multiple facets. Short-barrelled versions are also encountered. Additional silverwork may be inlaid into the barrel in the form of engraved rondels or rectangular plaques. The Dutch tulip is frequently encountered and this feature may be inlaid into the barrel, butt, or stock, of the pistol. The heart is another motif which is commonly found, while a broad band of engraved silver is often found at the junction between the heart butt and the stock proper. Engraving usually takes the form of scrollwork on the lockplate and cock, or, in the case of a snaphaunce, on the striker and pancover.

As the period covered by the heart-butt pistol is a fairly long one, from around 1650-1730, the angle of the butt relative to the barrel varies from being very shallow at the commencement of the period, to being almost a right angle, in the first quarter of the eighteenth century.

The fence is often dated with the year of manufacture of the pistol, and this date may be repeated on the barrel breech. These dates may not always agree, but this only signifies that the gunsmith has mounted a barrel or lock from stock, which has been constructed and engraved at an earlier date. The initials, and occasionally the full name of the gunmaker, are stamped on the lockplate. The practice of signing the lockplate with the full name of the maker did not become fully established until well into the eighteenth century, so that the researcher is faced with a formidable task in attempting to match the initials impressed on the pistol, with those of known gunsmiths of the period. James McKenzie of Brechin, for example, signed his pistols 'IA ★ MK', each pair of letters being separated by an asterisk or arrow, but pistols by this maker can often be recognised by their distinctive styling. William (Gulielmus) Smith of Inverness, who was active between 1670 and 1695, signed his pistols 'G.S.', or 'W.S.'. John Stuart, whose place of work is unknown, signed his pistols in full, 'I.O.Stuart', but the initials of many of the early Scottish gunsmiths remain unidentified.

Although almost always constructed of iron, heart-butt pistols are occasionally stocked in wood, presumably at the request of a particular customer, and attention should be drawn to a heart-butt pistol, stocked in rosewood, which was formerly in the Charles Whitelaw collection, but now in the Museum of Antiquities. Dating from about 1710, it has a doglock mechanism, with an unusually engraved ball trigger, and a matching false pricker. Its lock is of some elegance in respect of its construction and engraving, whilst the barrel is beautifully inlaid with silver. The pistol is by John Stuart and is a lasting tribute to that maker.

While some heart-butt pistols are relatively crude in construction, others, including the pistol by Stuart mentioned above, are beautifully decorated and constructed. It is necessary only to handle such a weapon, to realise that only in the English duelling pistol of some 80 years its junior, does one experience the same feeling of balance. Light in weight, the pistol comes up to the aim with such ease and accuracy, that it becomes a natural extension of the outstretched arm in exactly the same way as a high quality duelling pistol by such prestigious makers as Robert Wogdon or Durs Egg.

With the increasing popularity of the ramshorn-butt pistol, the heart-butt pistol began to lose favour, until, by about 1730, the ramshorn-butt had completely replaced it.

LOBE-BUTT PISTOLS

There are two varieties of lobe-butt pistols—early and late. Of the former, only three examples are known to exist, one of which can be seen in the Museum of Antiquities in Edinburgh. This pistol is a snaphaunce and is dated 1647. It has a 5-stage barrel, the barrel bands being inlaid with brass. As the lock is a left hand one, the pistol, which is unsigned, is obviously the sole survivor of a pair. The style would appear to be a development of the lemon-butt pistol, to which it bears a close resemblance. The others (owned by the W. Keith Neal Foundation) comprise a pair, also snaphaunces, and have 5-stage barrels inlaid with silver, the stages separated by silver barrel bands. They are signed "A.L.", possibly by Adam Lawson of the Canongate. Although of an elegant design, it would appear, to judge by the survival rate, not to have been a popular one. Although the fences are undated, all three pistols are of a similar period, the lockplates being brass.

FIG. 31. Early lobe-butt pistol, with left hand, late snaphaunce lock. Fence dated 1647. *Trustees of the National Museums of Scotland, 1996.*

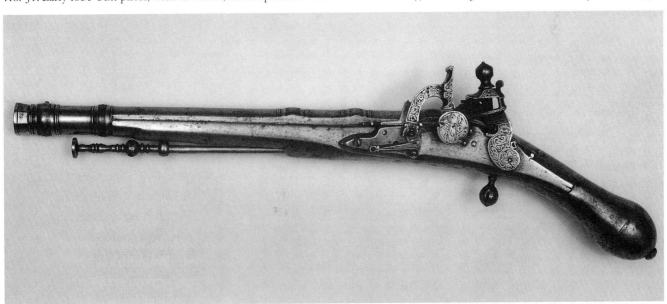

The second variety, the later lobe-butt pistols, seem to have been manufactured originally in Doune. Their styling was a marked deviation from the existing design of ramshorn pistol, which had, after about seventy-five years of manufacture, become firmly established in the public eye, and it must have taken a great deal of courage to introduce a weapon with an entirely different design. Thomas Murdoch must be given the credit for the new design of pistol, which, although retaining the Highland lock and the four-staged barrel of the more traditional Doune pistols, incorporated a butt which was of lobe shape, and so resembled more the conventional English pistol, with its more rounded butt. In designing his new pistol, around 1750, Murdoch may have been influenced by the decline in the gunsmithing industry in Doune after the '45, and was, perhaps, looking forward to new markets, since the demise of the clan system and the passing of the Disarming Act meant that gunsmiths could no longer look to the Highlander to purchase their wares.

Murdoch was not the only Doune gunsmith to manufacture lobe-butt pistols. Other gunsmiths included his namesake John Murdoch, John Campbell (son of the famous Alexander Campbell) and John Stuart. Thomas Murdoch was, however, the most prolific, and since the majority of surviving lobe-butt pistols bear his signature, it seems only fitting that Thomas Murdoch should be credited with their design. In about 1774, Murdoch moved to Leith, almost certainly with an eye to selling his pistols in the capital, where his market would be considerably enlarged. Leith, of course, was the port of Edinburgh, and consequently there would be greater scope for trade, not only with soldiers or sailors leaving Scottish shores, but with foreign buyers, including English merchants, and other travellers arriving there. Unfortunately, despite reaching the highest standards in the manufacture of Scottish lobe-butt pistols, Murdoch died in poverty in 1791.

The lobe-butt pistol was often constructed entirely of brass, although most examples are in steel. The pistols were engraved overall, from butt to muzzle, often in the form of stylised acanthus leaf, combined with scrolling foliage, which was a highly effective decoration. The trigger was always of ball form, but in view of the design of the butt, no pricker was fitted, while the belt hook was often nicely finished by means of the popular pierced and fretted finial.

FIG. 32. Close-up view of signature on lobe-butt pistol by Thomas Murdoch, c. 1750–75, illustrated in plate 7, with characteristic flourish of the R. John Murdoch, who was apparently unrelated, also incorporated this feature in his signature.

FIG. 33. Obverse side of the same pistol as fig. 32, showing belt hook with lyre-shaped finial.

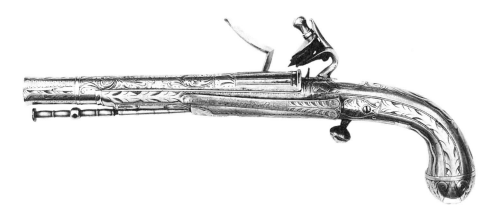

The all-steel version was equally attractive, due to the tasteful and intricate use of silver inlay in a very distinctive way on the butt pommel. At the centre of the pommel a small silver rondel was inserted, and four, or sometimes five, chevrons of inlaid silver were arranged around it, their apices pointing outwards, so that, from below, the appearance was of a four or five petalled flower of engraved silver decoration.

The butt itself had alternating longitudinal bands of wavy and straight lines, interspersed with bands of stylised acanthus foliage, achieved by the skill of the engraver's hand, a silver escutcheon being inserted in the spine, in a central position, behind the barrel tang. Other noteworthy features of these pistols are, the depth of the engraving, and the intricacy of the scroll-work, whilst the butts themselves are seldom offset.

The cock was of flat or round section, the pans usually oval, with rounded frizzens, whilst the barrels had octagonal, swamped, and engraved muzzles, and, often, fluted breeches. The trigger takes the form of a ball

FIG. 34. Lobe-butt pistol of small dimensions by John Murdoch of Doune, c. 1775. This pistol is sparsely engraved, and embellished only with a tiny silver escutcheon behind the barrel tang. Although furnished with a belt hook, its small size allowed it to be easily carried in an overcoat or breeches pocket, should its owner find it more expedient. Overall length 9″ (229mm), barrel 5¼″ (133mm), bore ½″ (13mm). *Private Collection.*

or sphere, constructed of brass, steel, or silver, and is engraved in keeping with the rest of the pistol, the commonest form being a rosette. It is secured by a screw which passes through it into the stock, inside the lock recess, so that the screw head is invisible from the outside. This is a point of difference from most Scottish pistols having ramshorn butts, in which the trigger suspension is almost invariably from a screw passing right through the stock behind the lock, and filed off flush with the surface of the metal.

Lobe-butt pistols were normally sold in pairs, and always with right hand locks. Although Murdoch continued to manufacture scroll-butt pistols, which still enjoyed a considerable degree of popularity amongst his clients, the vast majority of his pistols were of the lobe–butt variety.

RAMSHORN-BUTT PISTOLS

The ramshorn-butt, sometimes known as a scroll-butt, probably had its origins in the fishtail-butt pistol, by an elongation and attenuation of the upper and lower extremities of the butt of the latter, which were then folded round to form the horns. A pricker is inserted in a central position between the horns. The earliest ramshorn pistol known has a snaphaunce mechanism, and bears the date 1649 on its fence. In appearance, it is similar to the pistol worn by the Highland chieftain in Michael Wright's portrait, which has a doglock mechanism, and, as in most early pistols, the angle between butt and barrel is very shallow. The upper and lower spines of the butt are practically straight, and the scrolls which constitute the horns of the ram are full and circular. Many of the surviving examples of this type of weapon were made by the Caddell family in Doune. Despite their clumsy appearance, these pistols are light in weight and a delight to handle.

These early pistols have ball triggers and prickers, as well as the customary belt hook, and the earliest examples are always fitted with snaphaunce locks, each pair of pistols having right and left hand locks respectively. The belt hook has a finial, which is pierced and fretted in elaborate fashion. Towards the end of the seventeenth century, the lock mechanism was invariably of flintlock construction, having a laterally-acting sear which pierced the lockplate in the manner of the Highland lock.

These ramshorn pistols were at first relatively plain, engraving being generally restricted to some scrollwork around the lockplate and cock, but by about 1700, a type of ramshorn pistol had developed of extremely flamboyant design. The scrolls of the ramshorn-butt, although full and generous, lack the whorls of the earlier specimens. The barrels are long and have several stages or sections, sometimes as many as six or seven, each separated by a broad band of inlaid and engraved silver. The muzzle section is octagonal and flared, or swamped, whilst the breech is fluted. The ball trigger and pricker are usually of silver, which may be pierced and engraved. The pistols themselves are large, clumsy-looking weapons, and are liberally decorated with engraved silver plaques and other inlay, on the butts, forends, and barrels. This barrel inlay takes the form of squares, oblongs, rondels, or diamonds, each exhibiting 'punctate' engraving, consisting of punched dots, which considerably enhances their appearance. The forends and butt spines are inlaid with interlacing silver scrollwork, while the broad butt has star or heartshaped inlay. A recurring pattern is a stylised ramshorn motif, sometimes engraved, sometimes inlaid with silver. Frequently rosettes are engraved on the silver rondels inlaid into the barrel.

The barrels were originally heat-blued, providing a marked visual contrast against the extravagent silver inlay with which the pistols were adorned. This feature made such pistols extremely attractive to their prospective owners, and many of the pistols used during the '45 Rebellion must have been of this type. A good example is held by Glasgow Art Gallery and Museum (see fig. 36). Its maker was Patrick Buchanan, who is listed in the 'lockit-book' of the Incorporation of Hammermen of Glasgow, and is one of only two known specimens of his work. Buchanan was admitted to the Incorporation of Hammermen on 24 January 1718. His pistol has a multifaceted pan, a feature not uncommonly found in Scottish flintlock pistols. The cock screw has two slots, instead of the more usual single slot, running at right angles to each other, as a further embellishment.

FIG. 35. Pair of all-steel snaphaunce pistols of early ramshorn design by Alexander Logan of Leith Wynd. Dated 1660. Note the right and left hand locks. A pair of pistols by this maker was used in the assassination attempt on Archbishop Sharp in 1668.
The Trustees of the National Museums of Scotland, 1996.

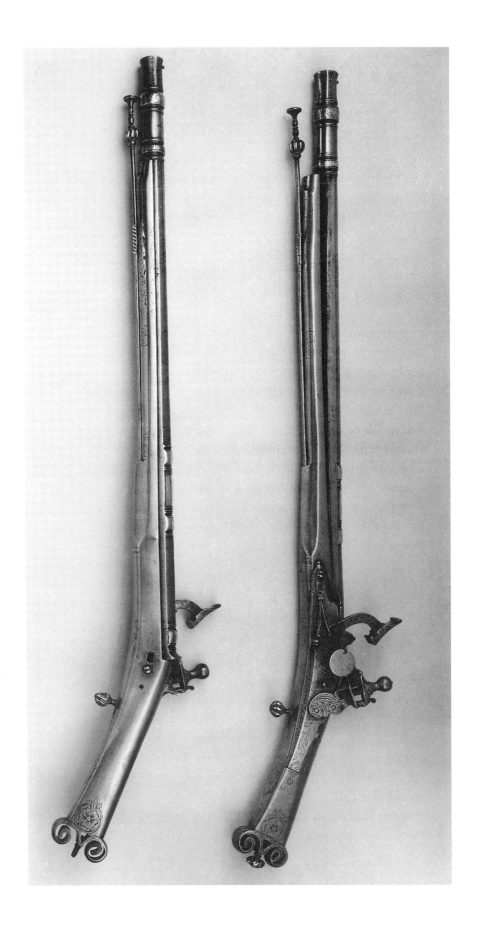

Many ramshorn pistols have butts which are offset for use in the right hand. This has already been noted as an occasional feature of heart-butt pistols, but it is an almost invariable feature of ramshorn-butts pistols throughout the eighteenth century. The practice was abandoned in the 1820s, with the production of the costume pistol, and, later, the percussion dress pistol.

As the skills of the Scottish gunsmiths developed, we find that barrel lengths become shorter, whilst bores enlarge. The angle between butt and barrel becomes progressively more acute, and the butt more rounded. The ramshorn pistol was now reaching its most elegant stage. In Doune especially the gunsmiths had developed the art of silver inlay to an incredibly high standard. Pistols by Alexander Campbell and John Christie were extensively inlaid with scrollwork, or engraved overall with great detail, usually in combination. Oval silver plaques were incorporated into the butts on either side, to which the owner could apply his crest or motto. The ball trigger would be of engraved silver, while the cock frequently had a flat disc behind the spur, which was pierced and engraved to form a star, often with circular holes between its points. Pairs of early ramshorn pistols are fitted with right and left hand locks, but this practice was soon abandoned, and the vast majority will be found to have only right hand locks.

The barrel was usually in four stages, having a fluted or multifaceted breech, a short second stage, a much longer third stage, and a fourth consisting of an octagonal swamped muzzle. The rounded sections of the barrel are scroll engraved, whilst the facets of the muzzle were often engraved with scrolls and borderline engraving. The ramrod does not have the heavy beading of the earlier pistols, being more delicately formed, and often retains the pierced ball amidst the gentler baluster turnings.

The lockplate is engraved with the maker's name, either in script or in Roman lettering, but consistency in spelling is not always found, for reasons discussed elsewhere in this book. Sometimes the town of manufacture is added. The cock may be of flat or round section, the frizzen mostly

opposite FIG. 36. Ramshorn-butt flintlock pistol by Patrick Buchanan of Glasgow, c. 1725. Note the Highland lock and the pierced ball trigger and pricker. The pistol is in the half-cock position. Overall length 15½″ (394mm), barrel 11″ (279mm), bore ½″ (12.7mm).
Glasgow Museums: Art Gallery and Museum, Kelvingrove.

pointed, although better quality pistols had coffin-shaped frizzens. The pans could be oval or multifaceted, but only the late flintlock Scottish pistols incorporated bridles to the frizzen.

Dimensions of these pistols can be variable, with the length being around 12½″ (317.5mm), with a barrel length approximately 7½″ (190.5mm) and a bore of about ½″ (15mm) or slightly less. As the century progressed, the barrels grew shorter, and the comb behind the cock disappeared completely, although the latter feature enjoyed a brief revival towards the end of the century. Throughout the century the locks retained the traditional laterally-acting, or horizontal, sear.

MILITARY PISTOLS

Scottish pistols of traditional all-metal construction were issued as a matter of course to all Highland regiments in the seventeenth and eighteenth centuries. Whitelaw makes no mention of these weapons, nor does his work contain any photographic record of military pistols. It must be assumed that, although he was undoubtedly aware of their existence, Whitelaw felt that they should not be included in his treatise, since they were both functionally inferior, and aesthetically less appealing when compared to the beautifully elegant specimens which comprised his own collection. Yet at the same time, there are several illustrated examples of Scottish pistols which have been badly restored and overcleaned and sometimes of fairly crude construction, which have nevertheless been included, due presumably to lack of availability of more perfect specimens.

Military pistols, forming, as they do, such an important part of Scottish history, cannot be excluded from a truly comprehensive classification of the Scottish pistol. Colonel Rogers states that Scottish pistols were first issued as Government weapons to the Independent Highland Companies of 1667–1717, and 1725–1739, later regimented to form the Black Watch or Highland Regiment in 1739.[1] Only one pistol per man was issued. It was suspended by its belt hook from a short belt or strap which passed over the right shoulder. The pistol butt was thus under the left armpit. If an officer chose to wear two pistols, the second would be suspended below the first, its belt hook slipping into the waist belt.

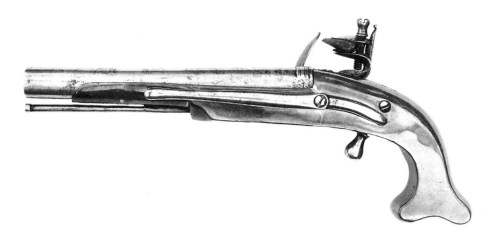

FIG. 37. Obverse side of a pistol by John Waters, c. 1780, illustrated in plate 11, showing belt hook, with downward-curving finial. See also fig. 38.

Alternatively, both pistols could be suspended from the shoulder-strap. It is unlikely that a double harness, capable of suspending one pistol above the other, existed at this time although it was available in the percussion era.

It has sometimes been stated that the use of Scottish military pistols was discontinued in 1786. That they were still in use in 1788 may be inferred from a request to Ordnance in April of that year by the colonels of the 74th and 75th regiments to supply pistols, and at the same time enquiring "whether they might be stocked in wood?"[2] The request was denied on the grounds that wooden stocks would be more vulnerable to breakage.

Not a great deal is known regarding the earlier military pistols, which probably resembled the more decorative specimens of the time, but were of much plainer and cruder construction, and their designation as military pistols can often be guessed at when examining these weapons. A typical example examined by the author has a ramshorn butt, with a stud-shaped trigger and ball pricker. The lock is of flattened section and Highland type, and the barrel has several stages, but lacks any moulding of the barrel bands separating them. The weapon is not engraved and is quite plain apart from the initials 'A.C.' engraved in script on the lockplate.

Of the later weapons, two distinct types of Scottish military pistols are recognised. Each is of all-metal construction, with flintlock action. The first type has a stock fabricated of bronze, but more commonly referred to as 'gunmetal'. The cock is flat in section, and the sear is laterally acting, holding the cock breast in the half-cock position. There is no pricker. The trigger is in the form of an elongated ball, or stud, whist the butt has contours vaguely reminiscent of the human renal pelvis, which has given rise to the description 'kidney-shaped'. However the butt shape could more appropriately be redefined as 'fishtail', since its shape more closely resembles, if anything, the tail of a fish than do the butts of the early wooden and brass stocked fishtail-butt pistols themselves. The ramrod pipe is brass, not bronze.

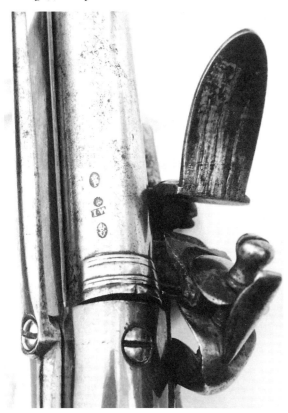

FIG. 38. Proof marks of the early Birmingham type, on a pistol by John Waters, c. 1780, with his initials 'I.W.' See fig. 37 and plate 11.

This form of pistol bears early Birmingham View and Proof Marks, with the stamp 'I. W.', of John Waters, between them. Although a contemporary London gunsmith was identically named, given that the pistols are known to have been manufactured cheaply in Birmingham, it seems likely that it was John Waters of Birmingham who was the gunsmith concerned. One example examined by the author is engraved 'J. WATERS, GUNMAKER, BIRMINGHAM', on the barrel.

The Waters military pistol is certainly plain and unadorned. Only occasional examples have some engraving, on the gunmetal stock, of running leaf scrolls, and perhaps a thistle on the butt spine, and wavy lines around the barrel tang screw. Silver inlay is absent, and the barrels themselves were apparently never blued.

On the other hand, such embellishments are hardly appropriate in a weapon designed for use by Highland regiments in the field. What was required was a robust weapon which would withstand hard usage. In fact, the brilliant designer who created this pistol, knew that the men of the Highland regiments, mainly Highlanders schooled in the

Highland discipline of warfare, wanted a sturdy, all-metal pistol, resembling those with which they were already quite familiar, while Ordnance, on the other hand, wanted a robust pistol which would be cheap to manufacture. Thus, the designer dispensed with engraving and other embellishments, the only concession being a stock fabricated in gunmetal, which allowed it to retain something of the flamboyance of the traditional Scottish pistol. The lock was still Highland in type, but the barrel was reduced to one stage, a simple round barrel with a little moulding at the breech, and a vestigial rear sight. The trigger became a simple stud, whilst the ramshorns, prone to damage if dropped, were removed, and the butt terminals rounded off to resemble a fish's tail. Even the belt hook was reduced to a functional level, gone being the elaborate and fretted finial, and instead there is a simple tang, curving slightly downwards, and secured by a stud and screw, the screw doubling also as a lock screw. The method of securing the barrel to the forend has been simplified. For the first time a slot appears in the forend, and a grooved wedge fitted to the underside of the barrel slides into the forend to hold the two parts together.

Another remarkable feature of these pistols is that, originally, the pistols must have been designed to have a pricker in the centre of the butt, similar to the scroll-butt pistols, but whether this proved unsatisfactory, or was deemed to be unnecessary, these were removed, and the holes filled in. The absence of blueing in surviving examples has many possible interpretations. It might merely reflect the hard usage to which the military pistol is subjected, similar to the absence of browning on English Tower pistols. Secondly, the original finish may have been deliberately removed by the soldier, in order to improve the appearance of the weapon, as is known to have been done in the case of the Brown Bess. The blueing may have worn off naturally with the passage of time, or been removed by inexpert cleaning, or lastly, the barrels may never have been blued in the first place. There is no doubt that the appearance of this military pistol is enhanced by bright steelwork and it may well be that the blueing process was never applied.

Two further points are, firstly, that the pistol is quite heavy in comparison to the average Scottish pistol, and, secondly, that the butt is of very small dimensions. It is true that men of 250 years ago were smaller in stature than those of the late twentieth century, but even making allowances for small hands, only the third and fourth fingers can grip the butt, the fifth either curling around the anterior edge of the butt terminal, or lying in the groove in the centre of the butt. Perhaps this may have been a factor in causing the removal of the pricker.

No regimental markings are in evidence on the barrels, a point of distinction between this type of military pistol, and the type which follows. Waters pistols were manufactured from 1766 until his death in 1781, when the firm became known as John Waters and Co., and production may have continued until as late as 1788.

The second type of Scottish military pistol is of the more traditional ramshorn design. It has a ball trigger and an elongated ball pricker with fully rounded butt horns. The pistol and its ramrod are all-steel, while the butt is engraved with a multi-petalled flower of daisy pattern. The lockplate is engraved 'Bissell', the pistol being the work of Isaac Bissell of Birmingham, who, it is believed, also had an office in Edinburgh. Sometimes the second 'l' is omitted from the signature on the lockplater.

The flat-section cock is engraved with a single border line at its peripheral edge, and this is repeated on both the front and tail sections of the lockplate. The barrel, which is 8″ in length, often has four stages, sepa-rated only by engraved lines rather than mouldings, and is frequently engraved 'R. H. R.', for Royal Highland Regiment, but single stage barrels are also to be found. The spine of the butt may carry further regimental markings in the form of company and rack numbers. Proof marks consist of crossed sceptres crowned, with identical view marks, used to denote Tower proof for private arms. The frizzen spring terminal is a simple point, compared to the Waters pistol in which the finial is trefoil in shape. The belt hook has a long and slightly downward-curving tang. Both types of mili-tary pistol have plain ramrods, which lack any elaborate or pierced turnings. Plate 12 shows a typical ramshorn-butt military pistol of Bissell type, although the lockplate is unmarked. As one of a pair, it probably belonged originally to an NCO in a Highland regiment.

Scottish military pistols are much maligned weapons, which have never quite recovered from the unjustified attack made upon them by the brothers Hay Allan, writing in 1892 in their notorious work entitled *The*

Costume of the Clans, when they described them in derogatory terms thus:

> . . . the pistols, unlike the finely formed productions of Campbell, Murdoch, Christie, Mackay, Macnab and Stuart, which united in an eminent degree elegance and strength, were coarse pop-guns, resembling more the tin toys of a bazaar than the weapons of an army.[3]

It is regrettable that these remarks have been quoted by successive authors ever since, and this has consequently downgraded the Scottish military pistol in the eye of the collector to be scarcely worthy of notice.

The two claimants to Royal ancestry—John Sobieski Stolberg and Charles Edward Stuart—were regarded even in their own time as imposters by many scholars, amongst them Sir Walter Scott himself. The apparent wealth of detail regarding the individual tartans displayed within the pages of *Vestiarum Scoticum* was allegedly based on a sixteenth-century manuscript in their possession, said to have been presented to Bonnie Prince Charlie at the Scots College at Douay, in France.

Many of these tartans, and also the archaic language which purported to be the original text of the manuscript, were quite clearly created by the brothers themselves, in an elaborate attempt to secure credibility in their chosen role as experts in the field of Scottish history and dress, and there is no doubt that the two enormous volumes must have appeared to many of their contemporaries as being the definitive work on that particular subject. As Mackay put it: "The claim of the Allans was at once audacious and preposterous".[4] The remarks quoted regarding the supposed inferiority of the Scottish military pistol can therefore no longer be given any credence, since the authors have themselves lost credibility, and the collector will search in vain for a lockplate which is marked 'Mackay', since no gunsmith of that name is known to have existed.

Further adverse publicity was attracted to the pistols when Colonels Montgomery and Frazer were raising their respective regiments, and made a request to Ordnance to supply them. It was agreed that these officers should supply the men, and would be reimbursed at £1-15-7 per pair. It was, however, discovered that the pistols were being supplied in Birmingham, and were "of a very bad sort, of which no more than 18s per pair is paid at that place."[5]

To sum up the situation with regard to military pistols, it is invidious to make comparisons between military pistols and the finer quality Scottish pistols, since one is not then comparing like with like. Military pistols must be seen as functional weapons, possessed of a large degree of robustness. They are not objects of beauty *per se*, but are designed as working weapons for everyday use by the ordinary soldier. One has only to examine a few of these pistols to see how much, indeed, they were used, and how effective they must have been, as witnessed by the vents enormously enlarged, and the bore of the muzzles much widened by repeated discharge. Specimens of military pistols encountered today, not surprisingly, tend to show evidence of considerable wear.

The more aspiring soldier, that is, officer class, could choose to indulge his aesthetic sensibilities, if he so desired, by the purchase from his own funds of pistols of a better quality than the standard issue. Such weapons, of course, cannot then be regarded as military pistols.

Thus we can now reappraise this pistol in a rather different light. What we have now is a functional military pistol, specifically designed as such, and of simple, and, in some cases, more modern lines. We have a weapon which is heavy and robust, with a barrel which has been proved, and, far from being a coarse pop-gun, was as deadly as any of its more illustrious colleagues. In fact, from a military standpoint and notwithstanding the deficiencies inherent in the Highland lock mechanism, it was in many ways superior to its wooden-stocked counterparts in the English armies. It is time for the military pistol both to be lifted from its century and a half of obscurity and placed alongside other and better-known pistols, and for it to share in the history of the Scottish regiments who carried it in battle.

COSTUME PISTOLS

After the formation of the Highland Society of London in 1778, and the election of its first president, Lieutenant-General Simon Fraser of Lovat, there began a revival of interest in the Highlands, and its customs and culture. The Disarming Act of 1746, in the aftermath of the Jacobite Rebellion, imposed severe penalties, not only for carrying and possessing arms, but for wearing the kilt, plaid, or any other tartan garment.[6]

FIG. 39. Costume pistol by McNab of Rannoch. Note the typically short barrel, with ring-neck cock and roller frizzen. *Perth and Kinross District Council, Museum and Art Galleries Department*

There followed, in 1782, a repeal of that section of the Act which prohibited the wearing of Highland dress, and, a few years later, members of the Royal family, including the Prince of Wales, later to become George IV, appeared in the kilt for the first time.[7] In 1822, George IV paid a State visit to Edinburgh, amidst great pomp and ceremony, and is depicted in Denis Dighton's watercolour in full Highland dress, including a pair of scroll-butt pistols, whilst receiving the Honours of Scotland.

Naturally, with the increasing popularity of Highland dress, in order to complete the attire it was essential that one, or more often a pair of pistols of Scottish design be provided. Until the 1820s, these pistols were flintlocks, but after this date, when the percussion system had shown its undoubted superiority over the flintlock, percussion pistols began to come into general use.

As the adoption of Highland dress became more widespread, so there was an increasing demand for these weapons. Such pistols were not intended primarily as weapons of offence or defence, but merely to be decorative objects used to put the final embellishment, or 'finishing touch', onto the dress or costume. Thus the gunmakers of the day began to produce cheap pistols which were functionally inferior, the policy being, that it did not matter how poorly constructed the pistols were, since they were never intended to be fired in anger. It is at this time, around the 1820s, that these poor quality Scottish weapons were being made, and they are certainly of no credit whatsoever to the gun trade of that period.

The pistols are flintlock, and any engraving on the metalwork is limited to a scroll or two on the lockplate, cock, and perhaps the butt. Not surprisingly, the maker's name is seldom in evidence on the lockplate, whilst the locks themselves do not function smoothly, and the ramshorn butts are inclined at a fairly sharp angle to the barrels, and have poorly curving horns. There is a ball trigger, and the pricker is usually in the shape of a thistle. The pistols are short, usually around 10½″ (266.5 mm) in length, although occasionally longer, whilst the barrels measure about 6″ (152.5 mm), and may have from one to three stages. The cocks have ring necks, and the internal lock mechanism is of the vertical sear type.

These pistols can always be recognised by the crudity of their construction. Not all so-called costume pistols, however, are of this poor quality. On the contrary, some are beautifully engraved, blued and gilt, and have locks of advanced design, incorporating rainproof pans and roller frizzens, which makes them equal, both in appearance and mechanical perfection, to any of the Scottish pistols made in the previous century. It is therefore clear that the term 'Costume Pistol' is undeservedly denigratory and should be reserved only for those crudely constructed pistols already described, intended solely as accoutrements for Highland dress.

PERCUSSION DRESS PISTOLS

By 1830, when the percussion era had become fully established, there was, in consequence, a demand for the new type of pistol as an accoutrement to enhance the Highland dress. Like the true costume flintlock pistols, percussion Scottish pistols were short, with barrels varying from one to three stages. Most were ramshorn in type, and incorporated a steel ball, or, more commonly, a thistle-shaped pricker, between the horns, which themselves tended to be poorly curved. The trigger was in the form of a ball, acorn, or thistle, and there would be a belt hook on the opposite side from the lock. The lock itself was of front-action percussion type, in which the mainspring is placed in front of the hammer. Whatever type of trigger or pricker is fitted, it was made from a solid piece of steel, and in this way differed from the weapons of the previous century, when these items were invariably hollow, being constructed in two halves, which were then brazed together.

Although some of these pistols are poorly constructed, many are of excellent manufacture, particularly with makers such as T. E. Mortimer of Edinburgh, or Westley Richards of Birmingham. Percussion dress pistols tend to be entirely covered in elaborate scroll engraving, often incorporating Scottish thistles or rosettes amidst the interlacing scrolls. They are usually to be found in pairs, and may have the maker's name engraved on the lockplate, although this may be absent. The barrels are often blued, and are stamped at the breech or undersurface with Birmingham Proof Marks of post-1813 type. Better quality examples have three-stage barrels, with fluted breeches and octagonal swamped muzzles. Sometimes the breech is octagonal, becoming rounded in the second stage, and cannon-barrel shaped in the third. Other examples have frames of nickel silver, and the pommel or butt may incorporate a cairngorm, this latter feature sometimes adorning the pricker instead.

In the United Services Museum in Edinburgh Castle, is an example of an un-named Scottish percussion dress pistol, with nickel silver frame and a steel barrel. A plaque in the shape of a sphinx is attached to the butt, with the word 'Egypt' underneath, confirming its regimental status. A similar pistol, by Mortimer of Edinburgh, is illustrated in *The Price Guide to Antique Guns and Pistols* by Hawkins.

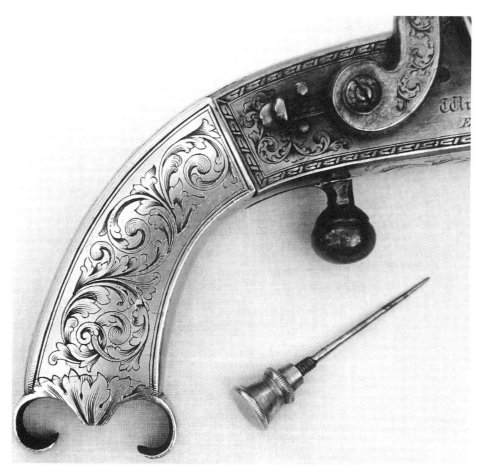

FIG. 40. The butt of a percussion-dress pistol by Wighton of Edinburgh, circa 1840–50, illustrated in plates 14 and 15.

Percussion dress pistols are occasionally set up in cases, together with accessories for cleaning and loading them. Although decorative, they are nevertheless perfectly functional, and quite capable of use in an emergency. Like the costume pistols described in the previous chapter, they are not considered seriously as examples of Scottish pistols by some collectors, since many are of Birmingham and even London manufacture. Nevertheless they remain as the last surviving examples of a type of weapon which was shortly to disappear for ever, and although far removed from their eighteenth-century forebears, they do have their place in the evolution of the Scottish pistol, albeit in its final and most debased form, and as such are deserving of more worthy consideration and appreciation by student and collector alike.

Plate 14 shows a pair of percussion dress pistols of the very highest quality. Barrels as well as frames are constructed of solid nickel silver, whilst the locks and other metal parts are heat blued, thus intentionally creating a marked visual contrast. The pistols are engraved overall, in a skillful yet restrained manner, with deeply-cut running leaf scrolls (see fig. 40). The locks incorporate safety bolts which operate in the half-cock position. The internal lock surfaces are highly-polished, and there is a vertical sear and a bridled tumbler, like high quality percussion locks of English manufacture.

The lockplates are marked 'Wighton, Edinburgh' (see plate 15) and each pistol is engraved with the crest and motto of its original owner. Many surviving examples of Scottish pistols are similarly engraved with crests and mottoes, so that the collector has a unique opportunity to identify the previous owner, or, at the very least his family name. Sometimes, after years of wear and, perhaps, overenthusiastic polishing, the inscription is indistinct or only partially visible due to the softness of the silver on which the engraving appears. Many hours in libraries and reading rooms can result in frustration in many cases, but the delight in achieving a successful outcome is ample reward for the hours spent in laborious research.

LATE FLINTLOCK PISTOLS

This category should be reserved for those pistols hitherto referred to as costume pistols, but whose quality of construction and mechanical refinements immediately separate them from the latter. In complete contrast to the typically short-barrelled costume pistols described in a previous chapter, the late flintlock Scottish pistols, on the other hand, can be recognised by their locks, which are of advanced form, having rainproof or semi-rainproof pans, roller frizzens and vents often lined with gold or platinum.

Late flintlock Scottish pistols were made between 1790 and 1820, and usually had ramshorn butts, the horns being full, yet without the elegant roundness of the pistols of the mid-eighteenth century. The locks may be of Highland type, but sometimes English-type locks with vertically-acting

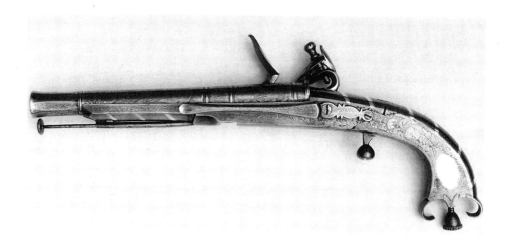

FIG. 41. Obverse side of late flintlock pistol by Macleod, circa 1820, illustrated in plate 16, showing the solid belthook finial of plain and abbreviated form. See also fig. 42.

FIG. 42. Lockplate of late flintlock pistol by Macleod, circa 1820. See also plate 16 and fig. 41.

sears are fitted, while the cock is of a form best described as 'pigeon-breasted'. They are usually well engraved, and sometimes etched with designs, including thistles and roses, while the figure of St Andrew, the patron saint of Scotland, is often found. Silver inlay may be a prominent feature, and several examples are inlaid with gold.

One maker who specialised in the production of late flintlock Scottish pistols was Macleod, who may have been trained in Doune, although his place of work has not been identified with certainty. A pair of pistols by him, and forming part of the collection of Sir Walter Scott, may be seen at Abbotsford, in the Scottish borders. The quality of these is such that they may well have originally belonged to an officer in a Highland regiment, or perhaps a laird who had purchased them to wear with his highland dress at Edinburgh in 1822.

In the collection of Scottish pistols at Blair Castle in Perthshire, is a pair of pistols which are designated as costume pistols. They are beautifully constructed of blued steel, with gold and silver inlay on the barrels and locks. Triggers and prickers are in the form of silver balls, probably gilded originally, while the pans are rainproof in type, and have roller frizzens. The barrels are four-staged, with fluted breeches and octagonal swamped muzzles, and the ramshorn butts are inlaid with enamel plaques bearing the Royal Coat of Arms. These magnificent arms are the work of a London gunsmith named William Watson. They are exquisite examples of the art of the gunsmith in relation to the Scottish pistol and to devalue such weapons by referring to them as costume pistols is to do them a gross injustice.

A similar pair by the same maker is on display at the Museum of Antiquities in Edinburgh, cased with accessories for loading and cleaning the weapons. Yet another pair, this time by the well-known Edinburgh gunsmith, Daniel Ross, is in the Blair Castle collection. The pistols are of ramshorn design, and have rainproof pans and sliding safeties. Such pistols, which are quite evidently of superior manufacture and quality, are better referred to as 'late flintlock Scottish pistols', and there is no doubt that many so-called costume pistols would fit more comfortably into this category.

PRESENTATION PISTOLS

The search for weapons and photographs necessary to complete the statistical data which forms part of this text, revealed a number of Scottish pistols which were of such opulence and magnificence that it was deemed proper to consider them separately from the others. These pistols are all of ramshorn design, and have, in the main, cannon barrels which are blued, and extensively inlaid with gold, sometimes taking the form of trophies of arms, which may be repeated on the lockplates, as well as foliate patterns. The stocks are of gilt brass, copper or silver, and are usually intricately engraved with a combination of foliate and floral patterns, together with a variety of complex borderline designs.

This engraving, although well executed and involving the entire stock, is quite shallow, lacking the boldness of that found in the earlier varieties of Scottish pistol, the weapon relying for its impact on the bright gilding of the stock, and the visual contrast between the latter and the blue barrel with its gold inlay.

The butts have enamel plaques on either side, which are adorned with the Coats of Arms of their titled owners. The pans are gold-lined, and the vents of solid gold, whilst even the ball triggers and prickers are often fabricated in gold, or in gilded silver. The pans may be rainproof or semi-rainproof, and the frizzen usually incorporates a bridle, for a smoother action, assisted by a roller which is fitted to the toe of the frizzen spring.

The lock may be of English type, with a vertical sear, the tumbler being held in position by an elaborate bridle, although some pistols retain the traditional Highland lock.

Such pistols are obviously of late manufacture, dating from between 1780 and 1810. They are overwhelming in their artistic appeal, and were intended as presentation pieces, to be given as gifts to persons of distinction.

In certain cases these pistols were constructed at the sole expense of the gunsmith concerned, as the *Edinburgh Evening Courant* records, with reference to Thomas Murdoch of Leith: "Last year he sent, at his own expense, a pair of pistols of the old Highland construction, to His Royal Highness the Prince of Wales." and this was no doubt with an eye to attracting future business from the Royal Court.

Two pairs of these presentation pistols are marked simply 'Watson', engraved within a pennant on the lockplate, one such pair being preserved in Blair Castle, and the second in the Museum of Antiquities in Edinburgh. Two further pairs are engraved 'Murdoch' in Roman lettering on the lock-plates, within a similar pennant. Since both John and Thomas Murdoch are known to have been responsible for the manufacture of gold-inlaid pistols for "the first nobility of Europe", the true identity of the manufacturer might have remained in doubt, but fortunately, in one pair of pistols, those presented by George III to Sir Henry Clinton, the letter 'J' appears, above the surname 'Murdoch', and the same prefix appears on the lockplates of yet another pair of Murdoch presentation pistols. Thus it can be safely assumed that John Murdoch of Doune was responsible for the manufacture of these beautiful examples of Scottish pistols (see plate 17).

As long ago as 1936, Ian Finlay, author of several articles on the subject of Scottish pistols, disputed that John Murdoch was indeed the maker of these presentation pieces. In an article entitled 'The Pistols of Macdonell of Glengarry', he pointed out that the pistols had barrels of cannon-barrel form, very unlike those of Doune manufacture.[8] In addition, the locks had refinements not found in Doune pistols, and even the style of engraving was substantially different from that normally employed by John Murdoch. However, cannon barrels had in fact been manufactured in Doune from the beginning of the eighteenth century, particularly by Thomas Caddell and John Campbell, so that their use in presentation pistols merely represented a reversion to the old style of barrel.

It has already been noted how Thomas Murdoch created a new design of pistol to accommodate a changing market, and it is quite feasible that John Murdoch adopted a similar attitude, designing what were, after all, exceptional pieces, intended to be presented to Royalty, or the nobility. It is therefore hardly surprising that these pistols of late manufacture should be designed more in keeping with the English taste, with its liking for cannon barrels and locks of improved construction and finish, rather than those previously demanded by the Scots.

For the same reason, the engraving lost the generously flowing scroll-work of the traditional Scottish pistol, becoming more subdued in order to cater for a vastly different clientele. It is also a distinct possibility that the pistols marked 'J. Murdoch' were not known to Finlay, as he makes no mention of them in his commentary.

It may be presumed that the London gunsmith Watson, modelled his weapons on the Murdoch pistols, to which they bear a close resemblance, as there is no reason to believe that the two ever worked in association with one another. It has been suggested that Murdoch might have manufactured the pistols, and that these were then gilded and inlaid in London, but this is pure speculation, and is not based on factual evidence. It is however, ironic, that amongst the very finest examples of Scottish pistols in existence, are two pairs which were manufactured and proved in England.

Presentation pistols are sometimes fitted with conventional barrels rather than cannon barrels, and this can be seen in a pair presented and inscribed to Lord Amherst in 1780, following service in the North American War. These pistols are signed "J. Murdoch" and have enamel butt plaques adorned with the arms of the Amherst family.

CHAPTER TWELVE ⤬

A Survey of Scottish Pistols

S COTTISH PISTOLS ARE TO BE FOUND SCATTERED THROUGH-
out the collections of museums in England as well as in Scotland,
whose collections vary from the solitary pistol to as many as thirty-
eight weapons. It was decided to visit as many of these museums as possible,
and, where permissible, to handle the weapons themselves, in order to gain
some appreciation of the weight and balance of the pistols, as well as iden-
tifying similarities in their construction, or any distinguishing features of
individual pistols. However, since many fine and rare examples of Scottish
pistols are to be found in museum collections abroad, for example, in
France, Sweden, Germany, Denmark, and the North American Continent,
it became apparent that the analysis would be more complete if these
weapons also, could be included in the survey (see Table I below).

Although, a comprehensive analysis of all surviving examples of the
Scottish pistol would provide the researcher with an enormous amount of
detailed information on such aspects as numbers, butt styles, makers and
construction, making a survey of such magnitude is obviously quite imprac-
tical. It was therefore decided to choose representative examples of these
weapons, and subject them to a close scrutiny, in order to see what conclusions could be made regarding the many different aspects of the Scottish
pistol (see Table II below).

Table I
Sources of Scottish Pistols Examined by the Author

1.	Private Collections	92	PISTOLS
2.	Glasgow Art Gallery and Museum	38	
3.	Edinburgh Castle	37	
4.	Museum of Antiquities, Edinburgh	29	
5.	Blair Castle	16	
6.	Inverness Museum and Art Gallery	16	
7.	Royal Armouries, HM Tower of London	15	
8.	Marischal Museum, University of Aberdeen	14	
9.	Arms Fairs	11	
10.	Victoria and Albert Museum, London	10	
11.	Perth Museum and Art Gallery	8	
12.	Sir Walter Scott Museum, Abbotsford	5	
13.	Drumlanrig Castle	5	
14.	Smith Art Gallery and Museum, Stirling	5	
15.	Musée de l'Armée, Paris	5	
16.	Warwick Castle	3	
17.	Montrose Art Gallery and Museum	2	
18.	Inverary Castle, Argyll	2	
19.	Fyvie Castle, Grampian	2	
20.	Dunvegan Castle, Skye	2	
21.	Black Watch Museum, Perth	2	
22.	Hancock-Clarke House, Lexington, Mass., USA	2	
23.	Burrell Collection, Glasgow	1	
24.	Dundee Art Gallery and Museum	1	
25.	West Highland Museum, Fort William	1	
26.	Dean Castle, Kilmarnock	1	
27.	Fort George, Inverness	1	
28.	Forres Museum	1	
29.	West Point Military Museum, New York, USA	1	
		328	TOTAL

Nevertheless, as a visual inspection at the very least was considered essential to the statistical exercise, mere knowledge of the existence of a particular weapon or weapons was not considered sufficient grounds to allow it to be included in the survey, and in all cases a photograph, or, in occasional instances, a drawing, was deemed essential in order to permit its inclusion. An example of the latter situation would be one of Drummond's illustrations in *Ancient Scottish Weapons*.

Table II
Statistical Analysis of Scottish Pistols Included in Survey

DESCRIPTION	TOTAL	PAIRS/SINGLES	%AGE OF TOTAL
Total number of pistols	760	164 pairs, 432 single	
Number illustrated	432		
Number inspected	328		
Type of Pistol			
Ramshorn-butt	474	106 pairs, 262 single	62.4%
Heart-butt	84	11 pairs, 62 single	11.1%
Lobe-butt	104	30 pairs, 44 single	13.7%
Lemon-butt	36	10 pairs, 16 single	4.7%
Fishtail-butt	23	7 pairs, 9 single	3.0%
Pommel-butt	9	all single	1.2%
Kidney-butt	30	all single	3.9%
Costume	54	incl. 15 pairs	7.1%
Late flintlock	42	incl. 16 pairs	5.5%
Military	98		12.9%
[of which ramshorn	68]		
Presentation pistol	17	7 pairs	2.2%
Foresights	42		5.5%
Un-named pistols	105		13.8%
Type of Lock			
Flintlock	590	120 pairs, 350 single	77.6%
Snaphaunce	80	23 pairs, 34 single	10.5%
Percussion	64	16 pairs, 32 single	8.4%
Doglock	22	4 pairs, 14 single	2.9%
Micquelet	3	1 pair, 1 single	0.4%
Perc/flint	1	single	0.1%
Construction			
All steel	567		74.6%
All brass	51		6.7%
Brass and steel	49		6.4%
Wood and brass/steel	17		2.2%
Steel/silver	52		6.8%
Brass/silver	1		0.1%
Steel/gold inlay or silver gilt	23		3.0%
Date of manufacture			
before 1650	67		8.8%
1650–1700	54		7.1%
1700–1750	131		17.2%
1750–1800	357		47.0%
1800–1850	151		19.9%

Such a large number of pistols represents the bulk of Scottish pistols in existence, since most of the remaining pistols are either in private hands or have not been illustrated in any source known to the author. It is, unfortunately, quite impossible to give any estimate of the number of Scottish pistols in private hands, which, in the main, consist of the occasional single pistol or pair of pistols, held as representative examples in the collections of antique firearms enthusiasts, and many such weapons have been included in the survey. In addition, there are a small number of much larger private collections, both in Scotland and abroad. As these weapons become increasingly more expensive, it is unlikely that in future large numbers of Scottish pistols will be found outside the great museum collections.

Many of the weapons examined had actions which were faulty, due either to missing or broken mainsprings, or worn or absent lock parts. Ramrods were often missing, or rusted in position. Triggers and prickers were frequently absent, as were strikers and striker springs. The distal attachment of barrel to forend was not uncommonly insecure, whilst cocks, topjaws and screws, were also sometimes lacking, all of these features serving to indicate the general wear and tear of the weapons concerned.

Out of 760 pistols examined, approximately 13% were military, and of these, only one pair could be identified with certainty. One of these, illustrated in plate 12, has the usual floral motif on the both sides of the butt, together with simple fern-like engraving on the locks and cocks. The latter are of the ring-neck variety. While true pairs amongst military pistols cannot generally be confirmed, since all Bissell or Waters pistols look more or less alike, the ones under discussion resemble Bissell pistols in only a general way and the similarity of their engraving, together with the matching cocks, confirm their status as a true pair. These ramshorn pistols are to be seen in Inverness Museum, and were probably originally owned by an NCO, who, although perhaps unable to afford the more expensive pistols of the higher ranking officers, nevertheless chose to purchase weapons of slightly higher quality than those of standard quality.

Very few of the pistols examined had foresights, and many lacked any sighting device whatever, both of these factors emphasising the employment of the pistol by the clansmen as a close range weapon. Two pairs of pistols were encountered with rifled barrels, but it is possible that this modification was carried out at some time subsequent to their original manufacture. Yet another pair of pistols, lemon-butt in style, was fitted with left and right hand micquelet locks, and a third pistol, a heart-butt, also had a lock of this type. These locks were probably replaced during the working life of the pistols, due to the loss of, or damage to the originals. Another pair, having lobe butts, by Thomas Murdoch of Leith, had spring bayonets fitted at the side of each barrel. Only five pistols were fitted with trigger-guards, one of which was probably carried out subsequent to its manufacture to suit the taste of the owner, but the others were undoubtedly fitted at the time of manufacture, and had conventional triggers of English type. A most beautiful pair of costume pistols, having nickel silver frames, is in the Inverness Museum. These pistols, by W. Mills, have no triggerguards, but are fitted with conventional triggers instead of the usual ball.

A further factor is that, although many of the pistols, especially those manufactured around 1700, appear relatively clumsy, the ease with which they were handled belied the apparent crudity of their construction, and these weapons were astonishingly light and well-balanced.

Although strenuous efforts have been made by the author to trace the present whereabouts of Bonnie Prince Charlie's pistols which had been given by him into the safe-keeping of Hugh Macdonald of Armadale, each fresh lead unfortunately ended in disappointment, and as yet they remain undiscovered. Were these the same gold-mounted pistols the Young Pretender had worn on his triumphant entry into Edinburgh? And were they the self-same pistols which Logan described in 1845, as being preserved in Clunie Castle, amongst other artefacts belonging to Charles Edward, and now unfortunately dispersed? Time and further research may someday provide the answers to these fascinating questions.

Preserved in Browseholme Hall, near Clitheroe in Lancashire, is a pair of scroll-butt pistols by John Murdoch of Doune. According to tradition, these pistols were presented by Bonnie Prince Charlie to the Master of Sinclair. George Sinclair of Geese was twenty-nine at the time of Culloden, and a Muster Roll of Charles' army lists his name as a 'Gentleman Volunteer' in the Earl of Cromartie's Regiment. Charles would not have been best pleased to learn that the recipient of his generous gift, captured on the eve of the battle, had been discharged after turning King's evidence.

149

A further pair of pistols, short heartbutts of around 1730, with safety-bolted locks, the lockplates signed 'Jas McRay', is traditionally said to have belonged to the Young Chevalier, and is preserved in Beaufort Castle, the former home of the Lovats.

Yet another pair of pistols of considerable interest is included in the survey. Constructed of brass, they are fully 23″ (584mm) in length, and were made in 1614 by James Low. The pistols are fitted with left and right hand locks of snaphaunce construction, and both barrels and fences are dated. The pistols have lemon butts, which unscrew, and can be drawn out to form rod extensions to a distance of just over four inches. It is hard to imagine what practical purpose this device may have served. The length gained in extending the pistols was insufficient to constitute a true shoulder stock, yet may have made sighting easier if the weapons were deployed using both hands. These pistols are certainly amongst the few to possess a foresight. On the other hand, extending the pistols would take a little time, and perhaps the device merely represents a vagary in lemon-butt construction. One theory propounded is that the extending butts would make the weapons easier to manipulate when on horseback. A further feature of these pistols, is that the trigger tension can be altered to suit the firer, by adjustment of a screw passing through the lockplate, and is believed to be the earliest known example of such a device.

One of the most interesting of the pistols examined, was that reputedly owned by Colonel John Roy Stuart, who was in command of a Regiment of Edinburgh men during the '45 Rebellion, and fought at Culloden. He succeeded in escaping to France along with Bonnie Prince Charlie and a number of others, and was one of the heroes of the '45. His pistol, a large weapon with ramshorn butt, and with considerable inlay on the barrel, having broad barrel bands, showed evidence of much hard usage. This pistol is almost certainly by Thomas Caddell 3rd., although the signature on the lockplate is now scarcely legible. The thrill experienced in holding the pistol formerly in the possession of such a man, and one which was certainly fired during the Battle of Culloden, may easily be imagined.

Another pair of Scottish pistols was also of great interest. Whilst lacking any original finish, the weapons were in magnificent condition, with elegant scroll butts of generously rounded proportions. The lockplates were marked 'I. Murdoch', and the butt plaques engraved with the initials and armorial bearings of their original owner, Sir Allan Maclean of Brolas, the 6th Baronet, who died in 1783. His pistols are of the period 1750–1775. The interesting feature about the weapons is that the locks have been altered from their original Highland form, to English-type locks, with vertical sears, the holes in each lockplate being now filled, and large safety bolts added. In addition, the barrels have been extended by about half an inch, by the addition of a moulded muzzle. Whether these modifications were carried out at the instigation of their original owner, or subsequently, is a matter of conjecture, but the likelihood is, that at some stage during the working life of the weapons, the owner decided to alter the guns in this way for purely personal reasons.

Probably the finest pistols examined were those marked only 'Murdoch', on the lockplates. These have been referred to in the chapter on Doune pistols and again in the commentary on presentation pistols.

These magnificent weapons are of late manufacture and design, and their locks have refinements which would do credit to any contemporary English pistols. Having enamel plaques on each butt, bearing the arms of William Henry, Duke of Clarence, later to become William IV, on one side, and those of the Order of St Andrew on the other, the pistols have gold inlaid and blued barrels, with gold ball triggers and gilded butts of ramshorn design. One pistol (plate 17) bears the following inscription:

> To His Royal Highness Wm Henry Duke of Clarence
> A Prince who from early Youth on various and arduous
> Military Service Has given signal proofs of Inheriting
> The virtues the valor and magnanimity
> Which so eminently distinguish
> His Illustrious Family
> As a testimony of pure Respect and Gratitude
> This piece of Highland Armor
> Is humbly presented
> By Lieut Coll John Small Comdr 2nd Battn
> of His Majestys Late 84th British Infantry 1790

The earliest known Scottish pistols are those in the Historisches Museum in Dresden (see fig. 43). This pair is dated 1598, and is probably the work of John Kennedy of Edinburgh. The pistols have snaphaunce locks, and wooden stocks with fishtail butts. Their steel barrels are blued and gilt. The interesting feature, in these early pistols, is that the vulnerable extremities of the fishtail butt are not protected, as in all other wooden-stocked pistols of this type, by the application of engraved brass mounts, and that the fishtail butt itself is very poorly shaped. This leads to the inevitable conclusion that the pistols were restocked, at some time past, in a manner approximating to that of the original stocks, which may have been destroyed by the ravages of woodworm, or even by fire. If this is the case, it is a pity that an attempt was not made to utilise the original brass mounts, although possibly these too, were destroyed or lost before the reconstruction took place.

In much better condition is the pair of fishtail butt pistols in the Tojhusmuseet, Denmark. These, too, are stocked in wood, rather unusually, at this time, in walnut. They are by James Low of Dundee, and the butts incorporate inlay in the form of lilies, a pot of lilies being the insignia of the City of Dundee. The pistols are dated 1602, on both barrels and locks. They were formerly in the possession of the last Count of Oldenburgh, who bequeathed them to the Kings of Denmark.

Also in Denmark in the National Museum is a pair of wooden-stocked lemon-butt pistols, known as the Sinclair Pistols. The lockplates are signed 'P.H.', probably representing Patrick Hamilton, of the Canongate, Edinburgh, and date from 1600–1625. The locks are snaphaunce and the stocks are of the more usual brazil wood. Their pommels are covered in thin, engraved brass plates.

Captain George Sinclair was an officer in a Scottish mercenary expeditionary force attempting to reach Gustavus Adolphus, in Sweden. In 1612, the Scots were ambushed and murdered by Norwegian farmers at a place called Kringen. Sinclair himself was not the leader of the mercenaries, who were commanded by Lieutenant-Colonel Ramsay. Although the pistols are old enough to have been used during the battle, unfortunately Sinclair's own initials do not correspond to the monogrammed 'A.S.', engraved in a shield on the barrels. The pistols were presented to King Christian V by Lieutenant General Johan Wibe, GOC North Norway, in 1690.

The earliest known pistol fitted with a ramshorn butt is to be found in the Burrell collection in Glasgow. It has a snaphaunce lock, and the fence

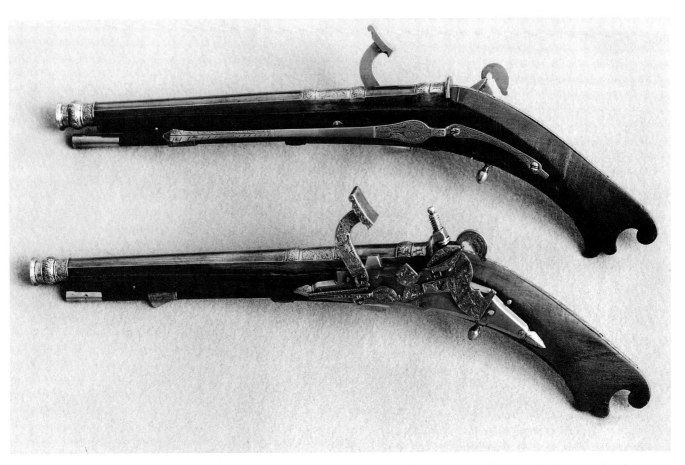

FIG. 43. The earliest-known Scottish pistols. Signed 'I.K.', possibly John Kennedy of Edinburgh. They are dated 1598, and have wooden stocks. *Historisches Museum, Dresden, Germany.*

has the date 1649 engraved upon it. The maker's mark, consisting of a monogrammed 'T.D.', is stamped within a rectangle on the lockplate.

Of the 760 pistols surveyed, one, designated as a costume pistol, had a dual system of ignition. This weapon, dating from around 1820–30, was fitted with a conventional flintlock mechanism and ring-neck cock, to which had been added a percussion arm, while a nipple was fitted to the left side of the barrel breech. It was thus possible to select the desired form of ignition before firing the weapon. This pistol was manufactured at a time when the percussion system was still new, and some customers undoubtedly had reservations regarding the superiority of the new system. The existence of alternative firing mechanisms in a single pistol clearly demonstrates these reservations, and at the same time raises an important issue regarding all costume pistols, which are generally regarded as purely decorative objects, not seriously intended as offensive weapons. It should therefore not be forgotten that such pistols were quite capable of being used to deadly effect if so desired.

Recently returned to their native Scotland, is a fine pair of heartbutt pistols with doglock mechanisms. They are reputed to have belonged originally to John Hay, Lord Inverness, Secretary to the Old Pretender. These long-barrelled weapons are wonderfully well-preserved, and are signed 'W.L.', beneath a crown, on the lockplates. The pistols, dating from about 1680, were beautifully inlaid with engraved silver, not surprisingly, since they were the work of the renowned Montrose silversmith, William Lindsay the elder. Although seen at a Jacobite Exhibition at Forres Museum, one pistol is expected to be displayed permanently in Montrose, the other in Edinburgh.

Three hybrid pistols were encountered during the survey, one pair, and a single pistol. The pair, manufactured from gilt bronze, were described in the chapter on the Doune pistol. Although presentation pistols of the highest quality, they lacked belt hooks and ball triggers, having instead conventional triggers with guards. The metalwork was chiselled and engraved, whilst the butts terminated in grotesque masks. The lockplates of the pistols were marked 'Christie, London'.

The remaining hybrid pistol was amongst the finest of all the pistols examined. It was formerly in the possession of Sir Alan Cameron of Erracht, who raised the 79th Regiment-the Cameron Highlanders, in 1793, and is exhibited at Fort George, Inverness. This magnificent weapon is double-barrelled, of over-and-under type, and has a ramshorn butt. The pistol mechanism is flintlock, with a pigeon-breasted cock, roller frizzens, and folding triggers. It has no belt hook, but is beautifully and extensively inlaid with gold, incorporating mottoes, crests, and trophies of arms. The scrollwork is of English type, and the pistol itself is the work of the famous London gunmaker, Durs Egg, and is a permanent tribute to his expertise in the craft.

Undoubtedly the most fascinating of all Scottish pistols is the one in Marischal Museum, Aberdeen (see the frontispiece). This pistol, of all-steel construction and early ramshorn design, is dated 1662, and is stamped only with the dagmaker's mark:

recently postulated to represent John Ochterlonie of Montrose. The remarkable feature of the weapon, however, is the five-flanged mace head which has been added to the muzzle. In eastern European countries, particularly Poland, this type of mace head was used as symbol of authority by its army officers, and is known as a budzygan. Many expatriot Scots served in the Polish army, and it seems highly significant that one Scots officer chose to embellish his pistol, already regarded as a symbol of authority in his native land, in a manner more appropriate to his adopted country.

CHAPTER THIRTEEN

The Makers of Scottish Pistols

TABLE III BELOW GIVES A LIST OF THE MAKERS OF SCOTTISH pistols. This does not purport to be a complete list of all such makers, as this is a subject which is quite comprehensively covered in Whitelaw's *Scottish Arms Makers*. Whitelaw's list is, however, comprised of cutlers, armourers, lorimers, swordslippers, bowers and gunners, in addition to gunsmiths and dagmakers, and may be confusing to those interested solely in the latter. The list which follows is comprised only of those makers whose pistols were encountered in the present survey, and totals 124.

A short supplementary list comprising a further nineteen gunsmiths has, however, been added, in order to take account of certain makers whose names have been verified as having appeared on Scottish pistols by past researchers, including Whitelaw, Hoff, and Stalin, but whose names were not actually encountered during the survey.

The earliest Scottish pistols, those of snaphaunce construction, may be either un-named, or merely stamped with the initials of the maker on the lockplate. This sometimes takes the form of a monogram, eg. Vb or Jb, or initials such as 'R.M.', 'I.L.', or 'D.H.' Determining the full names of these early dagmakers is best described as an educated guess. We cannot be absolutely certain, for example, that 'I.L.' represents James Low, but we do know that James Low worked in Dundee during the period concerned, and no other gunsmith is known to have existed around that time with identical initials, so that it appears logical that James Low made the pistols which have been attributed to his hand, and similar detective work can be applied to other sets of initials. Robert Mosman, Archibald Gibson, and John Kennedy, are others whose names have been attached to corresponding initials on these early pistols.

Whitelaw's *Scottish Arms Makers* is extremely helpful when attempting to associate initials with particular makers, but unfortunately there remain many sets of initials to which it is at present impossible to ascribe the name of a particular gunsmith, for example, 'I.D.', 'I.H.', 'D.H.', and 'J.O.' Where no name can be ascribed, only the initials appear in the list of gunsmiths which follows. The monogrammed initials Vb, representing a gunsmith of the period 1615–30, and reputedly to be found on the lockplates of two Scottish pistols of that period, may have been misread by past researchers, and are probably more accurately interpreted by the monogram Jb, and appear as such in the list, whilst the initials 'I.G.', are badly struck, and may possibly represent instead, 'I.C.'

Table III
Makers of Scottish Pistols

Alison, Charles	Dundee	1619–30
Alison, John	Dundee	1613
Alison, Robert	Dundee	1615–35
Allan, William	Edinburgh	1750
Ancell, Robert	Perth	1840
B.,I.		1630
B.,J.		1615–30
Beattie, James	London	1840
Bell, George	Glasgow	1840–50
Bissell, Isaac	Birmingham	1750–75
Brown and Rodda	London & Calcutta	1840
Buchanan, Patrick	Glasgow	1717–29
Burgess, John	Elgin	1695–1710
Byers, B.		1775–1800
Caddell, Robert	Doune	1700–25
Caddell, Thomas 2nd	Doune	1678
Caddell, Thomas 3rd	Doune	1700–25
Caddell, Thomas 4th	Doune	1725–50

Caddell, Thomas 5th	Doune	1750–75
C., A.	Doune	1740–50
Cameron, Alexander	Doune	1725
Campbell, Alexander	Doune	1730–50
Campbell, John	Glenelg	1725
Campbell, John	Doune	1700–20
Campbell, John	Doune	1750–75
Campbell, John	Edinburgh	1815–50
Christie, James	Perth	1750–75
Christie, James	Perth	1800–20
Christie, John	Doune & Stirling	1750–75
Christie	London	1810
Christie and Murdoch	Doune	1750
Clarke, J	London	1840
Clerk, James	Edinburgh	1630
D., C.		1680
D., I.		1619
D., T. [monogram]		1649
D. Thomas		1710–20
Dougal, John	Glasgow	1840
Egg, Durs	London	1770–1830
Forbes, Alexander	Elgin	1685
F., T.		1720
G., I.		1670–80
Gibson, Archibald	Canongate	1622–34
Gray, James	Dundee	1627–30
H., D.		1680–1700
H., I.		1615
Hamilton, Patrick	Canongate	1634
Heriot, William	Edinburgh	1820
Hunter		1814
Hunter, John	Stirling	1700–25
Hunter, William	Stirling	1720–30
I., D.		1800
Jb [monogram]		1613
Key, Alexander	Stirling	1820–30
Kennedy, John	Edinburgh	1598–1611
Lawson, Adam	Canongate	1660
Lindsay, William	Montrose	1670–90
Lochiel		1750
Logan, Alexander	Canongate	1660
Low, James	Dundee	1602–34
Low, Richard	Dundee	1589–1611
M., A.		1680
M., I.		1775
Marshall and Sons	Edinburgh	1820–30

Macleod		1820
McCulloch, Charles	Inverness	1715
McKenzie, David	Dundee	1700–20
McKenzie, James	Dundee	1690–1710
McKenzie, James	Dundee	1730
McKenzie, James	Brechin	1720–30
McL., K.		1725
McNab, Patrick	Dalmally	1820
McNab, Patrick	Dalmally	1730–50
McNab	Rannoch	1830
McNeil, Hector	Mull	1733
McRay, James		1730
Michie, James	Doune	1740–60
Michie, James	Perth	1800
Michie, John	Doune	1800
Mills, William	London	1830
Mortimer, Thomas Elsworth	London & Edinburgh	1840
Mosman, Mungo	Canongate	1621–31
Mosman, Robert	Canongate	1625
Murdoch, John	Doune	1750–98
Murdoch, Thomas	Doune & Leith	1750–91
Murdoch		1820–40
Naughton, Robert	Inverness	1820–30
⊶		1662
O., I.		1630
O., I.	Edzell	1730
O., .J		1613
Ogilvie, George	Glasgow	1716
Parker, William	London	1790–1820
Parker, Field, and Sons	London	1830–40
Paterson, James	Doune	1800–25
Patton and Walsh	Perth	1840
Pitcairn, John		1750–75
Playfair, Charles	Aberdeen	1820–50
R.		1690
Reilly, J.S.		1840
Richardson	Edinburgh	1840
Ross, Daniel	Edinburgh	1820
S., H.	Brechin	1700–25
Shiels, John		1750
Shires, Alexander	Old Meldrum	1700
Smith, William	Inverness	1671–95
Steuart, Daniel	Perth	1690
Strachan, Andrew	Edzell	1690
Stuart, John		1683–1701
Stuart, John	Doune	1750–75

Thomson, John	Edinburgh	1820–40
Tipping and Lawden	London	1840
W., H.		1650
Walker, Daniel	Dumbarton	1700–25
Walker, D.		1740–60
Walker, D.L.		1750–75
Waters, John	Birmingham	1750–81
Waters, John & Co.	Birmingham	1781–1810
Waters and Gill		1800–25
Watson, William	London	1800–20
Westley-Richards, William	Birmingham	1840
Wilson, Alexander	Canongate	1670
Wighton, Alexander G.	Edinburgh	1839–50
Winfield		1840

Supplementary List

Alison, John	Dundee	1613
C., E.		1627
C., W.		1750
D., A.		1650
Dunbar, David		1790
Forbes, Alexander		1775
G., W.		1750
H., I. [monogram]		1615
H., I.		1725
Innes and Wallace	Edinburgh	1800
M., A.		1611
McAllan		
McRosty, J.		
Mitchell, John		1725–50
Murdoch, Alexander		1750–75
Scott, Andrew		
Sutherland, James		
W., A.		
Wallace and Co.	Edinburgh	1820

Analysis of the large number of pistols examined permitted a further breakdown of the statistics, to indicate which of the 124 gunsmiths listed were the most prolific in terms of surviving specimens. Table IV below represents the results of this breakdown, the first time such an analysis has been made. The two Birmingham gunsmiths, Bissell and Waters, who produced large numbers of military pistols to specific patterns (forty and thirty respectively) have not been included.

Table IV
The Most Prolific Makers of Scottish Pistols

	PISTOLS	PAIRS	SINGLES	%AGE OF TOTAL
Thomas Murdoch	81	23	35	10.7%
John Murdoch	58	20	18	7.6%
John Campbell (2nd)	42	18	6	5.5%
Caddells	(35)			
I	–	–	–	
II	1	–	1	
III	7	–	7	
IV	12	1	10	
V	15	3	9	
Alexander Campbell	25	4	17	3.3%
James Low	21	8	5	2.8%
Macleod	21	7	7	2.8%
John Christie	19	4	11	2.5%
John Campbell (1st)	19	3	13	2.5%
John Stuart	16	3	10	2.1%
T. E. Mortimer	9	3	3	1.2%
John Campbell (Ed)	8	3	2	1.1%
William Smith	7	2	3	
Tipping & Lawden	7	2	3	
John Thomson (Ed)	6	2	2	
Jas McKenzie (Br)	6	–	6	
A. C.	5	1	3	
D. Ross	5	2	1	
D. H.	5	1	3	
James Michie	4	–	4	
C. Playfair	4	–	4	
J. Burgess (Elg)	4	–	4	
J. Gray	4	–	4	
Marshall & Sons	4	–	4	
W. Watson	4	2	–	
Christie & Murdoch	4	2	–	
W Lindsay	4	2	–	
J. Pitcairn	3	–	3	
Murdoch (?Wm)	3	1	1	

Table V below gives the geographical locations of the gunmakers of Scottish pistols, insofar as this can be ascertained from an examination of the lock-plates of the pistols, and a knowledge of hammermen records. In some cases, due to the obliteration of signatures on the lockplates by the ravages of time, it was not possible to identify makers, and therefore locations, and such pistols were listed in the 'unascribed' section. In this latter category were placed principally the large number of pistols which were unmarked with either the name or location of any gunsmith. The number of surviving pistols manufactured in each location is also indicated.

Table V
Geographical Locations of Scottish Pistol Makers

SCOTLAND

Aberdeen	4	
Brechin	7	
Dalmally	2	
Doune	199	
Dumbarton	4	
Dundee	36	
Edinburgh	130	(incl. Canongate and Leith)
Edzell	3	
Elgin	5	
Glasgow	5	
Glenelg	1	
Inverness	11	
Montrose	4	
Mull	1	
Old Meldrum	2	
Perth	12	
Rannoch	2	
Stirling	23	

ENGLAND

Birmingham	79
London	19

UNASCRIBED	211

THE MAKERS OF SCOTTISH PISTOLS
a selective list

John Burgess of Elgin, working during the period 1695–1710, manufactured four pistols amongst those surveyed. All were heart-butts, and either flintlocks or snaphaunces. His pistols are signed 'I. BURGESS', 'I.B.E.' or 'IOHN BURGES'.

'A. C.' are the initials of an unknown gunsmith who was responsible for the construction of five of the pistols surveyed, including one pair. All are ramshorn in type. He was active during the period 1740–50, and was probably one of the Doune gunsmiths, to judge from the appearance of the pistols. The pistols making up a pair are extensively inlaid with silver interlace and scrollwork, albeit of relatively primitive form. A further two of his pistols are of military type.

The Caddell family was a dynasty of gunsmiths, successive generations of which used the forename 'Thomas'. They manufactured thirty-five pistols in the series. Deciding which of them was responsible for which pistols is purely arbitrary, and the time scales given below are best considered as a useful working guide. No pistol of the series can be definitely attributed to **Thomas Caddell 1st.**, although it is vaguely possible that a pistol presently in the museum at Neuchatel, in Switzerland, was manufactured by this maker, but more likely by his son, **Thomas Caddell 2nd.** This, the earliest known Caddell pistol, has a dog lock, and, unusually, is signed in full on the lockplate, 'Thomas Caddell', in flowing script. The date 1678 is stamped at the bottom edge of the lockplate.

    Thomas Caddell 3rd., c. 1700–1725, manufactured seven pistols. **Thomas Caddell 4th.**, c. 1725–1750, manufactured twelve pistols including one pair. **Thomas Caddell 5th.**, c. 1750–1775, manufactured fifteen pistols, including three pairs.

The early Caddell pistols are normally signed 'THO CADDELL', in Roman lettering, whilst the later examples are signed 'THO:CADDELL', or 'Thos Caddell', in script.

Alexander Campbell was the second generation of Campbell to carry on his trade in Doune. He was responsible for twenty-five pistols in the survey (3.3%) including four pairs and seventeen single pistols. His pistols can be readily recognised by his use of inlaid silver interlace on the butts and spines of the weapons to a quite elaborate degree. Rarely, however, he abandons his normal practice, and reverts to the more traditionally engraved type of adornment. One of the most prestigious of all the Doune gunmakers, he invariably signed his pistols in script, 'Alexr Campbell'. Sometimes the words '*Duni fecit*', '*Fecit*, Doune', or '*Fecitt*, Doune' appear as well.

John Campbell, Alexander's father, was the first of three generations of his family to settle in Doune. He is described in the First Statistical Account of Scotland as having been trained in his art by Thomas Caddell 1st., and was active during the first quarter of the eighteenth century. He manufactured nineteen pistols in the survey (2.5%), including three pairs, and thirteen single pistols.

His pistols are long-barrelled, graceful weapons, having either cannon barrels, or the more popular four stage barrel with octagonal swamped muzzle. His signature took the form 'Io Campbell', or 'John Campbell', in script, and the latter may be found in Roman lettering. Sometimes the word 'Doune' appears in addition.

John Campbell (2nd) was the son of Alexander Campbell of Doune. Working in the third quarter of the eighteenth century, he is the third most prolific maker of Scottish pistols in the series. He made forty-two pistols of those surveyed (5.5%) including six single pistols and eighteen pairs. His signature is invariably engraved in script on the lockplate.

John Campbell of Edinburgh, working between 1815 and 1850, manufactured both flintlock and percussion pistols, sometimes with frames of nickel silver. He made eight pistols of those surveyed, including three pairs.

John Campbell of Glenelg was active during the eighteenth century, and in Warwick Castle is a pistol by this maker, with ramshorn butt and long cannon barrel, dating from around 1725, and signed in full on the lockplate in Roman lettering, along with the place of manufacture, Glenelg.

John Christie of Doune, and later Stirling, made nineteen pistols in the series (2.5%) comprising eleven single pistols, and four pairs. In addition, two pairs of pistols were manufactured by him in conjunction with John Murdoch. Signatures encountered with this maker include:

Jon CHRISTIE	Io CHRISTIE
Stirling	*Io Chrystie* DOWN

Sometimes the form 'Chrystie' is used instead.

One of Christie's pistols in the survey is a military pistol of ramshorn design, but of superior quality. The barrel is engraved 'RO H R 2d B', for '2nd Battalion, Royal Highland Regiment', with Company and Rack numbers, 'C4 N20', on the butt spine.

Christie habitually dated his pistols inside the locks, and is the only Doune gunsmith known to have done so. His pistols were of the very finest quality. One pair, formerly in the collection of the well-known portrait painter, Sir Noel Paton, and now in the Museum of Antiquities, in Edinburgh, were described by him thus: 'I have nowhere seen pistols more, or, indeed, so, beautiful as these'. These pistols are dated 1754 on the inner surface of each lockplate.

Another wonderful example of Christie's work, is in the Queen's collection at Windsor, and has gold butt plaques, ball trigger and pricker, as well as a gold ramrod pipe. Engraved beneath the belt hook is the Latin inscription: "*Totum hoc opus sua manu perfecit Joannes Christie*", which is translated as "John Christie carried out all this work by his own hand". The pistol was probably presented to George III on his accession to the throne in 1760, and is certainly amongst the finest Scottish pistols in existence.

A pair of ramshorn-butt pistols (illustrated in plate 2) is another splendid example of Christie's work. The lockplates of the pistols made in collaboration with John Murdoch, are marked 'Chrystie and Murdoch *Duni Fecit*' in script. Christie should not be confused with James Christie, who worked as a gunsmith in Perth around the same period. The solitary example of his work examined by the author was of inferior quality to that of his namesake, and its lockplate was marked 'CHRISTIE PERTH'. James had a son, also called James, who worked in Perth about 1820, and manufactured costume pistols.

James Gray of Dundee was working in the period 1627–30. He manufactured lemon-butt pistols with snaphaunce locks, and was responsible for four pistols in the series.

'D.H.' are the initials of a gunsmith who was working around 1680–1700. He manufactured heart-butt pistols and so was established somewhere on the east coast of the country. Five of the pistols in the series are stamped with his initials. They are all flintlocks, although one has been converted from snaphaunce.

William Lindsay, who was a prestigious silversmith in Aberdeen as well as Montrose, between 1670 and 1690, produced four pistols of the series, two pairs. All are heart-butts with snaphaunce locks, although one pair has been subsequently converted to doglock, and are of exceptional workmanship.

James Low of Dundee was responsible for the manufacture of twenty-one pistols in the series, including eight pairs and five single pistols, amounting to 2.8% of the total. His pistols were signed 'I.L.' Since he was working mainly in the first quarter of the seventeenth century, it is quite remarkable that so many examples of his work have survived. However the reason for this may be that his pistols were often presented as gifts to Royalty and foreign dignitaries, and have been preserved in their arms collections. His pistols were all originally of snaphaunce mechanism, although three have since been converted to flintlock, and each is dated. The earliest pair is dated 1602, and is in the Tojhusmuseum, Copenhagen. The stocks of these are, unusually, of walnut, and have fishtail butts. Low's pistols were either fishtail or lemon-butt in style. A fishtail-butt brass and steel pistol dated 1611, and stamped 'R.L.', for Richard Low, appears in the survey, and the two were almost certainly brothers.

Macleod was a gunsmith who flourished during the first quarter of the nineteenth century, and so was responsible for the manufacture of late flint-lock Scottish pistols, as well as costume pistols. Unfortunately, Macleod did not prefix the signature on his lockplates with the initial of his forename, and this has inevitably led to some speculation regarding the precise location of his place of work. Both Edinburgh and Perth have been suggested as possible bases for his gunsmithing business, and there has even been a suggestion that his pistols were manufactured in Birmingham, and that these were then marked with his name as the retailer. Whitelaw believed that Macleod was a cutler, who was working between 1813 and 1837 in Edinburgh and the Canongate. As such, he was not permitted to carry out gunsmithing without the submission of a further essay in his new craft, but this may have been difficult to enforce. Thus, Macleod may have been John Macleod, of 17 College Street, Edinburgh.

Yet another possibility is Alexander Macleod, who was a goldsmith in Inverness at the relevant time. Such craftsmen, who also belonged to the Hammerman craft, had been known to turn their hand to gunsmithing on occasion, for example, Robert and William Lindsay, both well-known silver and goldsmiths in Aberdeen, the former having been Deacon of Aberdeen Incorporation of Hammermen in 1659, and both Patrick and Thomas Ramsay of Dundee were goldsmiths as well as gunsmiths.

Although some pistols by Macleod are of costume type, others, including a pair in Sir Walter Scott's collection at Abbotsford, and another illustrated in plate 16, are of very advanced form, being skilfully etched and engraved, and of excellent workmanship. A solitary example of Macleod's work had a percussion lock, but in other respects was similar in form and engraving to his flintlock pistols. Macleod pistols are stamped at the barrel breech with post-1813 Birmingham View and Proof Marks, but it is of interest that these marks have been impressed on the barrels after the etching process has been carried out, which seems to indicate that Macleod fabricated the weapons himself, and had the barrels proved subsequently in Birmingham, to satisfy the demands of an increasingly discriminating Lowland clientele. Macleod made twenty-one pistols of those surveyed, including seven pairs and seven single pistols, amounting to 2.8% of the total.

❧

Marshall & Sons were Edinburgh gunsmiths, active around 1820. They produced four pistols in the series, including one pair. Costume pistols as well as late flintlock Scottish pistols were manufactured, sometimes with stocks of German silver.

❧

McKenzie is a name which recurs frequently in the survey. David McKenzie and his son James were both gunsmiths in Dundee during the first quarter of the eighteenth century. One pistol by the former, and two by the latter, are represented amongst those examined, their signatures appearing in Roman lettering. James signed his lockplates 'IAMES M^{c}KENZIE'.

Another James McKenzie is known to have been a gunsmith in Brechin about 1720–1740. He is probably not the same man, as his pistols are signed in a totally different manner, 'IAMK', or 'IAMK', probably in an effort to distinguish himself from his namesake. Although only six pistols can be definitely ascribed to him, a number of others which are unsigned or in which the signature is no longer decipherable, can almost certainly be attributed to him by virtue of the similarity of their design, being short weapons with angular butts and moderately large heart-shaped pommels.

Another James McKenzie, whose name does not occur in the records of the Dundee Hammermen, was in existence. This can be shown by the presence in the survey of two further heartbutt pistols, one with a doglock, which date from the late seventeenth and early eighteenth centuries respectively, and therefore are certainly of an earlier design than other James McKenzie pistols. These are signed 'I MᶜKENZIE', and 'IA MᶜKENZIE' respectively.

James McKenzie of Brechin had a son called David, who, to confuse the situation still further, also became a gunsmith in Dundee. This is exactly the type of scenario which faced Whitelaw and his researchers, when compiling his *Scottish Arms Makers*.

Michie is a name to which it is difficult to ascribe a particular location with any degree of confidence. One pistol in the series was clearly marked on the lockplate 'Io Michie, Doune', for John Michie. This pistol was a late flintlock Scottish pistol, dating from around 1800, although its cock still retained the starshaped comb. This feature, however, merely indicates a brief revival of the older style, which occurred in the early years of the nineteenth century. Most Michie pistols are signed 'IA MICHIE', for James Michie, and are typical, in their styling, of Doune pistols of the mid-eighteenth century. It is therefore likely that James Michie was, like John, one of the Doune gunsmiths.

James Michie of Doune produced good quality Scottish pistols, sometimes with star combs behind the cocks, during the mid-eighteenth century. Four pistols by him were encountered. One pistol marked in this way, however, is of much later design, with a rounded barrel and cannon muzzle, and a ring neck cock, bringing it into the category of the late flintlock Scottish pistol. There was therefore a third Michie in existence, who may possibly have been working in Perth around the turn of the century.

Thomas Elsworth Mortimer made high quality percussion dress pistols of the period 1830-1850. His pistols are signed in Gothic lettering, 'T.E. Mortimer, Edinburgh', on the lockplate. Nine pistols, some of which have nickel silver frames, were manufactured by him, including three pairs.

John Murdoch, who practised his trade as a gunsmith in Doune throughout his long life, was the second most prolific of the Doune pistol makers. He manufactured fifty-eight pistols of those surveyed (7.6%), comprising eighteen single pistols and twenty pairs. Forty-two pistols by John Murdoch had ramshorn butts, whilst sixteen were of the lobe-butt variety. His pistols were signed, 'MURDOCH', 'J.MURDOCH' or 'Io MURDOCH', the latter form being either in script or Roman lettering. The 'o' may occasionally occur as a capital letter, and sometimes the name 'Doune' appears in addition on the lockplate.

The most prolific of all the Doune gunsmiths in terms of surviving examples of his work was **Thomas Murdoch**, who later transferred his business to Leith. He manufactured eighty-one pistols of those surveyed, including twenty-three pairs and thirty-five single pistols, representing 10.7% of the total number of pistols. Although most (55) were of lobe-butt form, twenty-six of his pistols were ramshorn in type. Of his lobe-butt pistols, fourteen, or 25.5%, were constructed of brass. This refutes entirely the popularly held contention that Thomas Murdoch's lobe-butt pistols were 'normally constructed of brass'.

Thomas Murdoch signed his pistols 'T.Murdoch', in Roman lettering, and one example is marked 'Leith', on the upper edge of the lockplate. His pistols were engraved in two distinct styles. The first of these consists in the Celtic ornament common to the majority of Scottish pistols, and the second, and probably later style, involves the use of stylised acanthus leaf engraving, sometimes covering the entire surface of the pistol. Not infrequently, elements of acanthus engraving will be found amongst the more traditionally engraved pistols, as it does in examples by other makers. Late examples of Murdoch lobe-butt pistols also have abbreviated belt hook finials, and may also have barrels stamped with Tower Proof and View Marks for private arms.

A few examples were encountered of smaller pistols by both John and Thomas Murdoch, usually of lobe-butt form, but scaled down to the dimensions of overcoat pistols, yet still retaining their belt hooks, and a single example, by John Murdoch, of a small pistol with ramshorn butt.

William Murdoch was Thomas Murdoch's son, and after his death, continued to carry on working as a gunsmith at his father's old premises in Leith Walk, and is listed in the Edinburgh Directory of 1794. It is possible that he was the manufacturer of three pistols in the survey, marked only 'Murdoch'. One is a costume pistol with flintlock mechanism of around 1820, while the others are a pair of percussion dress pistols ten years its junior.

John Pitcairn appears to have manufactured solely military pistols, of plain appearance, clearly stamped 'JO PETCAIRN' on the lockplates. Three pistols by this maker were encountered in the series.

Charles Playfair of Aberdeen manufactured both flintlock and percussion dress pistols in the second quarter of the nineteenth century, all of costume type, and was responsible for four pistols in the series. The firm was still in existence in the 1920s.

Daniel Ross of Edinburgh, a prestigious manufacturer of pistols, contributed five pistols, costume as well as late flintlock Scottish pistols, with rainproof pans and roller frizzens, of the period 1820 or thereabouts. There were two pairs and one single pistol.

William Smith of Inverness, armourer to the Lairds of Grant at Bellachastel, the ancient name of Castle Grant, signed his pistols 'G.S', for Giulielmus Smith, or sometimes 'W.S.' He was responsible for seven pistols in the survey, including two pairs. All have heart-butts and snaphaunce locks. He was active during the last quarter of the seventeenth century.

John Stuart, working in an unknown location on the East coast of Scotland, manufactured sixteen pistols in the series, including three pairs, and ten single pistols. He was active during the period 1683–1701 and made heart-butt as well as ramshorn-butt pistols, fitted with either snaphaunce locks, doglocks, or true flintlocks. His pistols are signed 'Io STUART' on the lockplate.

John Thompson of Edinburgh contributed six pistols to the series, comprising two pairs and two single pistols. He was working during the period 1820–1840, and produced percussion dress pistols, as well as costume and late flintlock Scottish pistols.

Tipping and Lawden was a London firm, who were responsible for the manufacture of seven pistols in the series, including two pairs. All were percussion dress pistols, and silver-plating was sometimes employed in enhancing the appearance of the steelwork. They were active in the 1840s.

Walker is yet another name to which it is difficult to ascribe a particular location. One pistol, dating from the first quarter of the eighteenth century, is marked 'Daniel Walker, Dumbartan' (*sic*) on its lockplate. Other pistols, which date from 1740–1750, are marked 'D. WALKER', in Roman lettering, and a further single pistol, 'D. L. WALKER'. Thus two, and possibly three, gunsmiths named Walker were practising during the century, but whether all were related and worked in Dumbarton remains to be discovered.

William Watson of the Strand, London, was responsible for the production of high quality presentation pistols around 1820. He contributed four pistols to the survey, comprising two pairs.

Appendices

APPENDIX ONE

Historical References

"Pray cause thank John Currie Gun Smith in Glasgow for the pistolls he made wer extraordinar good. I mean the pistolls he made to the Company."

Robert Turnbull

THE HISTORICAL REFERENCES WHICH FOLLOW HAVE BEEN taken from a wide variety of sources. They commence in the year 1578, with a simple description of an armed band of Lowlanders, continue throughout the turbulent period of religious strife in Scotland during Covenanting times, and reach a climax in the Jacobite Rebellions of 1715 and 1745, particularly the latter. All references are reproduced as they appear in the original accounts, with the spelling, grammar, use of capital letters, place names and punctuation left unmodernised. Where marked differences occur from present usage, this has been indicated in the text. In each case the source of the reference has been given below the extract.

1. In 1578, the Lowland men appear "bodin with Jakkis, steilbonettis, pisto-lettis, speiris, lang hagbuts, and Jedburgh staffis."

From Privy Council Register (Scottish Records Office), in J. Drummond & J. Anderson, *Ancient Scottish Weapons* (Edinburgh and London: Waterson & Sons, 1881

2. Charles Whitelaw made a partial study of the inventories of, and debts owing to, deceased gunmakers. For example, in 1596, "Testament Testamentor and Inventory of umquile [deceased] George Richmount, dagmaker burgess of the Canongait died September 1596, Sum of Inventory £53–6–8." Amongst debts owing to deceased gunmakers were: "Walter Jak at the Kirk of Deir for ane pistowel vj lib. Wam. Rae dagmaker in the Canongait of lent money iiij lib. Mr George Frazer agent to the Earl Marschell for the rest of ane pair pisollath iij lib."

When David Clark dagmaker burgess of Edinburgh died in 1645, his inventory included: "Sex pair of Pistolls estimat all to £100, and warklumes [tools] in his buith £20." In 1767, "The Testament Dative and Inventory of the goods, etc., of deceased Thomas Caddell elder gunsmith in Doun in the parish of Kilmadock who died in the month of – 176–, Inventory two pistols to Jo: Caddell seven pounds four shillings."

From C. E. Whitelaw, *Scottish Arms Makers*, ed. S. Barter-Bailey
(London: Arms and Armour Press, 1970).

3. An inventory of the estate of one Peter Orem (Orme) citizen and trader of Cracow, Poland, one of a considerable number of Scottish tradesmen who settled in Poland in the late sixteenth and early seventeenth centuries and dated 1613, lists amongst his possessions:

Item 2 dozen simple wooden powder flasks. [*These were valued at 1½ zloty.*]
Item 2 plaid covers (Scotch) lined green
Item A pair of Scotch pistols
Item A third pistol.

From A. F. Steuart, *The Scots in Poland, 1576–1793*, Scottish History Society
(Edinburgh: Edinburgh University Press, 1915).

4. *The Compt Book of David Wedderburne, Merchant of Dundee, 1587–1630,*which contains the accounts of a Dundee merchant over a period of 43 years, has provided us with a valuable record in respect of exports, imports, and home trade, in a busy Scottish east coast port, at a time when such records are extremely scarce. The earliest entry in the account book occurs on 15 March 1587, the last on 12 December 1630. David Wedderburne was admitted burgess on 15 May 1582.

9 September 1594: "Giffen Patrik Ramsey smyth a crown of the sone in arrels of a pair pistolattis." This was the 'down payment' which was later followed by "£3 of silver", a further 2 "crowns of the sun" and a half-merk of silver", in order to clear the debt completely. [p. 43]

20 January 1594: "Item: to send my pistolattis or els to rander me thame agane in als gud a stait and gif thay feal to ware it as he dois the rest of his awn". [p. 46]

3 October 1597: "Send with John Scrymgeour merchant to Spane in the schip of St Andros:Item: Ane pair of pistolattis cost me xij lib. Giffen him commissione to sell the sam in Ingland or ony uther port he thinkis best to my proffit." [p. 87]

21 March 1608: "Sent out with Willaim Renkyn to Spane . . . 4 pistollatis and thair redschip." [p. 104]

15 March 1587: "I am restand awine to Dauid Wedderburne the sowme off tenne pundis money for his pistolet." [p. 183]

3 July 1612: "Lent James Alisone sone to Litel John Alisone my bandeler and tua velvit flasses coverit with Iron. Lent Alexr. Myln my puder horn." [p. 190]

9 August 1622: "Alexander Myln hes my pwder horn redy in borrowing." [p. 185]

From A. H. Millar, ed., The Compt Book of David Wedderburne, Merchant of Dundee, 1587–1630, Scottish History Society (Edinburgh: Edinburgh University Press, 1898).

5. On 6 July 1614, at a meeting of the Incorporation of Hammermen of Edinburgh,

Walter Smyth, servand to James Nasmyth, dagmaker, charged with coming to Thomas Glen dagmaker his buith with a pistolet in his lap and tuik ane gentillman away theirfra which was standit there in, which was proven by the brother of the said Walter.

Smyth was fined 20s, and discharged from work until he paid.

From C. E. Whitelaw, Scottish Arms Makers, ed. S. Barter-Bailey (London: Arms and Armour Press, 1970).

6. In 1618, Grant of Ballindalloch assaulted a house in Elgin, with men armed with "bowis, durkis, swerdis, Lochaber aixes, mailye coattis, Jedburgh staulfis, halbertis, guns, hagbutts and pistollets."

From J. Wallace, *Scottish Swords and Dirks* (London: Arms & Armour Press, 1970).

7. In 1623, Sir Robert Gordon recorded, that he had been given a commission "for punishing the wearers of pistols."

From I. Grimble, *Chief of Mackay* (London: Routledge & Kegan Paul, 1965)

8. In 1624, the Clan MacIntosh took fought the Earl of Murray "upon foot, with swords, bows, arrows, targets, hagbuts, pistols, and other Highland arms."

From J. Logan, *The Clans of the Scottish Highlands*, 1845

9. "Thay keipit the feildis in thair Hieland weid vpone foote, with suordis bowis arrowis targis hagbuttis pistollis and vther Hieland armour."

From J. Stuart, *Memorials of the Troubles in Scotland and England, 1624–45*
(Aberdeen: Spalding Club, 1850)

10. In 1634, commissions were issued in Sutherland, bestowing powers "To apprehend and cause justice to be administered on these limmars, and for this cause to hold courts, etc., with power of fire and sword, and permission to bear hagbuts and pistols in the execution of this commission."

From I. Grimble, *Chief of Mackay* (London: Routledge & Kegan Paul 1965)

11. In *Memoirs of a Cavalier*, Daniel Defoe describes the soldiers in a Highland army which invaded England in 1639: "There were three or four thousand of these in the Scots army, armed only with swords and targets; and in their belts some of them had a pistol, but no musquets at that time amongst them."

From J. G. Mackay, *The Romantic Story of the Highland Garb and the Tartan*
(Stirling: Mackay, 1924)

12. *The Rout at Newburn Ford, 1640.* "Many of the horse were armed with lances, in addition to their swords and pistols; the dragoons had buff coats with large skirts, sword, pistol, and slung musketoon."

From J. Grant, *British Battles on Land and Sea* (London: Cassell, 1897)

13. The 1640 inventory of Sir Colin Campbell of Glenurchy [sic], set aside as his heirlooms, "field pieces of copper and iron, and a few muskets and pistols", as well as some body armour, swords, and targes.

From C. Innes, *Ancient Scottish Weapons* (London, Edinburgh: Drummond & Anderson, 1881)

14. A clergyman named Father Blackhall, writing in 1643, said "I had behind my saddle a great cloach bagge in which were my new cloathes—and at the bow of my saddle two Dutch pistolettes with wheele-workes, and at my side two Scots pistolettes with snap workes."

From J. Grant, *British Battles on Land and Sea* (London: Cassell, 1897)

15. When the Army of the Solemn League and Covenant was formed on 18 August 1643, all fencible persons between the ages of sixteen and sixty were ordered to present themselves within forty-eight hours at various rendezvous, along with arms and ammunition. The infantry were expected to have muskets, pikes, and swords, whilst the cavalrymen were to carry pistols, broadswords, and steel caps. Extensive lists of the arms supplied to the army are still in existence, and these confirm the issue of large numbers of pistols to regiments of horse.

Sir James Ramsay's regiment, for example, was issued with fifty pairs of pistols on 22 April 1645. Sir Frederick Hamilton's was issued with ninety pairs. Colonell Weldon's regiment of horse was issued with 110 pairs. Pistols were also issued to Regiments of Foot, but only in small numbers, and presumably to officers who had chosen not to supply their own weapons.

Of the arms delivered to the regiment of the general artillery, there were 471 muskets, and only four pairs of pistols, and Lord Sinclair's Regiment had 258 muskets, but only twenty-two pairs of pistols.

After the disbanding of the Army, Sir James Ramsay's Regiment surrendered only nineteen pairs of old pistols, out of fifty pairs originally issued, whilst Sir Frederick Hamilton's Regiment surrendered only thirteen pairs, of ninety pairs originally issued. It is interesting that the pistols were issued only in pairs, and not singly.

A note on 1 February 1644 contains a reference to three Powder Hornes, supplied by James Ridle of Berwick, the name of a gunsmith which recurs frequently in the lists. Contained in the papers relating to the Army, is the 'Accompt. of Sir Adam Hepburn of Humbie, Treasurer of the Armies from 1644–45'. On 5 February 1645 in his detailed account is listed:

> Item 10. Payed to Leuitenant Collonell [*sic*] Andro Hamilton by ordour of the Comittie for 176 pair of pistolls at 40s sterling each pair delyvered by him to severall regiments off horse conforme to the account theroff to be giffin in be him. £0352–00–0.
>
> Item 11. Payed by James Suord to William Frier for 250 pair of pistolls delyvered by him to severall regiments off horse conforme to the Comittie and the Generall his Excellence ordour and the Leuitenant Generall his resaitt theroff at 40s sterling each pair is £0500–00–0.

James Sword was Collector of Excise, whilst William Frier was secretary to Lord Leven.

From C. S. Terry, Papers Relating to the Army of the Solemn League and Covenant, 1643–1647,
Scottish History Society (Edinburgh: Constable, 1917)

16. When Montrose's army entered Aberdeen, it was described thus: "upon the morne, being Saturday, they came in order of battell, weill armed, both on horse and foot, ilk horseman having five shot at the least, with ane carabine in his hand, two pistols by his sydes, and other two at his saddell toir."

From J. S. Keltie, A History of the Highlands, 2 vols. (Edinburgh: Fullarton, 1875)

17. Grant describes the equipment of Montrose's army thus: "Their arms were the claymore, now basket-hilted, and the dirk or armpit dagger [*skene ochles*]; a target with a pike in its orb; a pair of steel pistols, and frequently a

long-barelled Spanish musket; a skene in the right garter was the last
weapon to resort to, if under a horse's belly or grappling on the earth with
the foe; and in addition to these were still occasionally used the pike and
the tremendous Lochaber axe, and even the bow and arrow."

From J. Grant, British Battles on Land and Sea (London: Cassell, 1897)

18. In *The Souldier's Accidence*, published in 1648, Gervase Markam makes the
following recommendations regarding the arming of cuirassiers: "For offensive arms, they shall have a case of long pistols, firelocks, (if it may be) but
snaphaunces when they are wanting." This led Hayward to suggest that by
the mid-seventeenth century, few wheellocks were available, and cuirassiers
were armed mainly with flintlocks.

From J. F. Hayward, Art of the Gunmaker, 2 vols. (London: Barrie & Rockliff, 1962).

19. *From the Dundee Court Martial Records.* "September. 23 1651 Phillip
Rakeham, corporall to Capt. Lingwood saw 2 troopers about halfe a mile
off driving 2 Scotchmen with their swords drawn before them. One of
these troopers haveing knock't one of the Scotchmen downe with his
pistoll 3 severall times." A witness of the above incident stated that one of
the troopers "set his pistoll to this deponent's brest, and said "You Scotch
roge, give's your mony!" He then stated that he would pistoll this deponent
if he would not deliver it presently."

From G. Davies, ed., Miscellany of the Scottish History Society, vol. 3 (Edinburgh: Constable, 1919)

20. *From the Dundee Court Martial Records.* 1 December 1651: "One Robert
Bell, with six more of his companie came to Blaire and entered the house
of Mr Walter Rattray, with swords drawne and pistolls cock't." The soldiers
had earlier that day entered the house of James Haliburton of Cowper in
Angus "with their swords and durkes drawne and pistolls cock't." The party
was pursued by Lt. Col. Gray, and "fireing uppon one of them the rest came
out and fired their pistolls, but made their escape in the darkenesse of the
night."

Bell was tried as a spy, as well as for theft, robbery and murder, and was sentenced to death by hanging.

From G. Davies, ed., Miscellany of the Scottish History Society, vol. 3 (Edinburgh: Constable, 1919)

21. *From the Dundee Court Martial Records.* 11 October 1651. James Mauley, the Lard [*sic*] of Melgun Junr. being examined under oath regarding the plundering of the house of Lady Arley, stated that "hee meeting a messenger from the Lady Arley nere unto the gate, coming in did find the gates shut and the garden gate and the inner gate both on fire, and then he found the souldiers with their swords and pistolls in their hands, with this word: "Noe quarter to man, woman, or child."

From G. Davies, ed., Miscellany of the Scottish History Society, vol. 3 (Edinburgh: Constable, 1919)

22. *From the Dundee Court Martial Records.* "Thomas Pitt, a trooper in Col. Grosvenor's troope of horse, stated 8/12/51 that he was one of a party sent to apprehend some Scotchmen in armes. This deponent went into the house, and seeing about half a dozen of them in a roome hee bid them call for quarter and deliver their armes. One began to draw his sword, uppon which the deponent firing his pistoll att his bodie, he struck itt downe and the deponent shott him into the thigh."

A second trooper testified that he had gone to the aid of Pitt, and "offered to fire uppon one of them, but his pistoll nott going off hee advised them to call for quarter."

From G. Davies, ed., Miscellany of the Scottish History Society, vol. 3 (Edinburgh: Constable, 1919)

23. *From the Dundee Court Martial Records.* On 20 December 1651, "2 troopers in Capt. Lee's troope began to quarrel, and Henry Thompson took off a pistoll from off the table and broke John Dodd's head with itt." Several witnesses verified this account.

From G. Davies, ed., Miscellany of the Scottish History Society, vol. 3 (Edinburgh: Constable, 1919)

24. *From the Dundee Court Martial Records.* A deserter called William Lambe was taken "when hee had noe armes with him, but uppon his taking hee told the dragoones that tooke him where his armes were, being a case of pistolls and a sworde."

From G. Davies, ed., *Miscellany of the Scottish History Society*, vol. 3 (Edinburgh: Constable, 1919)

25. 4 November 1658: Alexander Chrysteson violently robbed William Gordon of Balimore of "an ox, two pistols and a durk, and did violently wound him with the durk." On a separate occasion the same man was "violently invaded and robbed of a further pistol."

From W. G. Scott-Moncrieff, ed., *Justiciary Records 1669–78*, vol. 2. Scottish History Society (Edinburgh: Constable, 1905)

26. Francis Crichton and James Duffus attacked Alexr Gregory of Netherdale on 7/3/64, although he had given up his arms and thrown himself on their mercy. ". . . did basely and treacherously pursue him more eagerly than before, fired pistols at him, gave him severall wounds in his head and breast to the effusion of his blood in great quantity." Gregory later died of his wounds.

From W. G. Scott-Moncrieff, ed., *Justiciary Records 1669–78*, vol. 1. Scottish History Society (Edinburgh: Constable, 1905)

27. On 5 December 1666, during the trials held in Edinburgh, of the rebels who had participated in the uprising at Pentland Hills, the following statements were made:

1. Cristall Strang confessed that he had taken the Covenant and "was an horseman in arms with Sword and Pistolls."

2. John Ross also confessed to "being in Arms, having Pistolls with him."

3. James Hamilton confessed also "to have taken the Covenant and joined Barscobb's Troup with Sword and Pistolls."

4. John Lindsay, "indweller in Edinbr. did confess that he went away

with two out of this town, and being armed with sword and pistol did join with the rebellious party under the command of Mr George Crookshank, and was with them at Lanark where they took the Covenant, and that he was at the late fight with sword drawn and pistol shott."

All the accused were sentenced to be hanged, and thereafter "their heads and right arms to be cut off and disposed of as the Lords of the Privy Council should think fitt."

The Pentland Rising took place in 1666, when 3000 Covenanters marched from Lanark to Edinburgh, in an attempt to overthrow Episcopalianism. Encountering a large measure of hostility, they abandoned the scheme when within 3 miles of the capital, and set off across the Pentland Hills to return to their homes. The Covenanters were confronted by Royalist troops under the command of Sir Thomas Dalziel, at Rullion Green, where they were defeated.

From W. G. Scott-Moncrieff, ed., *Justiciary Records 1669–78*, vol. 1. Scottish History Society (Edinburgh: Constable, 1905)

28. Captain William Barclay was charged that upon the 28 March 1668, in he house of Paul Watt in Greenbrae, he attacked Alexander Sinclair, and "did strick him over the head with a pistoll, and then shot him thro' the leg, and then three of the Captain's accomplices by his command, fired several shots at him, and one of these shots was by Robert Ogilvy with a blunderbush [*sic*] which shot the Defunct in the side, and thereafter the Captain did wound him with a broadsword in the head, of which wounds he dyed immediatly."

The Defendents pleaded self-defence, and were acquitted, the Justices being satisfied that the Defunct (deceased) Sinclair and his accomplices were the first aggressors, that he had wounded the Defendent's brother or servants, and thereafter pursued the Pannel (defendant) "with a drawn sword or bended pistol." (Note: a 'bended' pistol is taken to mean a fully cocked pistol, whilst a pistol which is 'half-bent' is on half-cock.)

From W. G. Scott-Moncrieff, ed., *Justiciary Records 1669–78*, vol. 1. Scottish History Society (Edinburgh: Constable, 1905)

29. *The assassination attempt on Archbishop Sharp of St Andrews.* In 1668, the Archbishop of St Andrews, James Sharp, Primate of all Scotland, was distributing alms to the poor from the comfort of his coach, when an attempt was made on his life. One of the crowd, a young and zealous Covenanter named James Mitchell, and himself a preacher of the gospel, fired a pistol at the Archbishop. The shot missed and struck instead the Archbishop's fellow cleric, Mr Honeyman, Bishop of Orkney, who was badly wounded and later died. Mitchell was seen to enter a nearby house, and later emerged wearing different clothes, apparently diverting suspicion from himself by assisting the crowd in their efforts to find the assassin. However, he was apprehended and charged with contriving the murder of the Archbishop. The record states:

> in order thereto, having provided yourself with a pair of long scots iron pistols near musket bore you did etc. and you having a charge pistol with powder and ball, did fire and discharge and shott the saids pistolls upon them. Furthermore having another charged and bended pistol in your hands of purpose and design to have killed any person who should have offered to take and apprehend you.

During the trial, in Edinburgh on 12 March 1674, John Bishop of Galloway

> Deponed [swore under oath] that the first time he saw the Pannell, was in Sir William Sharp's outter room, where he saw a pistoll, which was said to be taken from him, out of which, (as he supposes) there were three balls taken, and that the pistoll was like the pistoll produced.

Mitchell admitted "that he had shott the pistoll at the said Archbishop when the Bishop of Orkney was hurt." He declared that he had "bought the pistoll which was about him, charged with three balls, when he was apprehended, about the time when the Bishop was shott, from Alexander Logan dage maker [*sic*] in Leithwynd." He was condemned "to be hanged on a Gibbett till he be dead, and all his moveable goods and gear to be escheat [forfeit] and inbrought to His Majesty's use, which was pronounced for Doom [sentence]." The "moveable goods" presumably included his Logan pistols.

*From I. A. Lang, *A History of Scotland*, vol. 3 (Edinburgh: Blackwood, 1909) and W. G. Scott-Moncrieff, ed., *Justiciary Records 1669–78*, vol. 2. Scottish History Society (Edinburgh: Constable, 1905)*

30. A letter from the Duke of Hamilton to the Duke of Queensbury reads: "... Some others told that some gentlemens houses were provydt with arms far abov the condition of pryvett families; that in some wer 20 pair off pistols, 20 carbyns, besyd mussquets and fyerlocks."

From J. B. Elder, *The Highland Host of 1678* (Aberdeen: Aberdeen University Press, 1914)

31. On 16 September 1672, "Four men were charged with having been with the Rebells in the fight of Pentland Hills, and were accused of attacking the house of Alexander Ramsay, minister of Affleck, armed with Swords, Pistolls, etc, and did carry away the money and beat the said Mr Alexander with a Pistoll and wounded him with a sword."

From W. G. Scott-Moncrieff, ed., *Justiciary Records 1669–78*, vol. 2. Scottish History Society (Edinburgh: Constable, 1905)

32. Grant states that during the Battle of Drumclog, in 1679, the antagonists "grappled hand to hand with their assailants in the morass, fighting with swords shortened, or with clubbed steel pistols seeking to beat out each others' brains."

From J. Grant, *British Battles on Land and Sea* (London: Cassell, 1897)

33. *The Surrender of Arms.* In February 1679, arms belonging to the Maclean clan surrendered to Campbell of Inveraw amounted to: "185 swords, 95 guns, 3 pistolls, 5 Lochabur axes and ane two handed sword."[1]

Although this might be interpreted as indicating that very few pistols were in use by the Highlanders at that time, it is much more likely that pistols, being more valued and easily concealed, were in consequence not given up, and that only rusted and useless arms were surrendered. In this context it is interesting to read the account given to Bishop Forbes by Captain Roy Macdonald of Bonnie Prince Charlie's army, who admitted having made a "sham surrendry" of his arms.

A report to Lord Albemarle from Campbell of Airds after the 1745 Rebellion reads: "They have still plenty of arms for, when they surrendered, they gave up only some rusted useless arms, and still kept the good fresh arms."[2]

On 17 May 1746, forty-four Stratherrick people surrendered and handed in "27 guns 3 swords 6 pistols and a single dirk." On the same day, twenty-five men of Daviot and Dunlichty parishes handed in their arms to Mr John Campbell, minister.

These arms comprised "10 guns 4 swords 12 pistols and no dirk." Another group consisted of twenty-three Mackintoshes, Frasers, and others of the Parish of Moy. They surrendered "14 swords 4 pistols and 2 dirks." However, twenty McMartins surrendered sixteen guns and two swords to the Earl of Loudoun, but no pistols, and twenty Camerons at Moy gave up sixteen guns and one sword, but again no pistols. Seventy-seven men of the Glengarry Regiment surrendered sixty-five guns, twenty-six swords, and four dirks, but again no pistols, and ninety-eight men of Keppoch's Regiment surrendered ninety-eight guns, twenty-two swords, and a dirk, but no pistols.

It therefore seems highly probable, from these statistics, that pistols were held back, being much easier to conceal than any long gun, and dirks were probably also withheld for the same reason. After the Battle of Culloden, the English soldiers received the following orders: "French or Spanish firelocks or bayonets and cartridge boxes to be delivered by the train to Ensign Stewart of Lascelles Regt.; he is to distribute them to the Prisoners of our Army released here." Half a crown was paid for each firelock and one shilling for each broadsword.[3]

Intelligence received from Appin, 29 October 1746: "That on the 10th of Octr. last, every private man who did not deliver up his Arms in Appin and neighbouring countries received five pounds sterling reward . . ." The cash was provided by Clunie, Chief of the Clan MacPherson, to be taken from the treasure of Loch Arkaig, of which he was custodian.[4]

In a letter from Alexander McDonald of Glencoe to the Duke of Cumberland, he writes: "I have ordered such of my people as live in Glenco to meet of you, and to deliver all there arms to you as an evidence of my submission. I have sent by my son one gun one sword one pistill and durk which I beg you'll please lay aside by themselves." It is not difficult to imagine the Duke's reaction.[5]

After the Rebellion of 1715, Robert Low, Armourer in Inverness, surrendered 70 swords, as well as "Three Gunns, a pistol, ane two handed sword, valued at £1–10–8." Patrick Grant, Gunsmith, of the same town, surrendered, amongst other items, "Four side pistols at £0–15–0.", whilst Charles McCulloch, also gunsmith in Inverness, surrendered, with other arms "Six Gunns valued at £4–0–0. Six side pistols at £4–13–4."[6]

1. D. H. Caldwell, ed., *Scottish Weapons and Fortifications* (Edinburgh: Donald, 1981).
2. B. Seton and J. Arnot, *Prisoners of the Forty Five*, 2 vols. (Edinburgh: Edinburgh University Press, 1929).
3. Cumberland's Orders, 19 April 1746.
4. C. S. Terry, *Albemarle Papers*. Scottish History Society (Aberdeen: Aberdeen University Press, 1902).
5. Sir J. Fergusson, *Argyll in the Forty Five*. Scottish History Society (Edinburgh: Faber & Faber, 1895).
6. C. E. Whitelaw. 'Culloden Papers, 1716', *Scottish Arms Makers*, edited by S. Barter-Bailey (London: Arms & Armour Press, 1977).

34. A graphic account of the Battle of Bothwell Brig is given by Crichton, an officer in the Scots Guards, who was in command of thirty horse and fifty dragoons.

> One of the rebels ran me through the small of the back with his broadsword and at the same instant two more wounded me under the ribs with their small ones. Then I threw myself over the head of my horse, taking the far pistol out of the holdster [*sic*] in my left hand and holding my broadsword in my right; and as one of the rebels was coming hastily up to me his foot slipped and before he could recover himself I stuck my sword into his skull, but the fellow being big and heavy, snapped it asunder as he fell, within a span of the hilt. One of them made a stroke at me which I guarded off with the hilt of the sword that was left in my hand, but the force with which he struck the blow brought us both to the ground. However, I got up before him, clapped my pistol to his side, and shot him Dead.

From R. M. Barnes, *The Uniforms and History of the Scottish Regiments*
(London, Sphere Books, 1956)

35. Murder of Archbishop Sharp. On Saturday, 3 May 1679, Archbishop James Sharp of St Andrews, and the highest prelate in Scotland, was out driving with his daughter. When the coach reached Magus Muir, only two miles from the town, it was overtaken by a party of Covenanters, headed by Balfour of Kinloch. One pistol was discharged so close to the Primate, that his daughter rubbed off the burning wadding from his gown. However, "wounded by a ball between the second and third ribs, the Archbishop was immediately after stabbed with a small sword."

From M. Napier, *Memoirs of Dundee*, 3 vols. (Edinburgh: Stevenson, 1859)

36. During the persecution of the Covenanters by Graham of Claverhouse, some of his men tortured a suspect by "tying a cord about his head–and both ends of it were wreathed about the butt of one of their pistols; they then twisted it about the upper part of his head with the pistol so hard, that the flesh was cut round into the skull. His cries were heard at a great distance."

From M. Napier, *Memoirs of Dundee*, 3 vols. (Edinburgh: Stevenson, 1859)

37. Colonel James Douglas, brother to Graham of Claverhouse, attacked some Covenanters, and was himself nearly shot dead, but "the Whig's carbine misfired, whereupon Douglas pistolled him presently."

From M. Napier, *Memoirs of Dundee*, 3 vols. (Edinburgh: Stevenson, 1859)

38. During Covenanting times, the soldiers "found out a house in a hill, under ground, that could hold a dozen of men, and there were swords and pistols in it."

From M. Napier, *Memoirs of Dundee*, 3 vols. (Edinburgh: Stevenson, 1859)

39. In 1684, one Peter Pearsone, curate, was said to have "keept fyre arms in his house". One of the four men sent to apprehend the curate, knocked at the door, which was opened a little, "on which James McMichael fyred ane pistoll at some distance, least Mr Pearsone should have fyred first; with which shot the curat was killed deade."

From M. Napier, *Memoirs of Dundee*, 3 vols. (Edinburgh: Stevenson, 1859)

40. In Dalry, one of a group of four Presbyterians who became involved in an argument with some soldiers, drew his pistol to defend himself. He discharged the weapon "which contained no bullet but a piece of tobacco pipe, and hurt one of the soldiers."

From W. Mackenzie, *The History of Galloway*, vol. 2 (Kirkcudbright: Nicholson, 1846)

41. After the descent of the Highland Host of 1678, it was said that "many a man with but two cows, was eager to sell one of them for a pair of pistols."

From J. R. Elder, *The Highland Host of 1678* (Aberdeen: Aberdeen University Press, 1914)

42. In 1685, the Earl of Argyll was confronted near a stream by two militiamen. He grappled with them both, and fell from his horse, dragging one of his antagonists to the ground:

> On rising, he took out his pistols, and the two men rode off. As Argyll came out of the water, a local weaver, armed with a broadsword, took him prisoner. The Earl offered him money which he refused, and he then drew his pistol and endeavoured to fire it at his antagonist; but the water had wet the powder and it would not ignite.

From J. Wilcock, *A Scots Earl in Covenanting Times* (Edinburgh: Elliot, 1907)

43. A list of prices for arms supplied to the army at the time of Charles II reads: "for a pair of horseman pistols furnished with snaphaunces, mouldes, scowrer, worms, flask, a charger, and cases, ii–o–o", while "for a pair of firelock pistols, furnished with a key, mould, scowrer, worm, flasks and cases of leather, iii–o–o."

From F. Grose, *A Treatise on Ancient Armour and Weapons* (London: Hooper, 1786)

44. On the eve of the Battle of Killiecrankie, Menzies of Pitfoddels is described as "a lusty black man riding on a grey horse, with sword and pistol."

From M. Napier, *Memoirs of Dundee*, 3 vols. (Edinburgh: Stevenson, 1859)

45. Entries from the accounts of Sir J[ohn] Foulis:

[15 June 1692:] for dressing 3 pair pistolls 2–5–6.
[20 January 1699:] To david to buy lead and pouder 0–12–0.
[27 March 1705:] To rot. Henderson, Gunsmith, his count for a gun and
    a pair of pistolls helping and cleaning 7–0–0.

From A. C. Hallen, ed., *The Account Book of Sir J. Foulis of Ravelston, 1671–1707.*
Scottish History Society, vol. 16 (Edinburgh: Edinburgh University Press, 1874)

46. 13 August 1692: "The boy carrying the post–bag on its last stage from England was robbed by a person mounted on horseback with a sword about him, and another person on foot with a pistol in his hand, upon the highway from Haddington to Edinburgh . . . about ten hours of the night."

From R. Chambers, *Domestic Annals of Scotland* (Edinburgh: Chambers, 1885)

47. An inventory from 1698 states that, "of goods taken and plundered by Ewan Cameron and others from Isobel McLuckie", there appeared "It: Ane pistoll and a firelock estat to £10–0–0."

From Scottish Historical Review, vol. 10 (Glasgow: Maclehose, 1913)

48. 6 January 1697: The Committee of Improvements of the Company of Scotland trading to Africa ordered: "a contract to be drawn and signed the same with Francis Vanhagen Gunsmith in Leith Wind [Edinburgh], for fourti Mounted Guns at 20s p. s. and twenty pair Mounted Pistols at 17s pr."

From C. E. Whitelaw, 'Darien Papers'. Bannatyne Club. In *Scottish Arms Makers*,
ed. S. Barter (London: Arms and Armour Press, 1977).

49. 27 July 1704: ". . . by order from the Laird of Grant Younger, the said bailie ordaines and enacts that the haill tennantes, cottars, malenders, tradesmen, and servantes within the saidis landis of Skearadvie, Tulchine and Calender, that are fencible shall provyd and have in readiness against the eighth day of August nixt ilk ane of them Highland coates trewes and short hose of tartan of red and green sett broad springed and also with gun, sword, pistoll and durk, and with these present themselves to ane rendevouze when called upone 48 hours advertisement, within the county of Strathspey."

From J. G. Mackay, *The Romantic Story of the Highland Garb and the Tartan*
(Stirling: Mackay, 1924)

50. Lieutenant Robert Turnbull went to Central America as a member of the original Darien Colony, arriving there in November 1698. The Darien Scheme was an effort to establish a trading centre on the isthmus of Darien and so restore Scotland's fortunes. The project was doomed to failure, hund-reds of Scots perishing from shipwreck, famine, disease, and fighting with the Spaniards as well as the native Indians. Lt Turnbull wrote: "Pray cause thank John Currie Gun Smith in Glasgow for the pistolls he made wer extraordinar good. I mean the pistolls he made to the Company. Rot. Turnbull."

From G. Pratt, *Darien Shipping Papers, 1696–1707* (Edinburgh: Constable, 1924)

51. A Commission was presented to one Captain Andreas, a local Indian, by the colonists at Darien. It was delivered to him "with a broad basket-hilted sword and a pair of Pistolls, with which he solemnly promis'd to defend us to the last drop of his Blood against all our enemies."

From G. Pratt, *Darien Shipping Papers, 1696–1707* (Edinburgh: Constable, 1924)

52. An attempt was made by Arthur Rose, of the Rose family of Kilravock in Inverness-shire, to relieve the town of Inverness, which was held by the Highlanders during the Rebellion of 1715. Rose was guided into the Tolbooth by a traitor, who allowed him to gain entry, carrying "a drawn sword and a pistol", only to shout "An enemy, and enemy!". The guard rushed to the door and Mr Rose was shot through the body "with a pair of balls", and was so squeezed between the door and the stone wall, "that he could not have lived, although he had not received the shot".

From C. Innes, *The Family of Rose of Kilravock* (Edinburgh: Spalding Club, 1848)

53. During the Jacobite Rebellion of 1715, the rebels arrived in Lancaster. "During their continuance in this towne the gunsmiths here were well employed in cleaning guns and pistols, and received pay for their work."

From 'Clarke's Journal'. *Scottish History Society Miscellany*
(Edinburgh: Edinburgh University Press, 1873)

54. At the Battle of Sheriffmuir in 1715, it is reported that, regarding the troops of the Earl of Mar, the first line "consisted of ten batallions of infantry, all clansmen in tartan, armed with claymore and dirk, pistols and target."

From J. Grant, *British Battles on Land and Sea* (London: Cassell, 1897)

55. *The Tragedy of Steele's Close.* In this strange incident, a Mrs. McFarlane, "a young woman of extreme beauty who had been married to an old man" was visited by a suitor, a Mr Cayley, who was a Commissioner upon estates forfeited in the Rebellion of 1715. After an apparent quarrel, "Mrs McFarlane seized a pair of pistols which lay loaded in a closet, her husband intending to take them on a journey, and with them shot Mr Cayley dead."

From A. Fergusson, *Major Fraser's Manuscript*, vol. 2 (Edinburgh: 1889)

56. One story concerns Major Fraser of Castle Leathers, when he had travelled to France in search of his chief. Their meeting, at an inn in Normandy, was interrupted by the sounds, in an adjacent room, of a man in the process of being robbed by his travelling companion, who was a clergyman. The chief seized his pistol, and was about to shoot the thief, but Major Fraser" got hold of the pistoll", and managed to dissuade his chief from killing him, offering instead "to horse wheep him to an inch of his life."

From A. Fergusson, *Major Fraser's Manuscript*, vol. 2 (Edinburgh: 1889)

57. An Act of George I decreed that: "No Person in the said Highlands, shall use or bear Broad-swords or Target, Poynard, Winger, or Durk, Side-pistol or Gun." However, those with an income of 400 Scots pounds, were allowed "two Firelocks, two Pair of Pistols, and two Swords."

From The Life of Dr Archibald Cameron (London: Cooper, Reeves and Sympson, 1753)

58. "An English Officer, being in Company with a certain Chieftain and several other Highland gentlemen, near Killimuchen, had an Argument with the great Man; and, both being well warmed with Usky, at last the dispute grew very hot. A Youth who was Hanchman, not understanding a Word of English, imagined his Chief was insulted, and thereupon drew his Pistol from his Side, and snapped it at the Officer's Head; but the Pistol missed Fire."

From E. Burt, *Letters from a Gentleman* (London, 1754).

59. In 1725, General Wade issued licences to:" the forresters, drovers, and dealers in cattle and other merchandise belonging to several Clans who have surrendered their arms, permitting them to carry gun, sword, and pistol."

From J. Wallace, *Scottish Swords and Dirks* (London: Arms and Armour Press, 1970).

60. *The death of Rob Roy.* In 1734, as Rob Roy lay dying, one of his enemies came to visit him. The chief insisted on being propped up in bed, with his broadsword, dirk, and pistols, at hand. When his visitor had departed, Rob Roy ordered his piper "to play the dirge". He died before it was completed.

Another account is given by Millar: "Though prostrated by age and infirmity, Rob insisted that his sons and attendants should raise him from his bed, clothe him in martial array as for the battlefield, and place him in his chair with his claymore and pistols beside him as became a Highland chief."

From L. G. Pine, *The Highland Clans* (Newton Abbot: David & Charles, 1972) and A. H. Millar, *The Story of Rob Roy* (Glasgow: Bryce, 1883)

61. Burt tells the story of an officer who went to visit a local Laird, dressed in a fine suit. He was joined on his journey by a rough-looking Highlander, who took a fancy to his clothes, and declared: "Ah, 'tis ponny Geer! What an' I sho'd take 'em frae ye noo?" The Officer drew a pistol from his Breast, and said: "What do you think of this?" At the sight of the Pistol, the Highlander fell on his Knees and pleaded that: "she was but shoken." Burt, who travelled through Scotland with General Wade, was received everywhere with the warm and generous hospitality for which the Highlander is renowned, yet repaid his former hosts by writing about them and their customs in a blatantly sarcastic and deprecatory fashion.

From E. Burt, *Letters from a Gentleman* (London, 1754)

62. The arms of the Black Watch were described by Stewart of Garth in 1740: "The arms were a musket, a bayonet, and a large basket-hilted broadsword. These were furnished by the Government; such of the men as chose to supply themselves with pistols and dirks were allowed to carry them, and some had targets after the fashion of the country."

From General Sir David Stewart, 'Sketches of the Character, Manners and Present State of the Highlanders of Scotland', in J. Drummond & J. Anderson, *Ancient Scottish Weapons* (Edinburgh and London: Waterson & Sons, 1881)

63. In the weeks before the outbreak of the Rebellion of 1745, "a letter was immediatly dispatchd to Mr Murray of B., then att his own home, where he had been for some weeks very much upon his guard against a surprise, haveing gott intelligence that a warrant was ishued to apprehend him, and had sleepd for three weeks with loaded Pistoles by his bedside."

From R. F. Bell, *Memorials of John Murray of Broughton, 1740–47*, Scottish History Society (Edinbugh: Edinburgh University Press, 1898)

64. Murray of Broughton, Secretary to the Young Pretender, became separated from his servants and was stopped by a band of suspicious Highlanders, "upon which he immediately run aside, thinking to gett into a bog, where he could not be followed on horse back, but judging that impossible he stopp'd whille the other, with his pistole coked, asked him who he was, and desired a small sword he had gott in his hand." In the trials which followed the supression of the Jacobite Rebellion of 1745, Murray turned King's evidence in order to save his own life. For this he became known for ever after, as 'Evidence' Murray, and lost, not only his fortune, but his wife, his family, and the respect of his former comrades in the Jacobite army.

From R. F. Bell, *Memorials of John Murray of Broughton, 1740–47.* Scottish History Society (Edinburgh: Edinburgh University Press, 1898)

65. Letter from Lady Jane Nimmo to an unknown correspondent, 11 October 1745:

> On Wednesday the 9th of Octr. after it was dark bounces in at the Door some hiland Gentlemen with 3 pistols each. The first thing they did was to clap a Pistol to Laubrecht's breast and demanded Horses and arms... They found ninety one very old Firelocks which Mr Carre thought not worth sending to Berwick.

The firelocks were impounded by the Highland army.

From W. Angus, ed., *Miscellany of the Scottish History Society* (Edinburgh: Constable, 1933)

66. In a report submitted to the Lord Advocate regarding the Prince's force, one James Mor MacGregor stated that he saw "22 Field Pieces about the size of one's leg, that were brought in a boat from Kenlochmoydart's [*sic*] house up Loch Shiel to Glenfinnan, with a number of Barrells of Powder and Ball and about 150 Pair of Pistolls."

From Sir H. F. Maclean, *Bonnie Prince Charlie* (London: Weidenfield & Nicholson, 1988)

67. The sloop 'Hazard' was captured by the Highlanders after the Battle of Falkirk. "The Highlanders immediately climbed up the vessel, and took possession of it, but knowing nothing of navigation, they compelled their prisoners, with pistols at their breasts, to steer the vessel into the port of Montrose."

From Chevalier de Johnstone, *A Memoir of the Forty Five* (London: Folio Society, 1958)

68. Following the retreat of two regiments of dragoons from Colt Bridge, near Corstorphine, "the road to Dunbar was strewed with swords, pistols, and firelocks, which were gathered together, and carried in covered carts to Dunbar; so that the flight of the two regiments was very little known to the army."

From J. Home, *History of the Rebellion in the Year 1745* (Edinburgh: Ballantyne, 1802)

69. The Chevalier de Johnstone tells of a Highlander during the Battle of Prestonpans, who captured "10 Redcoats single-handed, herding them forward like sheep, with a pistol in one hand and a sword in the other."

From Chevalier de Johnstone, *A Memoir of the Forty Five* (London: Folio Society, 1958)

70. After the capture of Edinburgh by the Highland army, "almost all wore the tartan, sported the cockade, claymore, and pistols."

From D. M. Rose, *Historical Notes* (Edinburgh: Brown, 1897)

71. On the first appearance of Prince Charles Edward Stuart in Edinburgh, he is described by Logan as "wearing a short Highland coat of tartan, but no plaid, a blue velvet bonnet, having a gold band around it, in which was a white cockade and cross of St. Andrew, carrying an elegant silver-hilted sword, and gold-mounted pistols."

From R. R. McIan, *The Clans of the Scottish Highlands*, A. Fraser, ed. (London: Pan Books, 1980)

72. Whilst the Highland army was going through Carlisle, one rebel entered the house of a Mr Hewit, with a drawn sword in his hand: "[the] strange looking individual in tartans sheathed his sword, drew his dirk and pistol, stuck the former in the table and placed the latter beside it." The Sassenach occupants were unable to interpret his request for food, and screamed until the unfortunate Highlander was forced to leave the house.

From D. M. Rose, *Historical Notes* (Edinburgh: Brown, 1897)

73. As the Highland army retreated through Derby, the Duke of Cumberland's footman was captured. The prisoner testified that his master would have been killed, "if the pistol, with which a Highlander took aim at his head, had not missed fire."

From Chevalier de Johnstone, *A Memoir of the Forty Five* (London: Folio Society, 1958)

74. A description by Chevalier de Johnstone of the Battle of Falkirk reads: "Many used their pistols, but there were few that had elbow room to be able to use their swords." The account is taken up by Alexander Macdonald: "As the enemys dragoons rode off to their right betwixt the lines, our men ran eagerly in pursuit of them, but were much surprised to find themselves stopt by our generals and officers who with difficulty restrained them with their drawn swords and cocked pistols conjuring them to return to their ground or they would be undone."

From D. Daiches, *Charles Edward Stuart* (London: Thames & Hudson, 1973)

75. The English rearguard which had been left behind at Corstorphine was observed by the approaching Highland army. "The insurgents . . . sent forward one or two of their number on horseback to take a view of them, and bring a report of their number. These gentlemen, riding up pretty near, thought proper to fire their pistols towards the party; and the poor dragoons, in the greatest alarm, wheeled about, without returning a shot."

From D. Daiches, *Charles Edward Stuart* (London: Thames & Hudson, 1973)

76. On 16 February, 1746, Charles Edward spent the night at Moy, and an attempt was made to capture him by the Earl of Loudoun's Regiment. During this affray, in which the hereditary Piper of the Lairds of Macleod was killed, five men, amongst them the blacksmith of Moy, forced a regiment of two thousand men into retreat, by creating the impression during the darkness, of a much larger force. "Mr Gib, upon the alarm, having been sleeping in his clothes, stept out, with his pistols under his arms." James Gib was Charles's Master of the Household.

From R. Chambers, *Jacobite Memoirs of the Rebellion of 1745* (Edinburgh: Chambers, 1834)

77. Mr Francis Buchanan of Arnprior was taken prisoner before the Battle of Culloden, charged with the murder of Stewart of Glenbucky. After a quarrel between the two men on the previous night, Stewart had been found dead in bed on the following morning, a pistol in his hand. Arnprior was found guilty, despite the complete absence of any evidence against him, and was duly hanged at Carlisle.

From Rev. R. Forbes, *The Lyon in Mourning*, ed. H. Paton
(Edinburgh: Edinburgh University Press, 1895)

78. An account is given of Murdoch Macleod, the son of Donald Macleod, who was the Prince's pilot during his flight by sea after Culloden. Murdoch was fifteen years of age, and a schoolboy in Inverness. When he heard about the coming battle, "having got himself provided in claymore, durk, and pistol, he ran off from the school, and took his chance in the field of Culloden Battle."

From Rev. R. Forbes, *The Lyon in Mourning*, ed. H. Paton
(Edinburgh: Edinburgh University Press, 1895)

79. The night attack planned by Lord George Murray and the Duke of Perth on Cumberland's troops on the eve of the Battle of Culloden, and which might have altered the entire course of that battle, but which was destined to founder due to the nature of the terrain, and the difficulty of travelling with a large force at night, was intended to be made "with sword and pistol".

From Rev. R. Forbes, *The Lyon in Mourning*, ed. H. Paton
(Edinburgh: Edinburgh University Press, 1895)

80. During the Battle of Culloden, when the Macdonald Regiment retreated without apparently having attempted to attack, Macdonald of Keppoch himself advanced "with his drawn sword in one hand, and his pistol in the other; he had got but a little way from his regiment, when he was wounded by a musket shot and fell."

From J. Home, *History of the Rebellion in the Year 1745* (Edinburgh: Ballantyne, 1802)

81. After the Battle of Culloden, the Chevalier de Johnstone attempted to seize a horse whose bridle was grasped in the hand of a man who at first appeared to be dead. He was, however, alive, but in a state of abject fear, and refused to give up his horse. An officer of Lochiel's Regiment sprang to the Chevalier's assistance, and presented his pistol to the man's head, threatening to blow out his brains if he did not release the bridle.

From Chevalier de Johnstone, *A Memoir of the Forty Five* (London: Folio Society, 1958)

82. A description of Bonnie Prince Charlie whilst in hiding after the Battle of Culloden, at Locharkeig [*sic*] was as follows: "barefooted, had an old black kilt coat on, a plaid, philabeg and waistcoat, a dirty shirt and a long red beard, a gun in his hand, a pistol and durk by his side."

From Rev. R. Forbes, *The Lyon in Mourning*, ed. H. Paton
(Edinburgh: Edinburgh University Press, 1895)

83. Flora Macdonald had declared that "when the Prince put on women's cloaths, he proposed carrying a pistol under one of his petticoats for making some small defence in case of an attack." Miss Macdonald, however, declared against it, saying that, in case of a search, the pistol would only serve "to make a discovery".

From Rev. R. Forbes, *The Lyon in Mourning*, ed. H. Paton
(Edinburgh: Edinburgh University Press, 1895)

84. *Bonnie Prince Charlie's Pistols.* Donald and Malcolm Macleod, who were caring for the Prince in hiding, "agreed in saying that they had good reason to believe that Hugh Macdonald of Armadale in Skye (stepfather of Miss Macdonald) had a meeting with the Prince at Rushness in Benbecula, that he got the Prince's pistols in keeping, and that he had them still in his custody. They added further, that they were persuaded that he would sooner part with his life than with these pistols, unless they were to be given to their proper owner."

This account appears the more credible following Flora Macdonald's testimony regarding the Prince's unwillingness to part with his pistols until finally persuaded by her. When subsequently Captain Roy Macdonald, who had assisted the Prince in hiding, was interviewed by Bishop Forbes, the Bishop asked him "whether or not it was true that Armadale had the Prince's pistols in keeping?" "He told me it was a fact which might be depended upon, Armadale having received then from Macdonald of Milton, Miss Macdonald's full brother. Donald Roy said he saw the pistols in Armadale's house, and had them in his hands, but he could not inform me certainly who the person was who delivered them into Milton's hands, whether it was the Prince himself, O'Sullivan, or O'Neille."

Flora Macdonald herself confirmed that it was her brother, Macdonald of Milton, who delivered the pistols into Armadale's hands.

From Rev. R. Forbes, *The Lyon in Mourning*, ed. H. Paton
(Edinburgh: Edinburgh University Press, 1895)

85. Captain O'Neille complained that he had sent to General Campbell 450 guineas, "with my gold watch, broadsword, and pistols, all of which he has thought proper (to be sure consistent with his honour) to keep from me."

From Rev. R. Forbes, *The Lyon in Mourning*, ed. H. Paton
(Edinburgh: Edinburgh University Press, 1895)

86. Regarding the Battle of Culloden, one Fusilier Edward Lunn of the Royal Scots Fusiliers wrote: "A few Royals (mortars) sent them a few bombs and cannon-balls to their farewel, and immediately our horse, that was on the right and left wings pursued them with sword and pistol and cut a great many of them down so that I never saw a small field so thick with dead."

From Sir H. F. Maclean, *Bonnie Prince Charlie* (London: Weidenfeld & Nicholson, 1988)

87. "Mr Hunter of Burnside, an officer in the life-guards, narrowly escaped being made a prisoner. On firing his pistol at the enemy, he accidentally wounded his horse in the neck, who threw him; but at the moment the

English were on the point of seizing him, he sprung up behind a life-guardsman and they both saved themselves."

From Chevalier de Johnstone, A Memoir of the Forty Five (London: Folio Society, 1958)

88. Letter from Viscount Arbuthnott to the Earl of Albemarle, stating that his arms had been unjustly removed. Aug 8, 1746. ". . . and which were no more than what I am Priveleged to have by Law, viz a silver handled Sword, two mourning ones, two pair of pistols for my own use and my servants, and a fouling piece [*sic*] for my own diversion when I go to sport."

From C. S. Terry, The Albemarle Papers. Scottish History Society
(Aberdeen: Aberdeen University Press, 1902)

89. Letter from Colonel Warren to Waters, the Jacobite banker in Paris. When Prince Charles Edward Stuart escaped after the '45, he was dressed in "a threadbare short coat of coarse black frieze, tartan trews, and over them a belted plaid, a blue bonnet which he got from Cluns, and a dirk, pistol, and leather purse at his belt."

From J. S. S. & C. E. Stuart, The Costume of the Clans (Edinburgh: Grant, 1892)

90. After the defeat at Culloden, in the unremitting and determined search for Jacobite sympathisers, the minister of Glenelion (probably Glenisla) was

> . . . a sanguinary wretch who made a practice of scouring this moor every day with a pistol concealed under his great coat, which he instantly presented to the breasts of any of our unfortunate gentlemen who he fell in with, in order to take them prisoners.

The minister was later to meet his fate at the hands of Gordon of Abachie:

> Having found him in bed, they immediately performed the operation upon him, which Abelard formerly underwent, and carried off _____ as trophies, assuring him at the same time that if he repeated his nightly excursion with his parishioners, they would pay him a second visit which should cost him his life.

The Chevalier de Johnstone concludes his account by saying: "In this adventure his wife alone was to be pitied; as for himself, his punishment was not as tragical as the death on the scaffold which he had in view for Mr Gordon of Abachie."

From Chevalier de Johnstone, *A Memoir of the Forty Five* (London: Folio Society, 1958)

91. Cameron of Lochiel, in hiding with a few trusted friends in the aftermath of Culloden, saw a party of five men approaching. Believing them to be either soldiers or militia, it was decided that "they should be received with a general discharge of all the arms, in number twelve firelocks and some pistols." The approaching party, however, proved to be Charles Edward Stuart and other fugitives.

From J. Home, *History of the Rebellion in the Year 1745* (Edinburgh: Ballantyne, 1802)

92. "Captain Roy Macdonald, upon coming to the Isle of Skye after Culloden, had made a sham surrendry of his arms . . . the Captain having purchased some very indifferent arms to give up for his own good arms, which he took care to have safely conveyed to his brother in North Uist, for the preservation of them."

From Rev. R. Forbes, *The Lyon in Mourning*, ed. H. Paton (Edinburgh: Edinburgh University Press, 1895)

93. Major Donald Macdonald surrendered his arms on capture to Lord Robert Ker. When he was pulling off his pistol from his belt, he happened to do it with such an air that Hush [General Hush of Barrel's Regiment] swore the dog was going to shoot him. To which the Major replied: "I am more of a gentleman, Sir, to do any such thing. I am only pulling off my pistol to deliver it up."

When the Major at any time spoke to a friend about delivering up his good claymore and his fine [one] pistol he used to sigh and to mention Lord Robert Ker for his generous and singular civilities. Major Macdonald had become separated from his regiment at the Battle of Falkirk, and had been captured by the enemy. He was to meet his fate at the scaffold.

From Rev. R. Forbes, *The Lyon in Mourning*, ed. H. Paton
(Edinburgh: Edinburgh University Press, 1895)

94. "Mr Gordon, minister of Alvie, was summoned before the Duke of Cumberland for harbouring the rebels. He went without hesitation, equipped with sword and loaded pistols, to his highness, in answer to whom he asked, whether he was to obey the son of his heavenly, or his earthly, king."

From R. R. McIan, *The Clans of the Scottish Highlands*, ed., A. Fraser
(London: Pan Books, 1980)

95. A rebel, James Brand, who was quartermaster in the Highland army, was captured near Carlisle. The following is an account of his capture:

> . . . we saw the Rebels were coming all towards us—about 100 of them were at the bottom of the Hill—the Prisoner was before all the rest, and Kilpatrick and I were standing on the mountain and he bid me go down and see who this was—I went down and saw the white Cockade—came back and told Kilpatrick, and we all went up to him with our guns ready and ask'd who he was, and he said he belonged to Prince Charles, he laid his hand on one of his Pistols, and said he would fight for his Prince as long as he could stand—we surrounded him and told him we would shoot him if he didn't surrender—he did surrender and told us he was a Gentleman and hoped we would use him as such—Kilpatrick wouldn't let us rifle him—he had several Pistols—a tartan westecoat—Dragoon Boots—Broad Sword he took from Dragoons at Preston Pans.

The prisoner, Brand, claimed he had been "forced out" in the rebellion, and had tried to desert from the Highland army, but had been captured by the Highlanders, and imprisoned by them in a barn. This testimony was confirmed by another prisoner. Sentinels had been posted at the front and rear doors of the barn. However, his horse had been left tethered close by the barn door, his pistols and broadsword across its back. The prisoner "came out to make water—slipped his horse, mounted, and rode off." Brand stated that, had his pistols been loaded, he would never have been taken by the English. He was amongst the first to be hanged at Carlisle.

From R. C. Jarvis, *Collected Papers on the Jacobite Risings*
(Manchester: University of Manchester Press, 1971)

96. On 24th November, 1747, information was given against one James Davidson, a prisoner in the Tolbooth of Kerriemuir:

1 mo Upon the 21st day of November 1747 years. He invaded the house of Mr William Broun minister at Cartochie with ane other in Company called John Watt with cock'd Pistols in their hands which they did present at entering the door about eleven of the clock forenoon.

2 do About eight of the Clock said day, He with Watt and ane other whose name is not known, went to the house of Robert Patton at Bridgend of Cortachie, and after wounding him and servants with a sword and swearing them to secrecy, having a cock'd pistol in his hand, he plundered what was in his pocket, broke his doors, and carried off in haste from him in cash upwards of five pounds sterling, besides his Big Coat, a Web of Cloath, & Co.

3 tio He with the above accomplices went immediately to the house of Robert Clark, wright at the said Bridgend, where he robbed Robert Clark's wife (He being from home) of her money, being about five shillings sterling, held a cock'd pistol to her breast, which her daughter Isobell Clark endeavouring to divert from doing harm to her mother, he immediately discharged and shot the said Isabella Clark through the right arm, all of which can be clearly proven by Witness.

The said James Davidson was committed to, and detained prisoner at Perth. In his confession, Davidson admitted that he had fought at Falkirk with the rebel army, having been forced to enlist in the French Regiment, commanded by Lord John Drummond. At Culloden, he had been in charge of some English prisoners held at the eastern end of Loch Ness. He further declared that his father was John Davidson, gunsmith in Brecon (*sic*), now deceased.

From C. S. Terry, *The Albemarle Papers*. Scottish History Society
(Aberdeen: Aberdeen University Press, 1902)

97. Appearing in a list of Maintenance Charges in the House of Correction at Whitehaven in 1746 (at twelve pence per week) is one Thomas Hatch, who was captured at Carlisle. Hatch, who had formerly been a "Grocer at Preston", when taken was armed with "a Broad Sword, Brace of Pistols, and wore a White Cockade." He was acquitted "on lunacy".

From R. C. Jarvis, The Jacobite Risings of 1715 and 1745 (Cumberland C. C., 1954)

98. A letter to Ludovic Grant of Grant concerning the raising of a company in the King's service in 1746 states: "All the men of his company will have swords, and most of them pistols and dirks."

From W. B. Blaikie, Origins of the Forty Five. Scottish History Society
(Edinburgh: Edinburgh University Press, 1916)

99. During the '45 Rebellion, some volunteers, who had been driven out of Aberdeen by the rebels, tried to join up with a Macleod Regiment, but as "they could get nothing but pistols, they proved to be of no service."

From W. B. Blaikie, Origins of the Forty Five. Scottish History Society
(Edinburgh: Edinburgh University Press, 1916)

100. A letter from Lord Lewis Grant to Thomas Grant of Auchynuny in 1746, asks him to send "such a number of ablebodied men as will answer to the Valuation of your estate well cloathed in short cloaths, Plaid, new Shoes, and thrie pair of hose, and accoutred with shoulder belt, gun, pistol and sword", and in addition warned "I need not tell a man of your good sense and knowledge the hazard of not complying with the demand."

From W. B. Blaikie, Origins of the Forty Five. Scottish History Society
(Edinburgh: Edinburgh University Press, 1916)

101. *Lafayette Pistols.* When George Washington died in 1799, he bequeathed a pair of all-steel lobe-butt Scottish pistols by Thomas Murdoch of Leith, to the Marquis de Lafayette. Lafayette had become, at the age of nineteen, a

Major-General under Washington's command, serving 4½ years during the American War of Independence. He became a personal friend of the future President, and sought the aid of the latter whilst imprisoned during the French Revolution. Washington's will states: "To General de la Fayette I give a pair of finely wrought steel Pistols, taken from the enemy in the Revolutionary War." The pistols were valued for probate as: "1 pr Steel Pistols 50 Dollars." The oval silver butt plaques are engraved: "Washington to Lafayette Legaty." The weapons are now in the Chateau Lafayette, Haute-Loire, France.

From L. Sterett, 'A Pair of Pistols Bequeathed by Washington to Lafayette', *Journal of the Arms and Armour Society* (London) 1962–4

APPENDIX TWO

Scottish Pistols in Collections Abroad

I. Musée de l'Armée, Paris, France.
1. Pair of ramshorn-butt pistols by John Campbell, 1750–75.
2. Fishtail-butt pistol with wooden stock by Robert Alison, 1615.
3. Fishtail-butt pistol with wooden stock by Charles Alison, 1630.
4. Fishtail-butt brass pistol, with left hand lock, by James Low, 1620.

II. National Museum, Cracow, Poland.
Pair of lemon-butt pistols by Robert Alison, 1635.

III. Royal Armoury, Turin, Italy.
Pair of ramshorn-butt pistols by John Campbell, 1750–75.

IV. Metropolitan Museum, New York, USA.
1. Fishtail-butt pistol with wooden stock marked 'I.H.',1615.
2. Pair of heart-butt doglock pistols signed 'R', circa 1680.
3. Pair of lemon-butt pistols with micquelet locks, 1623,
4. Pair of heart-butt pistols signed 'T.F', circa 1720–30.
5. Heart-butt pistol by James McKenzie, circa 1730.
6. Ramshorn-butt pistol by Thomas Murdoch, 1775.
7. Pistol with lobe-butt by John Murdoch, 1775.

8. Military pistol with ramshorn-butt by Bissell.

9. Military pistol with kidney-shaped butt by Waters.

V. Art Museum, St Louis, Missouri, USA.

Pair of pistols with ramshorn-butts by John Murdoch, 1750.

VI. West Point Military Museum, New York State, USA.

Military pistol with ramshorn butt, 1775–1800.

VII. Hancock-Clarke House, Lexington, Massachusetts, USA.

Pair of ramshorn-butt pistols by John Murdoch, 1750–75. (Pitcairn Pistols.)

VIII. Tojhusmuseet, Copenhagen, Denmark.

1. Pair of wooden-stocked fishtail-butt pistols by James Low, 1602.

2. Brass fishtail-butt pistol by James Low, 1613.

3. Pair of pistols with ramshorn-butts signed 'Naughton, Inverness', 1820–30.

IX. Nationalmuseum, Copenhagen, Denmark.

Pair of lemon-butt pistols marked 'P.H.', 1620-30. (Sinclair Pistols.)

X. Livrustkammar, Stockholm, Sweden.

1. Pair of fishtail-butt pistols marked 'Vb' (or 'Jb')1613.

2. Pair of brass lemon-butt pistols marked 'J.A.', for John Alison, 1613.

3. Pair of lemon-butt pistols, 1629.

4. Pair of lemon-butt pistols by James Low, 1627.

5. Ramshorn-butt pistol with left hand lock, marked 'A.W.', 1670.

6. Pair of ramshorn-butt pistols by Thomas Murdoch, 1750–75.

7. Pair of ramshorn-butt pistols by John Murdoch, 1750–75.

8. Pair of heart-butt doglock pistols by John Stuart, c. 1695.

XI. Skokloster Castle, Sweden.

1. Pair of lemon-butt pistols, 1633.

2. Pair of lemon-butt pistols, 1633.

3. Pair of lemon-butt pistols, 1614.

XII. Historisches Museum, Dresden, Germany

Pair of wooden-stocked fishtail-butt pistols by John Kennedy, dated 1598. The earliest known pair of Scottish pistols.

XIII. Hermitage State Museum, St Petersburg, Russia.

1. Ramshorn-butt pistol by Thomas Murdoch, 1775–1800.

2. Pair of lemon-butt snaphaunce pistols with wooden stocks and mother-of-pearl inlay, by James Low, dated 1618.

3. Ramshorn-butt flintlock presentation pistol by Hunter, 1800–25.

Other, to date unspecified Scottish pistols, are in this collection.

APPENDIX THREE

The Care and Conservation of Scottish Pistols

SCOTTISH PISTOLS ARE BEST KEPT IN WARM, DRY SURroundings, preferably in zipped and padded cases. Sweaty hands will leave salt deposits on an all-metal pistol, which will cause subsequent rusting. Anyone handling pistols should wear clean cotton gloves. This unfortunately removes much of the 'feel' of the weapons, but is necessary to prevent any deterioration of the surface. Alternatively, the pistols should be wiped before being returned to their protective cases.

The lock mechanisms should be oiled occasionally and a few drops instilled in the barrel bores. From time to time, a light buffing with a clean duster will remove any tarnishing on the metal surfaces, and maintain that depth of shine which gives the Scottish all-metal pistol its unique appearance. Another technique consists in applying a smear of wax polish to the pistol, allowing to harden, and then polishing. This will produce a polished finish which is partly resistant to tarnishing and rust, but must be done *very carefully* in order to avoid clogging up the engraving.

It need hardly be said that collectors of these wonderful weapons are not only the owners but also the pistols' custodians. This brings with it a responsibility towards the future and those people and historians who will need the pistols to further understand their past. Proper conservation is an important issue of which any owner now should be aware.

APPENDIX FOUR ⤨

Fakes and Reproductions

AS LONG AGO AS 1923, WHITELAW, IN THE COURSE OF writing his famous treatise, so often referred to in these pages, included a chapter entitled 'Hints to Collectors', in which he described a few of the pitfalls facing the unwary collector. Today, more than seventy years later, the collector of Scottish pistols is beset by difficulties of even greater magnitude, ready to thwart him in his desire to accumulate genuine examples of the work of the Scottish gunsmiths. All collectors of antique firearms are aware of these dangers, yet despite this awareness, many are caught out by their failure to recognise that a particular item is a fake. As will be explained later, the position is greatly magnified in the case of Scottish pistols.

The reasons behind this proliferation in the creative activities of the faker are manifold. In the first place, antique guns in general have greatly increased in value in recent years, making it well worth the faker's time and effort to fabricate a piece. Secondly, many chemical agents are available which can artificially age metal, and the professional has, in consequence, little difficulty in transforming a newly-made weapon into one with the outward appearance of a genuine antique. The restorer of antique firearms himself uses these self-same chemicals to match a new cock or ramrod to the original gun, so the new parts do not alert the eye with the pristine appearance of the bright and shiny new metal, and this kind of sympathetic treatment of the restored weapon is to be applauded. When, however, it is carried out with the sole intention of deceiving a prospective customer, then this practice should not be condoned, and the seller should always point out the replaced part to him. On the other hand, when a reproduction piece is deliberately 'aged', in order to sell it later as a genuine antique, this is entirely fraudulent.

All collectors are aware that, even at the very highest level, where many thousands of pounds are paid by wealthy collectors for what they believe are rare and genuine weapons, fakes do occur, and often remain undetected in private collections for many years.

To compound this difficulty, several firms produce lists of do-it-yourself gun manufacturing, and pistols so assembled may be subjected to the usual process of artificial ageing, and then presented for sale as genuine antique pistols. Assembling such pistols requires considerable gunsmithing skills, and artificially ageing the piece is, by comparison, a relatively minor exercise. In the case of the Scottish pistol, constructed entirely from metal, manufacture by a gunsmith in a small workshop is relatively easy. After all, in days gone by, the dagmakers themselves were working in similar circumstances. The technique can be soon perfected, and suddenly a regular income is in prospect for the skilled artisan. Scottish pistols have, in recent years, become highly collectable and consequently extremely expensive. Relative rarity has served to increase the price still further, while at the same time creating the climate in which the faker best thrives—a market in which the demand cannot be satisfied by existing specimens. A few days spent in the fabrication of one such pistol is amply rewarded, and even if such pieces are produced purely as reproductions, the real faker is always there ready to complete the process.

One factor working to the advantage of the faker, is the fact that few collectors are entirely *au-fait* with the Scottish pistol. Because of their relative rarity, the collector will, in all probability, be unaccustomed to handling such (i.e. Scottish) pistols and therefore may have difficulty in recognising the fake before him. He may have seen a few pistols in a glass case in a museum, but he has no way of knowing how the pistol feels when handled, or how to compare the colour of the metal with that of genuine pistols.

The other factor militating against the collector is that, when the faker is at work, he generally chooses the plainer type of pistol, particularly the all-steel military version. Military pistols do not require to be finely engraved and inlaid with silver, or finished in the manner of the more elaborate and costly pistols, and their construction is much cruder than the latter. The sparse use of engraving on the military pistol, allows him to cut expenses to a minimum, engraving being very costly today, whilst at the same time it is extremely difficult to find an engraver capable of the standard of work consistently achieved by his 18th Century counterpart. The faker requires only to immerse the completed weapon in an acid solution, which causes it to become covered in red rust, and it is often in this condition that the pistol is presented to the potential customer. It is usual to concoct a good "cover-story", a sort of fake provenance. The customer is told, perhaps, that the pistol was discovered concealed in the stonework of a cottage which was being renovated in some remote part of Scotland, and that he, the seller, hadn't yet had time to clean it. The even cleverer faker will remove the cock and ramrod, to add credence to the story - after all, who would make a Scottish pistol, and then remove the cock? (Answer— the really canny faker!)

The unfortunate buyer then spends the next few months having a replacement cock and ramrod made to fit the pistol, and slowly and carefully removing the rusted finish, never realising for a moment that the metal from which it is fabricated is altogether too dull and lifeless to be really genuine. The amazing feature about scenarios such as that depicted above, is that almost everyone who examines the weapon accepts it as genuine. Occasionally one will be undecided. The really knowledgeable collector, however, doesn't say anything at all. He just knows. He knows by the feel of the gun and the way it handles. He is very suspicious of red rust, since he knows the multiplicity of defects it can conceal. He doesn't like the style of the engraving of the name on the lockplate, or the manner in which it was executed. He has noted the poor shape of the frizzen spring, and the pricker of incorrect pattern. He is, in fact, utilising all the knowledge he has accumulated through his study of his subject, all the photographs he has examined, all the pistols handled, pitting his own wits against the skill of the faker. Last of all, there is some indefinable instinct that the experienced collector acquires, usually in dotage, which rings bells in his head at the appropriate time, alerting him to the presence of any fake, and these warning bells must never be ignored.

A Scottish pistol which was made many years ago as a genuine reproduction was shown recently to the author. It had been beautifully engraved overall by the expert gunsmith who had fabricated it in his small workshop. The style of the engraving was, however, totally alien to a weapon purporting to be of Scottish origin, and would have been much more in keeping with an English pistol. This is the sort of clue which the collector must be alert to, if he is to avoid a disaster. Of course, there were other features about the pistol that did not weigh up, but the warning bells had already started to ring.

The shape of the pistol is another useful pointer, particularly the butt. It is very difficult for the faker to produce a well-shaped butt every time, as indeed it was for the gunmakers of the seventeenth and eighteenth centuries, and a really graceful curving butt is unlikely to be found in a fake Scottish pistol. In any prospective purchase, the collector is well advised to examine the butt shape closely, .

Many fakes of heart-butt pistols have been made but when these fakes are examined closely, the butts are usually very poorly shaped, having thin and flattened sides which lack the generous proportions of the genuine heart-butt pistol. However, in order to recognise the fake, the collector must have a mental awareness of the exact appearance of the genuine heart-butt.

Although the experienced collector should have acquired the knowledge to detect a fake relatively quickly, other factors may be operative which can influence his decision, usually, unfortunately, to his detriment. For example, the light may be poor, as it frequently is at Arms Fairs, and a good light is essential to the successful detection of the fake Scottish pistol. Another factor is the very circumstances of the deal in prospect, which can totally destroy one's judgement at the critical moment. One has allowed a good cover-story, similar to the one described, or the circumstances leading up to a prospective purchase, to affect the absolute necessity of detached and impartial judgement at the vital time.

Yet another pitfall to be avoided is the Victorian copy—copies made in Victorian times of genuine Scottish pistols, but which by now have aged naturally, so having the external appearance of the genuine pistol. One man in particular, an Edinburgh bagpipe-maker called Robert Glen, made excellent copies of Scottish pistols. Some time ago, a Scottish pistol of very early ramshorn design was examined by several enthusiasts. Most declared it to be a fine example of the work of a seventeenth-century Scottish dagmaker, and it was eventually sold for a considerable sum. The pistol was undoubtedly a fine example of the gunsmith's art, but he was certainly no Scot, and was working in the late twentieth Century, rather than 300 years previously! Conversions from one system of ignition to another are not often encountered with Scottish pistols. Whereas with English weapons the conversion most commonly found is from flintlock to percussion, with Scottish pistols this is extremely rare, and the conversions commonly met with are from snaphaunce to flintlock, or removal of the doglock mechanism which is effectively from doglock to true flintlock. As both of these last are quite rare outside museums, they are not likely to be encountered by the collector.

Weapons which are very worn are sometimes re-engraved, or the remaining engraving sharpened-up, to make the pistols more attractive to collectors. Such a practice does affect the subsequent value of the pistols, and this should be reflected in the price sought. However, if at all extensive, it virtually destroys the piece as far as the collector is concerned.

All replacement parts should be as like the originals as possible, and the collector should have no shortage of photographs from which to decide on patterns. If gunsmithing requires to be carried out, including the replacement of missing parts, these photographs should be passed on to the gunsmith himself, so that accurate copies can be made.

Any engraving necessary to the new part should match that on the rest of the pistol, both with regard to depth and style, and for this the collector is entirely dependent on the skill of the engraver. A perfectly matching cock can be ruined by poor engraving, and the collector is fortunate indeed who has the services available of a skilful and sympathetic engraver. The collector has to decide what parts, if any, have been replaced on the pistol he is examining. In the case of a cock, this may even have been replaced during the working life of the pistol, and, although perhaps of an incorrect pattern, may be more acceptable than a new cock fabricated in the correct pattern, and the same may be true of ramrods. Generally speaking, parts replaced during the working life of the pistol are perfectly acceptable in the eyes of the collector. More difficult is the situation where a cock has been replaced in recent times by a genuine old cock, and here the collector will have to make up his own mind, taking each case on its own merits.

Prickers and ramrods are easily lost, and may well have been replaced, particularly the latter, when the replacements are often much more elaborately turned than were the originals.

A weapon should not be rejected merely because certain parts have been replaced, but a decision must be reached as to whether the existence of such replacements is reflected in the price of the piece offered, and while an absence of replacement parts is desirable, most collectors have to settle for something short of this ideal.

How the collector of Scottish pistols can protect himself against the professional faker, or the equally unscrupulous dealer, who knows that the object in his possession, and which he is presenting for sale, is not what it appears to be, is a question which is difficult to answer. If there is any doubt in the mind of the purchaser, then he should decline to make the purchase. At the very least, he should seek the opinion of one who is perhaps better able to assist him in making a decision. It is always helpful to ask if the weapon is right, and to listen carefully to the reply. 'As far as I know', may sound very reassuring to a prospective customer, but in fact tells him precisely nothing. A receipt stating the age and price of the pistol, would be of value if attempting to obtain redress at a later date.

The collector must examine the pistol in close detail, assessing particularly the colour of the metal in relation to its age and condition, and comparing the colour match of the cock and ramrod with the pistol itself. It is useful to enquire specifically about replacement parts, since no reputable dealer would conceal such information. 'Know your dealer', is an axiom worth remembering, since good and bad exist in every profession. Another useful trick is to seek permission to remove the lock, and examine it from the inside. Any recent work will be immediately apparent, and alert the collector to the possibility of restorative work elsewhere.

There is no place for the amateur in the restoration of the Scottish pistol. The individual collector should restrict his activities to cleaning and

217

oiling the weapon, and perhaps the tidying-up of worn screws, but in general terms, these pistols are altogether too valuable to risk by indiscriminate over-cleaning or poor restorative work. Cleaning is best carried out using an oily rag. Too many Scottish pistols have been ruined by having been overcleaned in the past, usually using emery cloth or wet-and-dry sandpaper, to produce the bright finish so popular with many collectors. Such treatment is damaging to the pistol, and should never be undertaken. Far better to leave the honourable pitting resulting from the ravages of time and an unsuitable environment, than to obliterate all traces of engraving, and ruin the inlay, in an attempt to make a weapon more than two hundred years old, look like new again. Much better to leave that pistol where it lies. Someone else will come along who will love it for what it is, venerating its aged appearance, rather than attempting to remove it.

If any red rust is in evidence, wire wool will remove it, if soaked in oil and applied carefully, using one finger only, to the affected parts. In most case the pistol will look infinitely better if left with its grey, aged appearance, which will enhance the silver inlay by contrast, in the same manner as was intended originally, when the weapon was entirely blued.

Each newly-acquired pistol should be carefully examined for any remaining traces of bluing, so that this finish can be preserved during the removal of associated rust. Finally, using the point of a fine pin very carefully, the mixture of dirt, rust, and oil, which clogs up the engraving, can be removed, so transforming the appearance of the pistol, sometimes in quite dramatic fashion.

The faker of Scottish pistols can only be defeated by knowledge, and knowledge itself is based on study. As Whitelaw says:

> The most competent judge of the antique is he who, born with the gift of discrimination, has cultivated it, not only by the study of books and photographs, but, most necessary of all, by the careful study of the actual objects.[1]

Glossary

Barrel bands	Ridges or mouldings separating barrel stages.
Barrel tang	Metal tongue at barrel breech which allows it to be secured to stock.
Blueing	A type of finish often applied to stocks, barrels, and other steel parts of Scottish pistols, carried out by heating the polished surfaces to the requisite temperature. The treated metal resists further rusting.
Bore	Internal barrel diameter.
Bridle	Metal device which secures the tumbler inside the lock. Rarely found in Scottish pistols.
Buffer	A metal wedge fixed to the front of the lockplate of early snaphaunce locks, designed to arrest the fall of the cock.
Butt	Hand grip.
Cock	Metal arm which secures the flint.
Cock comb	The plume-shaped disc behind the cock in snaphaunce locks, or pierced in a star shape in some flintlocks.
Cock screw	Screw securing cock to tumbler.
Dog catch	The catch behind the cock in doglock pistols, which is moved manually to secure it at half cock.
Fence	A flat, circular or hexagonal disc, sometimes pierced, found at the lateral edge of the pan, which engages with the pan cover when closed, in snaphaunce locks.
Finial	The decorative terminal part of springs, belt hooks, etc.
Forend	The section of stock extending beyond the lock, which supports the front of the barrel.

GLOSSARY

Frizzen	Pan-cover struck by flint when pistol is fired.
Frizzen bridle	An added loop of metal on the lockplate which provides extra security to the frizzen pivot.
Frizzen spring	A spring fitted on the outside of the lockplate, which tensions the frizzen and holds it in the closed position.
Lock	Pistol firing mechanism.
Mainspring	Internal lock spring which tensions the tumbler.
Pan	The shallow receptacle at the breech which contains black powder.
Pricker	A sharpened point used to clear the vent of powder fouling. It is attached to a metal ball or thistle, and is screwed into the butts of many Scottish pistols.
Rainproof pan	A modification of the lockplate, which allows rainwater to be diverted on either side of the pan.
Ramrod	A metal rod used in loading.
Ramrod pipe	Tubular metal sheath, usually single, designed to accommodate ramrod.
Ring neck cock	Also known as throat hole cock, this type of cock incorporates a hole at the neck, and is only rarely found in Scottish pistols.
Roller frizzen	A tiny roller fixed to the front of the frizzen spring, found in late flintlock pistols, which speeds the opening and closure of the frizzen.
Safety bolt	A sliding safety device sometimes fitted at the rear of the lockplate in percussion dress pistols.
Sear	Internal lock part which engages the tumbler and is activated by the trigger plate. In the Highland lock the sear also passes through the lockplate, to hold the breast of the cock in the half-cock position.
Sear spring	An internal lock spring, which holds the sear under tension.
Swamped	A flaring of the muzzle.
Topjaw	Shield-shaped piece of metal securing the flint to the cock.
Topjaw screw	Secures topjaw to cock.
Tumbler	Internal lock part which engages the sear. Its axle pierces the lock-plate, and is attached to the cock.
Trigger plate	The proximal part of the trigger, inside the lock.
Vent	A hole connecting the barrel breech with the pan.

Notes

Dedication Page
'The Blessing of Highland Arms' translated from the Gaelic by Sheriff Nicholson. From
    J.Mackay, *The Romantic Story of the Highland Garb and the Tartan* (Stirling: Mackay, 1924).

Introduction
1. J. Elder, *The Highland Host of 1678* (Aberdeen: University of Aberdeen Press, 1914)
    p. 47.
2. J. B Kist, *Dutch Muskets and Pistols* (London: Arms & Armour Press, 1974) p. 35.
3. I. Eaves, 'Some Notes on the Pistol in Early Seventeenth-Century England', *Journal of the Arms and Armour Society*, vol. 6, no. 10 (June 1970).

Chapter One: The History of Scotland
1. Sir H. F. Maclean, *A Concise History of Scotland* (London: Thames & Hudson, 1970)
    p. 115.
2. J. Grant, *British Battles on Land and Sea* (London: Cassell, 1897) p. 281.
3. Elder, *The Highland Host*, p. 37.
4. Ibid., p. 46.
5. Ibid., p. 47.
6. Ibid., p. 123.
7. A. Lang, *History of Scotland* (Edinburgh: Blackwood, 1909) p. 317.
8. Maclean, *A Concise History of Scotland*, p. 145.
9. Mackay, *Highland Garb and the Tartan*, p. 177.
10. J. Prebble, *Culloden* (Harmondsworth: Penguin Books, 1967) p. 167.
11. R. R. McIan, *The Clans of the Scottish Highlands* (London: Pan Books, 1980) p. 118.

NOTES

12. Sir B. G. Seton and J. Arnot, *Prisoners of the Forty Five*, 3 vols. (Edinburgh, 1928) vol. 1, p. 289.
13. S. Wood, *The Scottish Soldier* (Manchester: Manchester Archive Publications, 1987) p. 13.
14. R. W. Munro, *Highland Clans and Tartans* (London: Peerage Books, 1987) p. 65.
15. Allan Breck Stewart.

Chapter Two: The Highlander and the Clan System
1. Mackay, *Highland Garb,* p. 113.
2. E. Burt, *Letters from a Gentleman*, 2 vols. (London, 1754), vol. 2, p. 105.
3. Samuel Johnson, *A Journey to the Western Islands of Scotland, 1773* (Edinburgh: Laurie & Symington, 1792) p. 63.
4. Munro, *Highland Clans*, p. 17.
5. Ibid., p. 42.
6. Anon, *The Loch Lomond Expedition, with some Short Reflections on the Perth Manifesto.* C. Blair, 'The Word Claymore', in D. H. Caldwell, ed,. *Scottish Weapons and Fortifications* (Edinburgh: Donald, 1981) p. 379.
7. Burt, *Letters*, vol. 1, p. 220.
8. J. S. Keltie. *A History of the Highlands*, 2 vols. (Edinburgh: Fullarton, 1875) p. 169.
9. Sir J. Fergusson, *Argyll in the Forty Five*, Scottish History Society (London: Faber & Faber, 1951) p. 56.
10. Mackay, *Highland Garb*, p. 84.
11. J. Drummond and J. Anderson, *Ancient Scottish Weapons* (Edinburgh and London, 1881) p. 15.
12. J. Wallace, *Scottish Swords and Dirks* (London: Arms & Armour Press, 1970) p. 8.
13. J. Robinson, *A Short History of the Highland Regiment* (Golden Lion Press, 1743).
14. Grant, *British Battles,* p. 244.
15. J. Campbell, *A Full and Particular Description of the Highlands of Scotland* (London, 1752) p. 4.
16. Prebble, *Culloden,* p. 42.
17. Burt, *Letters*, vol. 2, p. 183.
18. Drummond & Anderson, *Ancient Scottish Weapons*, p. 6.
19. Sir Walter Scott, *Notes on the Highland Discipline* (Edinburgh: Waverley, 1814) p. 483.
20. Sir H. F. Maclean, *Bonnie Prince Charlie* (London: Weidenfield & Nicholson, 1988) p. 41.
21. "Bullet mould": I feel sure that the Vicomte de Vaux intended to write powder flask as there could be no reason to wear a bullet mould as part of Highland dress.
22. J. S. S. and C. E. Stuart *The Costume of the Clans,* 2 vols. (Edinburgh: Grant, 1892) p. 85.
23. McIan, *The Clans of the Scottish Highlands*, p. 52.
24. Ibid., p. 190.

Chapter Three: Weapons Associated with the Scottish Pistol
1. From the Roll of Honour of the Clan Macrae. Mackay, *Highland Garb*, p. 132.
2. C. S. Terry, *The Last Jacobite Rising of 1745* (London: Nutt, 1903) p. 30.

3. Grant, *British Battles,* p. 386.
4. Campbell, *A Full and Particular History,* p. 4.
5. Chevalier de Johnstone, *A Memoir of the Forty-Five* (London: Folio Society, 1958) p. 41.
6. Ibid., p. 37.
7. Sir Walter Scott, *Tales of a Grandfather* (Edinburgh: Cadell, 1830) vol. 3, p. 169.
8. C. S. Terry, *The Last Jacobite Rising of 1745,* (London: Nutt, 1903) p. 30.
9. A. Lumisden, *A Short Account of the Battles of Preston, Falkirk, and Culloden. Origins of the Forty-Five.* Edited by W. B. Blaikie. Scottish History Society. (Edinburgh: University of Edinburgh Press, 1916) p. 408.
10. Mackay, *Highland Garb,* p. 84.
11. Keltie, *A History of the Highlands,* p. 169.
12. Burt, *Letters,* vol. 2, p. 177.
13. Johnstone, *A Memoir,* p. 88.
14. W. G. Scott-Moncrieff, *Judiciary Records 1669–78.* Scottish History Society (Edinburgh: Constable, 1905) p. 128.
15. A. Fletcher, *Letters of Andrew Fletcher of Saltoun and his Family 1715–16. Miscellany of Scottish History Society.* Edited by I. Murray. (Edinburgh: Constable, 1965) vol. 10, p. 153.
16. Burt, *Letters,* vol. 2, p. 220.
17. Grant, *British Battles,* p. 244.
18. W. McLeod, *A List of Persons Concerned in the Rebellion of 1745–46.* Scottish History Society (Edinburgh: University of Edinburgh Press, 1890) vol. 8, p. 252.
19. Campbell, *A Full and Particular History,* p. 4.

Chapter Four: Natural Resources

1. I. F. Grant, *Social and Economic Development of Scotland* (Edinburgh: Oliver & Boyd, 1930) p. 325.
2. M. C. Smout, *Henry Kalmeter's Travels in Scotland. Scottish Industrial History Miscellany* (Edinburgh: Constable, 1978) p. 19.
3. Grant, *Social and Economic Development,* p. 339.
4. H. Hamilton, *Economic History of Scotland in the Eighteenth Century* (Oxford: Clarendon Press, 1963) p. 185.
5. Ibid., p. 189.
6. Smout, *Henry Kalmeter's Travels,* p. 16.
7. Hamilton, *Economic History of Scotland,* p. xvi.
8. Sir J. Sinclair, *Statistical Account of Scotland,* vol. 6, p. 593.
9. Hamilton, *Economic History of Scotland,* p. xxviii.
10. Ibid., p. 185.
11. Smout, *Henry Kalmeter's Travels,* p. 16.
12. Grant, *Social and Economic Development,* p. 325.
13. Ibid., p. 290.
14. Smout, *Henry Kalmeter's Travels,* p. 4.

NOTES

Chapter Five: Shipping Lists

1. Sir A. Wedderburne, *The Shipping Lists of Dundee. The Compt. Buik of Sir David Wedderburne, Merchant of Dundee, 1587-1630.* Edited by A. H. Millar. Scottish History Society (Edinburgh: University of Edinburgh Press, 1898) p. xliv.
2. Grant, *Social and Economic Development,* p. 339.
3. Wedderburne, *The Shipping Lists of Dundee,* p. xliii.
4. Ibid., p. 226.
5. Ibid., p. 249.
6. Ibid., p. 228.
7. A. Campbell, *Scottish Industrial History Miscellany.* (Edinburgh: Constable, 1978) p. 19.
8. Wedderburne, *The Shipping Lists of Dundee,* p. 228.
9. Ibid., p.87.
10. Ibid., p.263.

Chapter Six: The Hammerman Craft

1. E. Bain, *Merchant and Craft Guilds: a History of the Aberdeen Incorporations and Trades* (Aberdeen: Edmund and Sparks, 1887) p. 210.
2. H. Lumsden and P. Aitken, *The History of the Hammermen of Glasgow* (Paisley: Gardner,1912) p. xxvii.
3. Ibid., p. xix.
4. Ibid., p. 2.
5. Ibid., p. 5.
6. Ibid., p. 6.
7. Ibid., p. 5.
8. Ibid., p. 3.
9. Ibid., p. 7.
10. Ibid., p. 9.
11. Ibid., p. 47.
12. Ibid., pp. 80–81.
13. Ibid., p. 98.
14. Ibid., p. 23.
15. Ibid., p. 62.
16. Ibid., pp. 20–21.
17. Ibid., p. 56.
18. W. C. Little, *Observations on the Hammermen of Edinburgh, Archeologia Scotica,* vol.1, (Edinburgh, 1792) p. 170.
19. Ibid., p. 172.
20. Ibid., p. 177.
21. Outred = finished.
22. Half bend lock = doglock.
23. ? Highland lock.
24. Little, *Observations,* p. 181.

25. Ibid., p. 171.
26. D. B. Morris, *The Incorporation of Hammermen of Stirling.* Stirling Natural History and Archeological Society (Stirling: Learmonth, 1927) p. 8.
27. Ibid., p. 6.
28. Ibid., p. 34.
29. C. E. W. Whitelaw, *Scottish Arms Makers.* Edited by S. Barter-Bailey. (London: Arms & Armour Press, 1970) p. 288.
30. Morris, *The Incorporation of Hammermen,* p. 28.
31. Ibid., p. 18.
32. D. H. Fleming, *An Account of the Hammermen of St Andrews* (Cupar, Fife, 1884) p. 43.
33. Ibid., p. 42.

Chapter Seven: Gunsmithing Techniques

1. Morris, *The Incorporation of Hammermen,* p. 16.

Chapter Nine: The Decoration of Scottish Pistols

1. R. & V. Megaw, *Celtic Art: from its Beginnings to The Book of Kells* (London: Thames & Hudson, 1989) p. 10.
2. C. Davis, *The Celtic Art Source Book* (London: Blandford, 1988) p. 46.
3. Ibid., p. 14.
4. Megaw, *Celtic Art,* p. 252.

Chapter Ten: The Doune Pistol

1. A. Campbell, *A Journey from Edinburgh through Parts of Northern Britain* (London: Longman & Rees, 1802) vol. 1, p. 101.
2. Drummond & Anderson, *Ancient Scottish Weapons,* p. 22.
3. Sinclair, *Statistical Account,* p. 86.
4. J. Arthur and D. H. Caldwell, 'The Doune Pistol Makers', *Guns Review* (April 1976) p. 184.
5. Ibid., p. 183.
6. Ibid., p. 184.
7. W. McLeod, *A List of Persons Concerned in the Rebellion, 1745–46,* Scottish History Society (Edinburgh: University of Edinburgh Press, 1890) vol. 8, p. 244.
8. Ibid., p. 244.
9. Arthur & Caldwell, 'The Doune Pistol Makers', p. 185.
10. Morris, *The Incorporation of Hammermen,* p. 40.
11. Whitelaw, *Scottish Arms Makers,* p. 154.
12. Ibid., p. 154.

Chapter Eleven: Classification and Design

1. Col. H. C. B. Rogers, *Weapons of the British Soldier* (London: Sphere Books, 1972) p. 101.
2. H. L. Blackmore, *British Military Firearms, 1650–1850* (London: Jenkins, 1969) p. 66.

NOTES

3. Stewart, *The Costume of the Clans*, p. 125.
4. Mackay, *Highland Garb*, p. 166.
5. Blackmore, *British Military Firearms*, p. 66.
6. Sir H. F. Maclean, *A Concise History of Scotland* (London: Thames & Hudson, 1970) p. 182.
7. Munro, *Highland Clans and Tartans*, p. 78.
8. I. Finlay, 'The Pistols of Macdonnell of Glengarry', *Connoisseur Magazine* (February 1939) p. 272.

Appendix Four: Fakes and Reproductions

1. C. E. Whitelaw, 'A Treatise on Scottish Hand Firearms of the xvith, xviith and xviiith Centuries' in H. J. Jackson and C. E. Whitelaw, *European Hand Firearms of the Sixteenth, Seventeenth, and Eighteenth Centuries* (Frome: Hillman & Sons, 1959; 1st ed. 1923) p. 77.

Bibliography

Books

Adam, F. *The Clans, Septs, and Regiments, of the Scottish Highlands*. Edited by Sir T. Innes. Edinburgh: Johnston & Bacon, 1955.

Angus, W., ed. *Miscellany of the Scottish History Society*. Vol. 5. Edinburgh: Constable, 1933.

Ascanius: An Impartial History of the Rebellion in Scotland in the Years 1745, 1746. London: Houlston & Sons, 1890.

Bain, E. *Merchant and Craft Guilds: a History of the Aberdeen Incorporations and Trades*. Aberdeen: Edmund and Sparks, 1887.

Barnes, R. M. *The Uniforms and History of the Scottish Regiments*. London: Sphere, 1956.

Bell, R. F. *Memorials of John Murray of Broughton, 1740–47*. Scottish History Society. Edinburgh: University Press, 1916.

Blackmore, H. L. *British Military Firearms, 1650–1850*. London: Jenkins, 1961.

Blaikie, W. B., ed. *Origins of the Forty Five*. Scottish History Society. Edinburgh: University Press, 1916.

Boothroyd, G. 'The Birth of the Scottish Pistol'. In *Scottish Weapons and Fortifications*, edited by D. H. Caldwell. Edinburgh: Donald, 1981.

Boswell, J. *The Journal of a Tour to the Hebrides with Samuel Johnson*. 8 vols. London, 1785.

Buckroyd, J. *The Life of James Sharp, 1618–79*. Donald, Edinburgh, 1987.

Burt, E. *Letters from a Gentleman*. 2 vols. London, 1754.

Burton, J. H. *History of Scotland*. London, 1853.

Caldwell, D. H. *The Scottish Armoury*. Blackwood, Edinburgh, 1979.

———, ed. *Scottish Weapons and Fortifications*. Edinburgh: Donald, 1981.

Campbell, A. *A Journey from Edinburgh through Parts of Northern Britain*. London: Honeyman & Rees, 1802.

BIBLIOGRAPHY

Campbell, A. *Scottish Industrial History Miscellany*. Edinburgh: Constable, 1978.

Campbell, Lord A. *Highland Dress, Arms, and Ornament*. London: Constable, 1895.

Campbell, D. *The Clan Campbell*. Macniven & Wallace, 1915.

Campbell, J. *A Full and Particular Description of the Highlands of Scotland*. London, 1752.

Carlyle, A. *Anecdotes and Characters of the Times*. Oxford: Oxford University Press, 1973.

Chambers, R. *Domestic Annals of Scotland*. Edinburgh: Chambers, 1885.

———. *Jacobite Memoirs of the Rebellion of 1745*. Edinburgh: Chambers, 1834.

'Clarke's Journal'. *Scottish History Society Miscellany*. Edinburgh: University of Edinburgh Press, 1873.

Daiches, D. *Charles Edward Stuart*. London: Thames & Hudson, 1973.

Davies, G., ed. *Miscellany of the Scottish History Society*. 3 vols. Edinburgh: Constable, 1919.

Davis, C. *The Celtic Art Source Book*. London: Blandford, 1988.

Drummond, J., and Anderson, J. *Ancient Scottish Weapons*. Edinburgh and London: Waterson & Sons, 1881.

Duke, W. *Lord George Murray and the Forty-Five*. Aberdeen: Milne & Hutchison, 1929.

Elder, J. R. *The Highland Host of 1678*. Aberdeen: University of Aberdeen Press, 1914.

Erskine, J. *Journal of J. Erskine of Carnock, 1683–87*. Scottish History Society, vol. 14. Edinburgh: University of Edinburgh Press, 1893.

Fergusson, A. *Major Fraser's Manuscript*. 2 vols. Edinburgh, 1889.

———. *Scots Brigade Papers*. Scottish History Society, vols. 32, 35, 38. Edinburgh: University Press, 1899–1901.

Fergusson, Sir J. *Argyll in the Forty Five*. Scottish History Society. London: Faber & Faber, 1951.

———. *John Fergusson, 1727–50*. London: Cope, 1948.

Finlay, I. *Scottish Gold and Silverwork*. Edited by H. S. Fothringham. Stevenage: Strong Oak Press, 1991.

Fleming, D. H. *An Account of the Hammermen of St Andrews*. Cupar, Fife, 1884.

Forbes, D. *Culloden Papers*. London: Cadell & Davies, 1815.

Forbes, Rev. R. *The Lyon in Mourning*. Edited by H. Paton. Scottish History Society. 3 vols. Edinburgh: University of Edinburgh Press, 1895.

Gibson, J. S. *Lochiel of the '45*. Edinburgh: University of Edinburgh Press, 1994.

Goldsmid, E. *The Massacre of Glencoe, 1695*. Edinburgh: Goldsmid, 1885.

Grant, G. *The New Highland Military Discipline of 1757*. 1757. Ontario: Museum Restoration Service, 1988.

Grant, I. F. *The Macleods: The History of a Clan 1200–1956*. London: Faber & Faber, 1951.

———. *Social and Economic Development of Scotland before 1603*. Edinburgh: Oliver & Boyd, 1930.

Grant, J. *British Battles on Land and Sea*. London: Cassell, 1897.

Grimble, J. *Chief of Mackay*. London: Routledge & Kegan Paul, 1965.

Grose, F. *A Treatise on Ancient Armour and Weapons*. London: Hooper, 1786.

Hallen, A. C. *The Account Book of Sir J. Foulis of Ravelston 1671–1707*. Scottish History Society, vol. 16. Edinburgh: University of Edinburgh Press, 1874.

Hamilton. H. *Economic History of Scotland in the Eighteenth Century*. Oxford: Clarendon Press, 1963.

Hawkins, P. *Price Guide to Antique Guns and Pistols*. Suffolk: Baron, 1973.

Hayward. J. F. *Art of the Gunmaker*. 2 vols. London: Barrie & Rockliff, 1962.

Henderson, G. D. *Chevalier Ramsay*. London, 1952.

Home, J. *The History of the Rebellion in the Year 1745*. Edinburgh: Ballantyne, 1802.

Hopkins, P. *Glencoe and the End of the Highland War*. Edinburgh: Donald, 1986.

Hume–Brown, P. *A History of Scotland*. Edinburgh: Oliver & Boyd, 1907.

Innes, C. *The Family of Rose of Kilravock*. Edinburgh: Spalding Club, 1848.

Jackson, H. J., and C. E. Whitelaw. *European Hand Firearms of the Sixteenth, Seventeenth, and Eighteenth Centuries*. London: Holland Press, 1923.

Jamieson, R. *Burts Letters from the North of Scotland*. 2 vols. Edinburgh: Paterson, 1876.

Jarvis, R. *Jacobite Risings of 1715 and 1745*. Cumberland C. C., 1954.

———. *Collected Papers on the Jacobite Risings*. 2 vols. Manchester: Manchester University Press, 1971

Johnson, S. *A Journey to the Western Islands of Scotland*. Edinburgh: Lawrie & Symington, 1792.

Johnstone, Chevalier de. *A Memoir of the Forty-Five*. London: Folio Society, 1958.

Keltie, J. S. *A History of the Highlands*. 2 vols. Edinburgh: Fullarton, 1875.

Kist, J. B. *Dutch Muskets and Pistols*. London: Arms & Armour Press, 1974.

Lang, A. *A History of Scotland*. 3 vols. Edinburgh: Blackwood, 1909.

———. *Prince Charles Edward*. Edinburgh: Goupil & Co., 1900.

Lenman, B. *The Jacobite Cause*. Glasgow: Drew, 1986.

———. *The Jacobite Clans of the Great Glen, 1650–1784*. London: Methuen, 1984.

The Life of Dr Archibald Cameron. London: Cooper, Reeves & Sympson, 1753.

Logan, J. *The Clans of the Scottish Highlands*. 1845.

———. *The Scottish Gael*. Edited by A Steuart. Edinburgh: Mackenzie, 1876.

Lumisden, A. *A Short Account of the Battles of Preston, Falkirk, and Culloden. Origins of the Forty-Five*. Edited by W. B. Blaikie. Scottish History Society. Edinburgh: University of Edinburgh Press, 1916.

Lumsden, H., and P. Aitken. *The History of the Hammermen of Glasgow*. Paisley: Gardner, 1912.

McIan, R. R. *The Clans of the Scottish Highlands*. 1845. Edited by A. Fraser. London: Pan Books, 1980.

Mackay, J. G. *The Romantic Story of the Highland Garb and the Tartan*. Stirling: Mackay, 1924.

Mackay, W. *The Letter-Book of Baillie John Steuart of Inverness, 1715–52*. Edinburgh: University of Edinburgh Press, 1915.

Mackenzie, Rev. W. *History of Galloway*. 2 vols. Kirkcudbright: Nicholson, 1846.

Mackenzie, W. C. *Duke of Lauderdale, 1616–82*. London: Kegan Paul, 1923.

Maclean, Sir H. F. *A Concise History of Scotland*. London: Thames & Hudson, 1970.

———. *Bonnie Prince Charlie*. London: Weidenfield & Nicholson, 1988.

McLeod, W. *A List of Persons Concerned in the Rebellion 1745–6*. Scottish History Society, Edinburgh: University of Edinburgh Press, 1890.

BIBLIOGRAPHY

Macphail, J. R. N. *Highland Papers. Vol. IV. 1296–1752*. Scottish History Society, 3rd Series, vol. 12. Edinburgh: Constable, 1934.

Marshall, R. K. *Bonnie Prince Charlie*. Edinburgh: HMSO, 1988.

Megaw, R and V. *Celtic Art: From its Beginnings to the Book of Kells*. London: Thames & Hudson, 1989.

Millar, A. H. *The Compt Book of David Wedderburne, Merchant of Dundee, 1587–1630*. Scottish History Society. Edinburgh: University of Edinburgh Press, 1898.

———. *Glamis Book of Records 1684–89*. Scottish History Society. Edinburgh: University of Edinburgh Press, 1896.

———. *The Story of Rob Roy*. Glasgow: Bryce, 1883.

Miscellany of the New Spalding Club. 2 vols. Aberdeen, 1890.

Morris, D. B. *The Incorporation of Hammermen of Stirling*. Stirling Natural History and Archaeological Society. Stirling: Learmonth, 1927.

Munro, R. W. *Highland Clans and Tartans*. London: Peerage Books, 1987.

Murray, I. *Miscellany of the Scottish History Society*. Vol. x. Edinburgh: Constable, 1965.

Napier, M. *Memoirs of Montrose*. 2 vols. Edinburgh: Stevenson, 1856.

Napier, M. *Memoirs of Dundee*. 3 vols. Edinburgh: Stevenson, 1859.

Peterson, H. L. , and R. Elman. *The Great Guns*. London: Hamlyn, 1971.

Pine, L. G. *The Highland Clans*. Newton Abbott: David & Charles, 1972.

Pratt, G. *Darien Shipping Papers, 1696–1707*. Edinburgh: Constable, 1924.

Prebble, J. *Culloden*. Harmondsworth: Penguin Books, 1967.

———. *Glencoe*. London: Secker & Warburg, 1966.

Reid, W. 'Scottish Firearms'. In *Pollard's History of Firearms*, edited by C. Blair. Northants: Country Life Books, 1983.

Rose, D. M. *Memoirs of Sir Ewen Cameron of Locheil. Historical Notes*. Maitland Club. Edinburgh: Brown, 1897.

Robertson, J. A. *Highlanders of Scotland*. Edinburgh, 1866.

Rogers, C. *Memoirs of the Earl of Stirling, and of the House of Alexander*. Edinburgh, 1877.

Rogers, H. C. B. *Weapons of the British Soldier*. London: Sphere Books, 1972.

Rose, D. M. *Historical Notes*. Edinburgh: Brown, 1897.

Scott, J. G. *European Arms and Armour*. Glasgow: Glasgow Museum & Art Galleries, 1980.

———. 'A Scroll-Butt Flintlock Pistol by Patrick Buchanan of Glasgow'. In *Scottish Weapons and Fortifications*, edited by D. H. Caldwell. Edinburgh: Donald, 1981.

Scott, Sir Walter. *Waverley*. Edinburgh: Cadell, 1814.

———. *Tales of a Grandfather*. 3 vols. Edinburgh: Cadell, 1830.

Scott-Moncrieff, W. G., ed. *Justiciary Records of Edinburgh 1669–78*. 2 vols. Scottish History Society. Edinburgh: Constable, 1905.

———. *Lady Grisell Baillie's Household Book, 1692–1733*. Edinburgh, 1911.

Scottish Historical Review, vol. 10. Glasgow: Maclehose, 1913.

Seton, B., and J. Arnot. *Prisoners of the Forty Five*. 2 vols. Scottish History Society. Edinburgh: University of Edinburgh Press, 1929.

Sinclair, Sir J. *Statistical Account of Scotland*. 21 vols. Edinburgh: Creech, 1791-99.

Skene, W. F. *Highlanders of Scotland*. London, 1837.

———. *History of the Highland Clans*. Edited by A. Macbain. Stirling: Mackay, [no year].

Snoddy, T. G. *The Life and Times of Sir John Scot, Lord Scotstarvit*. Edinburgh, 1968.

Steuart, A. F. *The Scots in Poland, 1576–1793*. Scottish History Society. Edinburgh: University of Edinburgh Press, 1915.

Story, R. H. *William Carstares. A Character and Career of the Revolutionary Epoch, 1649–1715*. London, 1874.

Stuart, J. S. S. , and C. E. *Costume of the Clans*. 2 vols. Edinburgh: Grant, 1892.

Stuart, J. *Memorials of the Troubles in Scotland and in England 1624–45*. 2 vols. Aberdeen: Spalding Club, 1850.

Taylor, A. & H. *1745 and After*. London: Nelson, 1938.

———. *Stuart Papers at Windsor*. London: Murray, 1939.

Taylor, I. C. *Culloden*. National Trust for Scotland. Aberdeen University Press. 1965.

Terry, C. S. *Life and Campaign of Alexander Leslie*. London: Longmans & Green, 1899.

———. *The Albemarle Papers*. Scottish History Society. Aberdeen: University of Aberdeen Press, 1902.

———. *The Last Jacobite Rising of 1745*. London: Nutt, 1903.

———. *John Graham of Claverhouse, Viscount of Dundee, 1648–89*. Aberdeen: University of Aberdeen Press, 1905.

———. *Papers Relating to the Army of the Solemn League and Covenant, 1643–1647*. 2 vols. Scottish History Society. Edinburgh: Constable, 1917.

Tweedsmuir, J. B. *Montrose*. London: Nelson, 1928.

Wallace, J. *Scottish Swords and Dirks*. London: Arms & Armour Press, 1970.

Whitelaw, C. E. *Scottish Arms Makers*. Edited by S. Barter-Bailey. London: Arms & Armour Press, 1977.

Whitelaw, C. E. 'A Treatise on Scottish Hand Firearms of the xvith, xviith and xviiith Centuries' in Jackson, H. J., and C. E. Whitelaw, *European Hand Firearms of the Sixteenth, Seventeenth, and Eighteenth Centuries*. London: Holland Press, 1923.

Wilkinson, F. *The Illustrated Book of Pistols*. London: Optimum Books, 1979.

Willcock, J. *A Scots Earl in Covenanting Times*. Edinburgh: Elliott, 1907.

Wood, S. *The Scottish Soldier*. Manchester: Archive Publications, 1987.

Periodicals

Note: *Dispatch, Journal of the Scottish Military Historical Society* is identified by the shortened title *Dispatch*.

Arthur, J. , and D. H. Caldwell. 'The Doune Pistol Makers'. *Guns Review*, vol. 16 (1976).

Beard, C. R. 'Two Disputed Portraits at the Royal Academy'. *Connoisseur Magazine* (February 1939).

Berg, G., and B. Lagercrantz. 'Scottish Soldiers in Swedish Service in the Sixteenth Century'. *Dispatch*, 119/120 (1988).

Blair, C. 'Scottish Firearms'. *Bulletin of the American Society of Arms Collectors*, vol. 31 (1975).

BIBLIOGRAPHY

Boothroyd, G. 'Scottish Pistols'. *Journal of the Arms and Armour Society*, vol. 6 (1969).
———. 'A Pair of Pistols for the Marquis'. *Dispatch*, 108.
Bracegirdle, C. 'The Pistols of Doune'. *Guns, Weapons, and Militaria*, vol. 1 (1992).
Caldwell, D. H. 'Scottish Pistols: A Celtic Style?' *Dispatch*, 103 (1983).
Claydon, R. T. 'The Traditional Pistols of Scotland'. *Canadian Journal of Arms Collecting*, vol. 8, no. 2 (1976).
Darling, A. D. 'Weapons of the Highland Regiments, 1740–80'. *Canadian Journal of Arms Collecting*, vol. 8, no. 3 (1970).
———. 'Early Scottish Basket-hilted Swords'. *Dispatch*, 109 (1985).
Dickinson, G. 'Some Notes on the Scottish Army in the First Half of the Sixteenth Century'. *Scottish Historical Review*, vol. 28 (1949).
Dillon, Viscount. 'Scottish Arms in the Tower of London'. *Chambers Journal* (December 1907).
Dondi, G. 'Scottish Pistols in the Royal Armoury of Turin'. *Dispatch*, 108.
Eaves, I. 'Some Notes on the Pistol in Early Seventeenth Century England'. *Journal of the Arms and Armour Society*, vol. 6 (1970).
Ferguson, J. 'The Mackay Targe'. *Dispatch*, 104.
Finlay, I. 'The Decoration of Scottish Pistols'. *Connoisseur Magazine* (November 1936).
———. 'Highland Weapons at the Royal Academy'. *Connoisseur Magazine* (February 1939).
———. 'The Pistols of Macdonell of Glengarry'. *Connoisseur Magazine* (February 1939).
———. 'Doune Pistols'. *Scotland's Magazine* (January 1953).
———. 'The Milne-Davidson Collection'. *Connoisseur Magazine* (April 1955).
———. 'Princely Pistols, Made from Old Nails'. *Everybodies Weekly*, 2 February 1957.
Forman, J. D. 'A Heartbutt Variation'. *Canadian Journal of Arms Collecting*, vol. 10 (1972).
———. 'The Dirk'. *Dispatch*, 120.
———. 'The Gunmakers of Doune'. *Man at Arms*, vol. 1, no. 4 (July 1979).
Gordon, G. A. 'Numbered and Dated Scottish Pistols'. *Dispatch*, 128 (1992).
Grancsay, S. V. 'Scottish Pistols in the Metropolitan Museum'. *The American Rifleman* (November 1947).
Gwynn, R. T. Letter in *Apollo Magazine* (August 1942).
Hamilton, J. G. 'Scottish Highlanders'. *Gun Report* (December 1959).
Held, R. 'Scottish Micquelet Pistol'. *Dispatch*, 112 (1986).
Hendry, C. 'A Brace from the Balkans'. *Guns Review* (January 1988).
Hoff, A. 'Scottish Pistols in Scandinavian Collections'. *Journal of the Arms and Armour Society*, vol. 5 (1953).
Kelvin, Martin. Letter on Numbered and Dated Scottish Pistols. *Dispatch*, 131 (1993).
Little, W. C. 'Observations on the Hammermen of Edinburgh'. *Archeologia Scotica* (Edinburgh), vol. 1 (1792).
Longfield, G. M. 'Ancient Firearms of Scotland'. *American Society of Arms Collectors Bulletins*, no. 45 (October 1981).
McAllister, R. 'The Pistols of Doune'. *Scotland's Magazine* (May, June, July, 1983).
Macnab, S. 'The Flintlock Pistols of Doune'. *Classic Arms and Militaria* (March 1994).

Mayer, J. R. 'Celtic Art on Scottish Pistols'. *Arms and Armour Club Papers* (New York), no. 1 (1940).

———. 'A Further Note on the Decoration of Scottish Pistols'. *Connoisseur Magazine* (February 1937).

Maxwell, S. 'A Highland Pistol by Hector McNeill of Mull, 1733'. *Proceedings of the Society of Antiquaries of Scotland*, vol. 100 (1902).

Millar, A. H. 'Notice of a Steel Pistol with the Dundee Mark'. *Proceedings of the Society of Antiquaries of Scotland*, vol. 22 (1888).

'Note on a Fishtail Butt Pistol of 1619 at the Tower of London'. *Proceedings of the Society of Antiquaries of London*, vol. 17 (1897–9).

'Note on a Pair of All-Steel Pistols by John Murdoch of Doune'. *Journal of the Arms and Armour Society*, vol. 10 (1962–4).

Owen, A. G. 'Scottish Military Pistols'. *Antique Arms and Militaria*. No. 11 (August, 1979).

Reid, W. 'Lady Seafields Scottish Pistols'. *Connoisseur Magazine* (July, 1962).

———. 'The Heart-butt Pistols of East Scotland'. *Scottish Art Review* (February 1963).

Scobie, I. H. M. 'The Regimental Highland Pistol'. *Journal of the Army Society for Historical Research*, vol. 7 (1928).

Scott, J. G. 'A Scroll-Butt Flintlock Pistol by Patrick Buchana of Glasgow'. *Dispatch*, 100 (1982).

Sloane, H. 'The Fish-Scale Pistol, 1613'. *Dispatch*, 109 (1985).

———. 'The Sinclair Pistols'. *Dispatch*, 111 (1986).

———. 'The A. G. Pistols'. *Dispatch*, 113 (1987).

———. 'A Pistol by R. Alison of Dundee, 1615'. *Dispatch*, 117 (1988).

———. 'A Pistol by C. Alison of Dundee, 1630'. *Dispatch*, 117 (1988).

———. 'A Pair of Pistols by R. Alison of Dundee, 1635'. *Dispatch*, 118 (1988).

———. 'A Pistol by Daniel Steuart of Perth, c. 1690'. *Dispatch*, 119 (1988).

———. 'A Pistol by James Low of Dundee, 1620'. *Dispatch*, 122 (1989).

———. 'A Scottish Bissell Pistol'. *Dispatch*, 123 (1989).

———. 'Thomas Caddell'. *Dispatch*, 123 (1989).

———. 'Thomas Caddell Pistol, circa 1700'. *Dispatch*, 123 (1989).

———. 'Thomas Caddell Pistol, 1700–25'. *Dispatch*, 123 (1989).

———. 'Thomas Caddell Pistol, 1750–75'. *Dispatch*, 123 (1989).

———. 'A Macleod Pistol'. *Dispatch*, 124 (1989).

Sloane, H., and J. B. Mackay. 'Scottish Pistols 1'. *Dispatch*, 99 (1982).

———. 'Scottish Pistols 2'. *Dispatch*, 100 (1982).

———. 'Scottish Pistols 3'. *Dispatch*, 101 (1982).

———. 'Scottish Pistols 4'. *Dispatch*, 102 (1983).

———. 'The Peoples Palace Pistol'. *Dispatch*, 102 (1983).

———. 'The 1602 Pistols'. *Dispatch*, 102 (1983).

———. 'Scottish Pistols 5'. *Dispatch*, 103 (1983).

———. 'A Pair of John Murdoch Pistols'. *Dispatch*, 103 (1983).

———. 'Scottish Pistols 6'. *Dispatch*, 104 (1983).

BIBLIOGRAPHY

———. 'A Cut-down Pistol'. *Dispatch*, 104 (1983).

———. 'Scottish Pistols 7'. *Dispatch*, 105 (1984).

———. 'Scottish Pistols 8/9'. *Dispatch*, 106 (1984).

———. 'A Waters Pistol. Scottish Pistols 10'. *Dispatch*, 107 (1984).

'Some Notable Weapons and Accessories, including inscribed Powderhorns'. *Journal of the Society of Antiquaries of Scotland*, vol. 86 (1954).

Stalin, G. 'Notes sur un Pistolet Écossais, suivi dine Liste de Noms de Fabricantes de Pistolets Écossais de 1592–1850'. *Bulletin de la Société d'Études Historiques et Scientifiques de l'Oise* (Beauvais), vol 2 (1907).

Sterett, L. 'A Pair of Pistols Bequeathed by Washington to Lafayette'. *Journal of the Arms and Armour Society* (London), vol. 10 (1962–4).

'Tartans'. *The Journal of the Scottish Tartans Society* (summer 1980).

Wallace, J. 'Scottish Pistols'. *Discovering Antiques*, vol. 4 (1970).

Webster, D. B. 'The Highland Pistol of William McGillivray of the North West Company'. *Canadian Journal of Arms Collecting*, vol. 31, no. 1 (February 1993).

Index

'A.C.', 129, 163
Adolphus, Gustavos, 3, 18, 152
Albemarle, Earl of, 202
Appin murder, 19
apprentices, 64–66, 78, 91
Arbuthnott, Viscount, 202
Argyle, Duke of, 12, 190
arms, surrender of, 186–188, 203
Atholl, Marquis of, 3, 13, 15, 28

Bissell, Isaac, 132, 148
blueing, 72, 85, 110, 130–131,137, 142
Bonnie Prince Charlie, 27, 133, 150, 200
    See also Chevalier; Stuart, Prince Charles
        Edward; Young Pretender, The
Bothwell Brig, Battle of, 14, 188
Boyne, Battle of the, 14
Brand, James, 204–205
brass, 85
Brechin, Bishop of, 11
broadsword, 1, 4, 17, 23–24, 26–28, 38–41, 61
Brown Bess, 1, 2, 131
Buchanan, Francis, of Arnprior, 199
Buchanan, Patrick, 86, 124
Burgess, John, 163

Burt, Edward, 21, 23, 26–27, 42, 195

Caddell family, 3, 95, 123, 163–164
Caddell, Robert, 95
Caddell, Thomas, 86, 95, 150, 163–164
Cameron, of Lochiel, 15, 16, 203
Cameron, Sir Alan, of Erracht, 154
Campbell, Alexander, 3, 87, 95, 120, 127, 164
Campbell, Charles, of Lochlane, 34
Campbell, Donald, 95–96
Campbell, John (Edinburgh), 165
Campbell, John (1st), 3, 93, 95, 164
Campbell, John (Glenelg), 165
Campbell, John, of the Bank, 36
Campbell, John (2nd), 96, 120, 164
Celtic art, 42, 49, 79–84, 110, 170
Chevalier, 16, 150
    See also Bonnie Prince Charlie; Young
        Pretender, The; Stuart, Prince
        Charles Edward
Christie, James, 99
Christie, John, 67–68, 87, 98–100, 127,
    165–166
Christie, (London) 100, 154
Christie, William, 67

INDEX

clans, gathering of, 12, 22
claymore, 1, 23–24, 38–40
Cope, General Sir John, 15
Covenanters, 3, 12–14, 184, 189–190
Cromwell, Oliver, 12
Culloden, Battle of, 2, 17–18, 25, 37, 149–150, 199–203
Cumberland, Duke of, 16, 198–199, 204

'D.H.', 166
dag, 28, 66
dagmakers, 60, 66–67, 80, 94, 111, 114, 156
    See also gunmakers; gunsmiths
Davidson, James, 205
Davidson, John, 205
Defoe, Daniel, 178
Dighton, Denis, 32, 50, 135
dirk, 1, 4, 17, 23–24, 26–28, 34, 41–43, 61, 79
Disarming Acts,
    of 1715, 18
    of 1746, 17, 25, 42, 46, 68, 99, 120, 134
doglock, 117–118, 123
Doune, 18, 87, 91–100, 120, 123, 127, 141, 143
dragoons, 1, 3
dress, Highland, 26–27, 49, 135–137
Drumclog, Battle of, 14, 186
Dundee Court Martial Records, 181–183

East India Company, 19
Edinburgh Evening Courant, 99, 142
Egg, Durs, 154
engraving, 72, 88–89
etching, 89

Falkirk, Battle of, 16–17, 40, 43, 196, 198, 204
Ferrara, Andrea, 39–40
flintlock, 3, 13, 19, 75–77, 117, 136
Forbes, Duncan, Lord President, 25
foresights, 72, 115, 148, 150
Fraser, Major James, 28, 193
Furnace, 4, 56

gemstones, 89

Gibson, Archibald, 157
gilding, 85, 110
Glen, Robert, 216
Glen, Thomas, 177
Glencoe, Massacre of, 14–15
gold, 90
Gordon, Sir Robert, 178
Graham, John, of Claverhouse, 14, 22, 189
Grant, Ludovic, of Grant, 206
Grant, Patrick, 188
Gray, James, 11, 114, 166
gunmakers, 2, 5–6, 61, 68, 116, 136, 164
    See also dagmakers; gunsmiths
gunsmiths, 61–63, 67, 69, 72, 78–79, 156, 167
    Doune, 91, 94, 120, 127, 163, 170
    Dundee, 65–66, 114, 167, 169
    early, 5
    Edinburgh, 168, 171
    Perth, 166
    St Andrews, 68
    See also dagmakers; gunmakers

Hamilton, Duke of, 186
Hamilton, Patrick, 114, 152
hammermen, 4, 62–68, 111
'Hazard' (ship), 196
Highland Host, The, 13

inlay, 72, 86–87
Ironworks, Carron, 56

Jacobites, 14–15, 17–18, 22–23, 95, 175, 193, 196, 202
John Waters and Co., 132
Johnson, Samuel, 21
Johnstone, Chevalier de, 38, 43, 196–198, 200
Kalmeter, Henry, 55–57, 60, 69
Kennedy, John, 107, 152, 157
Ker, Lord Robert, 203
Killiecrankie, Battle of, 14, 38, 40, 191

Leslie, General David, 12
Lindsay, Robert, 167

Lindsay, William, 66, 154, 166–167
lockit book, 66, 96, 124
Logan, Alexander, 185
Logan, James, 32, 34, 37, 92, 94, 149, 197
Loudoun, Earl of, 198
Low, James, 11, 110, 113, 150, 152, 156–157, 166–167
Low, Richard, 167
Lumsden, Major Sir Robert, 12
Lunn, Edward, 201

Macdonald, Captain Roy, 201, 203
Macdonald, Flora, 200–201
Macdonald, Major Donald, 203–204
Macdonald, McIan, of Glencoe, 14
Macdonald, of Clanranald, 15
Macdonald, of Keppoch, 15, 199
MacDonell, of Glengarry, 15, 56, 143
Macleod, 141, 167–168
Macleod, Murdoch, 199
Macpherson, Cluny, 16, 36
Mar, Earl of, 15, 193
Marshall and Sons, 168
matchlock, 3, 13
McCulloch, Charles, 188
McIan, Robert R., 32, 34, 36
McKenzie, David, 168
McKenzie, James (Brechin), 3, 118, 168
McKenzie, James (Dundee), 168
McRay, James, 150
mercenaries, 18
Michie, James, 100, 169
Michie, John, 100, 169
Mills, W., 149
Monk, General, 12
Montgomerie, Hugh (5th Earl of Eglinton), 34
Montrose, Duke of, 12, 24
Mortimer, Thomas Elsworth, 137, 169
Mosman, Robert, 113, 157
Muir, Drummossie, 16, 17
Murdoch, Alexander, 99
Murdoch, John, 93–94, 98, 120, 143–144, 149, 151, 170

Murdoch, Thomas, 3, 98–99, 120, 142–143, 149, 170
Murdoch, William, 99, 171
Murray, John, 4th Earl of Dunmore, 34
Murray, John, of Broughton, 195–196
Murray, Lord George, 15, 199
Murray, Lord Mungo, 28, 90
musket, 13, 24, 27, 37–38, 41

Nasmyth, James, 177
Naughton, Robert, 66
Nimmo, Lady Jane, 196

Oath
    after Culloden, 17
    of Allegiance, 14
Ochterlonie, John, 155
Old Pretender, The, 15, 66

Paterson, James, 100
Perth, Duke of, 32, 199
pistols, Scottish
    Bonnie Prince Charlie's, 149, 200–201
    care of, 211
    costume, 134–136
    fishtail-butt, 107–111
    geographical locations of, 162
    heart-butt, 114–118
    in collections abroad, 208–210
    Lafayette, 206–207
    late flintlock, 139–141
    lemon-butt, 111–114
    lobe-butt, 119–123
    mace, 155
    makers of, 157–160
    military, 128–134
    most prolific makers of, 161
    percussion dress, 137–139
    Presentation, 142–144
    ramshorn-butt, 123–128
    rat-tail, 2
    Scottish
    sources of, 146
    survey of, 147

INDEX

Sinclair, 152 (*see also* Sinclair, Captain George)
Pitcairn, John, 171
Playfair, Charles, 171
powderhorns, 28, 46–50, 79
Prestonpans, Battle of, 15, 38, 40, 197

Queensbury, Duke of, 186

Ramsay, Patrick, 65, 167, 177
Ramsay, Thomas, 66, 167
Redcoat, 1, 14, 16
Richards, Westley, 137
Rising, Pentland, 183–184, 186
Rose, Arthur, of Kilravock, 192–193
Ross, Daniel, 141, 171
Roy, Rob, 194

Scheme, Darien, 191–192
Scott, Sir Walter, 27, 32, 133, 141, 167
Seven Years' War, 18
Sharp, Archbishop James
    assassination attempt on, 185
    murder of, 14, 189
Shaw, Fearchar, 34
Sheriffmuir, Battle of, 15, 193
silver, nickel, 90, 139
Sinclair, Captain George, 152
Sinclair, Sir John, 92
skean dhu, 24, 46
skene ochles, 23, 46
Smith, William, 118, 171
snaphaunce, 3, 5, 13, 73–74, 79, 107–108, 111, 117
Solingen, 39
Stewart of Ardshiel, 15
Stuart, Colonel John Roy, 150
Stuart, James, of Aucharn, 19
Stuart, John, 3, 118, 171
Stuart, John (Doune), 100, 120
Stuart, Prince Charles Edward, 15–16, 197–199

See also Bonnie Prince Charlie; Chevalier; Young Pretender, The
Sutherland, Kenneth (3rd Lord Duffus), 28, 50

'T.D.', 153
tacksmen, 23
targe, 16, 23–25, 28, 41, 43–45, 79
Taynuilt, 4, 56
Thirty Years' War, 3, 18
Thomson, John, 172
Tipping and Lawden, 172
Tryst, Crieff, 24

Vanhagen, Francis, 191

Wade, General George, 21, 194–195
Waitt, Richard, 34
Walker, Daniel, 173
wapinschaws, 64
Watch, Black, 18, 26, 34, 128, 195
Waters, John, 130, 132, 148
Watson, William, 141, 143–144, 148, 172
Wedderburne, David, 176–177
wheellock, 3, 6, 107, 111
Whitelaw, Charles, 5, 100, 103–104, 107, 111, 113–114, 118, 128, 156, 169, 175
Wighton, Alexander, 139
Wilkie, Sir David, 33
William IV, 98, 151
William of Orange, 14, 22, 86
wood
    brazil, 4, 107, 152
    rosewood, 4, 107, 118
    walnut, 107
Wright, John Michael, 28, 90, 123

Young Pretender, The, 18, 149, 195
    See also Bonnie Prince Charlie; Chevalier; Stuart, Prince Charles Edward

ACKNOWLEDGEMENTS

Acknowledgements are due to the following publishers and authors:

Addison Wesley Longman for *Social and Economic Development of Scotland before 1603* by I. F. Grant (Oliver & Boyd, 1930).

Arms & Armour Press for *Scottish Arms Makers* by C. E. Whitelaw, edited by S. Barter-Bailey (1977) and *Scottish Swords and Dirks* by J. Wallace (1970).

Barrie & Jenkins for *Art of the Gunmaker* by J. F. Hayward (Barrie & Rockliff, 1962) and *British Military Firearms 1650–1850* by H. L. Blackmore (Jenkins, 1961).

Guns Review Magazine for 'The Doune Pistol Makers' by J. Arthur and D. H. Caldwell.

Constable Publishers for *Letters of Andrew Fletcher of Saltoun and His Family* by A. Fletcher (Miscellany of the Scottish History Society, vol. 10, 1965); *Darien Shipping Papers, 1696–1707* by G. Pratt (1924); *Miscellany of the Scottish History Society* (vol. 5, 1933); and *Henry Kalmeter's Travels in Scotland* by M. C. Smout (Scottish Industrial History Miscellany, edited by A. Campbell, 1978).

Cumbria Archive Service and Cumbria Record Office, Carlisle, for *The Jacobite Risings of 1715 and 1745* by R. C. Jarvis (Cumberland C.C., 1954).

John Donald Publishers for *The Loch Lomond Expedition, with Some Short Reflections on the Perth Manifesto* (unknown author) and 'The Word Claymore' by C. Blair in *Scottish Weapons and Fortifications*, edited by D. Caldwell (1981).

Edinburgh University Press for *Prisoners of the Forty Five* by B. Seton and J. Arnot (1929).

Faber & Faber for *Argyll in the Forty Five* by Sir J. Fergusson (1951).

Folio Society for *A Memoir of the Forty Five* by Chevalier de Johnstone, edited by B. Rawson (1958).

Little, Brown & Company for *The Uniforms and History of the Scottish Regiments* by Major R. M. Barnes (Sphere Books, 1956) and *Weapons of the British Soldier* by Colonel H. C. B. Rogers (Sphere Books, 1972).

Mackay Publishers for *The Romantic Story of the Highland Garb and the Tartan* by J. G. Mackay (1924).

Macmillan for *Clans of the Scottish Highlands* by R. R. McIan (Pan Books, 1980).

Manchester University Press for *Collected Papers on the Jacobite Risings* by R. C. Jarvis (1971).

Oxford University Press for *Economic History of Scotland in the Eighteenth Century* by H. Hamilton (Clarendon Press, 1963). Reprinted by permission of Oxford University Press.

Routledge & Kegan Paul for *Chief of Mackay* by I. Grimble (1965).

Secker & Warburg for *Culloden* by John Prebble (© John Prebble 1961), and reproduced by permission of Curtis Brown Ltd., London, on behalf of John Prebble.

Thames and Hudson for *Charles Edward Stuart* by D. Daiches (1973) and *A Concise History of Scotland* by Sir H. F. Maclean (1970), © the authors.

Weidenfeld and Nicholson for *Bonnie Prince Charlie* by Sir H. F. Maclean (1988).

Every effort has been made to contact all copyright holders and the author apologises to any authors and publishers where this has not proved possible.